PACIFIC RIM LETTERS

ROY K. KIY

EDITED AND WITH AN AFTERWORD BY SMARO KAMBOURELI

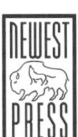

Copyright © Estate of Roy K. Kiyooka 2005
Afterword copyright © Smaro Kamboureli 2005

All rights reserved. The use of any part of this publication reproduced, transmitted in any form or by any means, electronic, mechanical, recording or otherwise, or stored in a retrieval system, without the prior consent of the publisher is an infringement of the copyright law. In the case of photocopying or other reprographic copying of the material, a licence must be obtained from the Canadian Reprography Collective before proceeding.

Library and Archives Canada Cataloguing in Publication
Kiyooka, Roy
Pacific Rim letters / Roy Kiyooka ; edited and with
an afterword by Smaro Kamboureli

ISBN 1-896300-70-7

I. Kamboureli, Smaro   II. Title.

PS8521.I9P28 2005   C818'.5408   C2004-903656-4

Editor for the Press: Smaro Kamboureli
Cover image: Roy Kiyooka, Small Magic Ring, 1965, acrylic on canvas, Vancouver Art Gallery, Gift of Ian Davidson VAG87.20 (Photo: Trevor Mills).
Interior images: *Okinawa*, 1984 25 silver prints 37" x 49".
Courtesy Catriona Jeffries Gallery, Vancouver
Cover and interior design: Ruth Linka

 Canada Council for the Arts   Conseil des Arts du Canada   Canadian Heritage   Patrimoine canadien   edmonton arts council

NeWest Press acknowledges the support of the Canada Council for the Arts and the Alberta Foundation for the Arts for our publishing program. We also acknowledge the financial support of the Government of Canada through the Book Publishing Industry Development Program (BPIDP) for our publishing activities. NeWest Press also acknowledges the assistance of the National Association of Japanese Canadians Endowment Fund with this project.

Every effort has been made to obtain permission for quoted material and photographs. If there is an omission or error the author and publisher would be grateful to be so informed.

NeWest Press
201-8540-109 Street
Edmonton, Alberta
T6G 1E6
t: (780) 432-9427
f: (780) 433-3179
www.newestpress.com

1 2 3 4 5   09 08 07 06 05

PRINTED AND BOUND IN CANADA

. . . this was the order of human institutions:
first the forests, after that the huts, then the villages, next the cities, and finally the academies.

. . . this axiom is a great principle of etymology, for this sequence of human institutions sets the pattern for the histories of words in the various native languages. thus we observe in the latin language that almost the whole corpus of its words had sylvan or rustic origins. for example, 'lex.' first it must have meant a collection of acorns. thence we believe is derived 'ilex' as it were 'illex,' the oak (as certainly 'aquilex' means collector of waters); for the oak produces the acorns by which the swine are drawn together. 'lex' was next a collection of vegetables, from which the latter were called legumina. later on, at a time when vulgar letters had not yet been invented for writing down the laws 'lex' by a necessity of civil nature must have meant a collection of citizens, or the public parliament; so that the presence of the people was the 'lex,' or *law*, that solemnized the wills that were made calatis comitiis, in the presence of the assembled comitia. finally, collecting the letters, and making, as it were, a sheaf of them for each word, was called 'legere,' reading. (78)

. . . finally, beginning with the idea by which every slight slope was called 'mundas' (whence the phrases in mundo est, in proclivi est, for 'it is easy'; and later everything for the embellishment of a woman came to be called mundas muliebris), when they came to understand that the earth and the sky were spherical in form and that from every point of the circumference there is a slope towards every other, and that the whole of things is adorned with countless varied and diverse sensible forms, the poets called this universe 'mundas' as being that which by a beautifully sublime metaphor, nature adorns herself. (275)

> from: Giambattista Vico, *The New Science of Giambattista Vico*
> translated by Thomas Goddard Bergin and Max Harold Fisch

CONTENTS

Pacific Rim Letters ~ 1

Afterword: *for what it's worth* ~ 330

Roy Kenzie Kiyooka: a chronology ~ 350

Index of Correspondents ~ 356

Acknowledgements ~ 358

~ ~ ~

Okinawa, 1984 (a grid of 25 silver prints) can be found between pages 152 and 153.

some thoughts concerning
a 2nd Book of Letters titled
The Pacific Rim Letters

'76/'85: the hive of those years:
the erstwhile politics as it veers in on
one man's life in art inside the
maelstrom of these covert ideological times.
together with (a matrix of) yes
love letters rooted in one man's erotic
confabulations. where 'polis' touches
'eros' and both touch 'art' is   to
say the least   where you find me. follow
the precincts of a chronology as posited
by the dated letters: enfold blocks
of other writings, obsessions, truculent
thoughts from other contexts to bear
in upon   callit a weaving/   wavering narrative.
ah! my mid-winter thoughts—you too
shall sieve a frost-bite thought through
the fecund seasons resounding inside
a prolix pagination. these hibernating words
want to plant a spring vowel inside
that endless processional of words they are
a humble heir of. . . . perhaps all the
letters i've ever written are addressed to
a fearful mute i carry around inside
my mundane self.

                the redemption of Language
                is a real issue mired within the tissue
                of scientific/   ideological
                gestalts. . . .   one finds here the necessity
                of periodically recovering the
                'beginnings,' the return to the 'origins'
                which characterizes the archaic world.
                begin with the body and its
                ah! myriad extensions.   test the in-
                explicable terror of muteness
                mouth your first cry . . .

these letters i've kept in duplicate

those that i never mailed
together with those i wrote ostensibly
to myself. all of them and
more: a biography of self cast upon
the study wall.
                        m.a.'s winter sun
                        all the 'dumbfounding' apparencies

April '75

Dear Daphne and Kit:
for the day he can read it if he wants to

    Sunday, 11.30 am
    Qualicum Beach after the tidal pools drain
    2 red-breasted robins preen in
    the foreground beside the Toyota truck.
    no sounds but the sundry sounds
    of my own late-morning
    ablutions. everything is 'as usual' that is
    i'm quite thoroughly at home
    with the likes of 'myself' and it gives me
    a delicious pleasure thinking
    that the birds and i have
    this simple thing in common. thus
    our interactions must be an indivisible part
    of the whole world's ongoing
    tidal/diurnal transactions.

    Dear Kit: i don't think i've ever had words
    that were not meant for your ears.
    there's a red and green sweatered young girl
    jumpin' across a fallen log   outside
    and to the left of the robins that have left
    and my Toyota truck. now her parents
    walk past my window and, turning, give me a nod.

    from cabin 8
    across Qualicum Bay past the furthest point
    of demarcation—Vancouver!
    and both of you are as close as my thots can clasp
    in a double hug. Dear Daphne:
    there's no place to be but at home in one's
    own body, even as we embrace. i mean
    it's taken 49 years to get there and yes!
    sing the neural-body, a live wire in your keeping.
    to go on simply taking the kinks out of
    it to let the message flow thru.

    love is a conduit
    robin red breast knows the absolute meaning of.
    the foreground the grassy patch
    in front of and behind the cabin is their domain.
    the ducks and the gulls have theirs
    even as i sit at my cabin window

        our domain will always be bigger than words

Nov. 21st   '75 AD

after hanging *Kiyooka 25 Years at the V.A.G.*
    rose   red
    sunset   snow

    greyslush
    rush-hour traffic

    —an endless
    processional of

    fossil fuel
    navigators humping

    across the
    Burrard Bridge.

    25 years of
    pictures prism'd

    in the V.A.G.
    solstice brine

    escarpment
    half-a-life of *soi*—

    distant images
    relegated—

    to a cantankerous
    silence . . .

    rose   red
    over Georgia Strait

    Kits point
    trove

    all a heartfelt
    illusion

    of an incomparable

plenitude

no more
no less than

the dwindling eco/bio
sphere

the tarnisht
nomenclature . . .

January 27th, '76

'a false spring day ... she had sd'

2 weeks ago: the unstirring
Yucatan jungle 25000 ft below hiding the Mayan ruins
the hieroglyphs of unrepentant sun-worshippers.
my fair lady recalls the exultations, the hypnagogic
Mayan-serpent, unmortared stone pyramid
flora and fauna translucencies. my fair lady divines
the horst of turquoise aqua while
i drive mindlessly along Spanish Banks towards U.B.C.

Daphne: mother and i are at Lionel and Maya's
she is eliciting mother's life, particularly her
childhood and youth in Kochi City way back
at the turn of the century. i seem to be on hand
to lend an ear and keeping an eye on the tape
deck. earlier, Lionel and i smoked some
weed and Lionel gladly hugged a tree. you and Kit
could fall by and have sushi and tea with us
if you want to take some time off. i cleared your
writing table while mother slept. it's patiently
waiting for your perusal.
                    from W.W.'s *Respondez!*
let the sympathy that waits in each man wait! or
let it also pass, a dwarf, to other spheres!

driving east on 4th past Primley's
the plain, unadorned, round-faced lady wearing granny glasses
smiled—i thot, for me, but it was really
for everyone crossin' the street towards her. Su Tung Po
sd 'lightly painted or heavily made-up i find all
women equally attractive.' lucky Su Tung Po.
lucky me. on Cornwall Street headin'
towards the Burrard Bridge after droppin' in at Elsie's for
a meat pie and a sweet cake the thot
that 'it' must be our everyday minds that partake of
whatever divinity there is to be had
gratuitously: that it is in its very substance an infinitesimal
speck of the very sun itself. no mind left
to praise or fault a nonetheless perfect equanimity
headin' 40 miles an hr over Burrard Bridge

these winter nights
a 60 watt incandescent light bulb
is my writing sun. 'i'
heap stones on sheets of paper
colour me 'yellow'

Dear Joy:

        as an erstwhile 'mentor' of those with geriatric problems i'm a most unlikely candidate. i mean i have lived the sometimes 'mean' even scurrilous life of an obsessed artist and that doesn't qualify me to be a family conciliator, tho i would hasten to add that i do have some know-how about the depth of the familial, coming as i do from a large family and having sired my own small brood. i am all for 'caring' for our aged ones though i am not at all comfortable with the ways and means we do it in this country. i mean given my own proximity to those who are already old and all the social/familial separation i see them put through, i have no intention of being cared for that way. still, in terms of our parents and the body politic, i'm all for doin' whatever we can to ease them into retirement. if that's what they want or need. think of all the unborn children who might never be able to play on their grandfathers' knees except for a few moments every other weekend. think of the waste of affections. a bunch of old geezers watchin' television together ain't my favorite notion of what happens to the trunk of the old family tree when it bears an ofttimes more plangent fruit. i don't seem to be one of those who are given to exercise the will-to-power political action propitiates for the so-called common good. my forum, if i could be said to have one, has to do with the authentication of all things large and small without recourse to ideological classifications. an artist, as much as any big-time political boss, is a permeable thing caught up in the penumbra of time. even as i write these words down, i am, as you will be when you come to read them, older than when i began. in my book of secret lore there's a huge, rambling, many-storied dwelling for all those who elect to be known as among the aged, and within its many-chambered corridors and rooms there are countless hidden doors and invisible windows wherein all the grand children played until their creaky old grandparents came to tuck them all in and even empty out their chamber pots. Joy: the N.A. style 'nuclear' family, despite its diminution, doesn't deserve a nuclear holocaust, let alone a separately constituted state especially for the acrimonious geriatrics. 'i' for instance pledge with every fibre of my being to be as nimble as i can be in my old age and when my time comes both 'body' and 'mind' will go off together. be ye gratuitously ebullient and let the devil take the hindmost.

        born at the beginning of the Showa dynasty and the first quarter of the 20th century i can see myself (plaintively) as an errant Child of the American Democratic Myth and all its virulent Technologies. need i add that i'm dumbfounded and, yes, appalled by my own naiveté.

    take good care of the roof over your head.

he had brought the panel of nine cibachromes home from the studio because he wasn't spending much time there and missed being able to look at them. now the panel sat on the floor up against the half-wall dividing the kitchen from the living room. he had only to turn his head slightly to the right when he sat at the oval table to peer intently at them. the panel consisted of nine eleven-by-fourteen cibachromes, each print comprising a partial view of a naked woman he had been commissioned to portray several years ago. he barely remembered all the unspoken sunlit moments of that photographic occasion and no doubt would have forgotten completely if he hadn't kept the panel within sight. she had been asked by her lover if she would consent to being photographed naked for his own sake and she had told him that for his sake and all that that meant she would. what they had going between them was not his business. his business began the summer afternoon she arrived at the studio for the photo session. the unspoken idea between model and photographer proposed that she would do what she felt like doing and that the photographer would in his turn simply take whatever pictures he felt like. as he sat one evening at the oval table he thought of that distant afternoon and in his mind he tried to recreate the exact sequence of events and thus reconstitute how both model and photographer enacted an ancient rite. again and again he had noted how her image got partially reflected in the tall mirror she lay beside. that mirror in which his own unobtrusive self disappeared into all the oblique shadows netting her naked body. 'i' am nothing but an eye witness to the manifold ways of the things of this world. i would be an unsullied mirror if i thought i could. the mottled light moulding her care-worn body, her voluptuous stare owing something to the dust-covered window, the half-open door letting an oblique zone of palpable heat in upon the ongoing depictions. he was certain that words had passed between them but nothing of it remained. no residua informed the panel's chiaroscuro. nothing he would photograph would equal 'this' bespoken occasion when a body made of itself a present for the unalloyed erotic eye. . . . he found himself mumbling as he got into bed and turned off the light. all the images of her nakedness disappeared into the depth of his sleep.

ALPHABET SOUP or
How the ABCs got to be rotund

for Kit Marlatt

                    hey! let's let all the sounds
                    our throats announce   / resound with
                    the names of the many things

    let Tom Dick and Mary
    the raucous Crow in the old Pear Tree
    animate our back alley

    let the many voices of the Ocean unseal
    the waxen gates of fear

heap up all the sounds to shape a midden plumbful
of the Heart's own   (ofttimes crazed)   artifacts

        talk your heart out!   laugh cry groan and shout!
        sound everything as if it were 3-D

            like our Pear Tree
            the fabled Language Tree proposes
            a Covenant with the 4
            Seasons underwriting the gist/s
            the husks of our nouns

June 11th, 1976

Dear Lynne Bell:
(Research Assistant to the Art Committee)

<u>YES</u> I'm responsible for all the 'Designs' on the Biology Bldg. Check w/ Gordon Arnott, architect, for exact dates tho I think it was abt '57/'58. Wow! It's 20 yrs ago already. Anyhow, I workt along w/ both architects and biologists. The former advised me abt materials and structure. The latter, motif. There's probably a few profs left in the dept. who might remember my visitations w/ them, et cetera. I hired a number of my students to assist me in laying up and packing them. Later I workt along-side of the tile contractors mounting them on the walls. You cld say I had an awful lot to do w/ every stage of it. I can't remember how much I got for it but it cldn't have been more than a few thousand dollars plus material and mounting expenses. I remember losing money on the project tho that wasn't anything new.

—Don't know any more where Biology has got to viz its *theoretical postulates* tho I believe that 'Mitosis,' the split-cell motif I used, still remains a verifiable phenomenon.
                    Is this of any use to you?

      Yrs truly

for Glady

    they are old friends
    in every way / they are always
    themselves: double-
    exposed they enact the old felicities
    the shadows round them
    unmask their words. these photos
    echo and re-echo their
    doubleness. listen—
    to their arcane conversation
    watch their myriad-faces

    speak from the divinatory-self
    the other mirrors

at La Push

she sd she thot she heard a plaintive bird
whilst walking in the trees beside the ocean. impossible
i sd, given its tumultuous uproar. tho i quickly
added that it might well have been a woodland thrush
meaning her own keening voice. it doesn't matter
if i've never seen or heard such a bird i know its warble
as only a brine-tongue can. this oceanic rock
outcropping these tidal flats these millennial indians
their corroding automobiles and trailers

                              this treetop raven

—for Daphne

June 15th / 1976

Dear Mike and Kim O

apropos reading at Glendon: can't of course speak for G.G. tho I am sure he wldn't say no. as for myself, it's ok with or without Gerry providing the reading isn't another of those in-class or noon-hour affairs that only last an hour and everyone disappears. ideally the occasion ought to last a long rambling evening with time to spare. to insist, I don't want to be another C.C. sponsor'd kultur-is-good-for-Canadian-University-Students poet. I am, as you know, more interested in dis-course. better hoarse and heard than a slot machine poet et cetera.

viz transcanadaletters: better a ripped pitcher than a pinch hitter or the proverbial snowball in Hell. yes, i have subsequent to yr letter seen W.W.'s review—WOW! i thot at last i've joined the Company of Peerless Letter-Writers, but it's not The Kid born in Moose Jaw, Saskatchewan. he died ignominiously: i am merely his prognostications, his ghost writer in the sky, et cetera.

            (didn't know porcupine quills
            were threaded   .

  do give us your news, whenever

. . . to begin: Here's a little deja-vu to introduce the 4th Vancouver Poetry Western Front Reading . . . a bit of callit angelic-stammerings to un-wind the Vocables of these, to say the least, eminent poets. . . . this will be my strut for all those keen ears out there .
driving serpent-wise back to town along south-east Marine late last night with a small harp on her lap and strummin' it, she sd it's too angelic for me: i want more raunch for the punk rocker inside me. i, fingering my zippy zither (on the seat between us), sd i'd like to think i'm still ballsy but it ain't as urgent as it used to be. ha! maybe that's why angelic chords make my ears wiggle. we talkt abt all the square pegs looking for round holes with all the oblique referentials both language and gender re-compose.

. . . o.k. now we've got a leg up on the ol' angelic ladder, let's get a leg up on the next rung . . . assuming, of course, there's only one way to go if you start from the bottom rung . . . assuming you all brought your pack-sack full of metamorphosis. . . . let's listen first to none other than Ed Dorn alias 'Gunslinger' who rode in via the pony express from Colorado to give us a piece of his jaw. i think of him as one of the original breed of poets-cum-iconoclasts 'who' steer a big car with one hand on the wheel, the other countin' the chips-of-fate. Ed's ofttimes trenchant views of kultur below the 49th peril constitutes what i call the 'real' news. then, we'll hear from Lionel Kearns whom i first met in the mid 60s stacking syllables with such an acute ear lyrical air . . . all the iambic stanzas got caught flat-footed with their end-rimes pointing towards Elysium. . . . while i haven't attended his verse lately, i go on honouring the outraged boy in him (grown to manhood) who can shout —LOOK! THE EMPEROR OF ICE CREAM IS WEARING ERMINE UNDERWEAR!

after the Intermission you'll be hearing from Daphne Marlatt   poet editor mother of invention   whom i met in the mid 60s along with other Tish poets whom i invited to read at the old Vancouver School of Art. she with whom i share bed board cat and son. one of our acute chroniclers. and last but certainly not least . . . you'll be hearing from Eli Mandel with whom i share a peculiar distinction—that of being Saskatchewan-born. talk abt alien passports and bucolic transports. i tend to think of Eli as one of our most adroit men-of-literature and a poet of distinction. one who exemplifies a civilized breadth of knowledge with, shall i say it, lotsa passion. . . . now, just to wind up my act at the foot of the ladder, i've collaged a poem, using a line from each of the writings of the 4 poets for all of you out there who believe that poetry spoken out loud bears both the small pleasures and outsized burdens of the intrinsicly humanoid. . . . get yrself another beer, scratch yr ass, lend me yr ear for another moment . . .

watch it driver!
there isn't any road   /   there's only the sound of
rubber in the night

the vanishing point of your un finisht
portrait

                in a superior   conjunction
                   back of   the sun
o! the fabulous laughter of the sea trappt in a jar   o!
the   tearing of water

                                        watch it driver!
                                  watchout for ol' Mother Midnight's
                                      angelic ladder
                                            rising up into Protean Night

Ladies and Gentlemen!
Here's Mister Ed Dorn . . .

                          June 24th, 1976

A Draft of
A Proposal to cause to be built
A giant Gate
              Archaic
              Entrance to Sky | Sea
                       mirror | fate

consult:
Geographers and Oceanographers
Local Tribal Lore
The Traditional Gate-Builders in the Orient
Local Tides and Winds
Native Indian Myths of Passages
consult lotsa Maps
topo/ geo/   meta-physical
Photograph   camp on   feel the scourings
of actual Site   /   Scale
Note prevailing Winds/   Lunations
Vegetation. attend to
Local superstitions to divine
The Precincts of
a once Hallowed Place to place it
Where it belongs

A Gathering together of
Modern / Ancient Lore for the sake of
The Sacral: without which
Architecture is bereft of Eloquence

            (All for the sweet Soul's Weathering/ s
            A lifetime Project   /   Predilection

                       Bare arsed to summer's
                       voluptuary winds

summer and smoke
for Daphne, '76

he took off his clothes
and sat down in an armchair with a mask
up to his face. he thot of
the heaptup rocks his own nakedness: the
shadows coveting both. he
tried to recall the exact expression he had
on his face . . . just as his
bare feet tripped the shutter-release.
if you look closely at the hand
holding the mask you'll notice that the
index fingertip is missing:
if you look closely at the mask you'll notice
how a mishap got mapped. he
had literally 100s of photoglyphs of
himself as others portrayed
him. he had upon occasion looked at one or
another of them and had often
wondered why they never corresponded to
the face he often looked at
in an uncrazed mirror. she: for her part held
her mask away from her face.

the heaptup rocks got their own
perdurable nakedness

3/4 July '76

Dear Phyllis

    ah   my 50th Summer, its dispersals: Daphne off to childhood hauntings in Penang Malaysia till the 19th of August with her father and favorite sister . Kit whose picture sits in front of me is with his father till early August when his grandmother takes over . I'm headin' up to Yellowknife N.W.T. for an art feast tho I don't know what to expect : it's been 30 yrs since I workt up there in the fishing industry and read Bertrand Russell and T.S. Eliot's J. Alfred Prufrock etc. The Northland in those yrs was a very real place—it's where I underwent my initiation into manhood viz gruelling work and gambling .

                                  count on us— we'll be there:
                                  tell D. Fitchew we'll take
                                  what the reading enables . no
                                  more or less than

    I had thot to take a year off to see if I can make a living via Art but have found out (again) I can't so it's back to U.B.C. and a layman's salary . you, too?

    love

mid summer '76

Dear Claudia Lapp
   is lazuli and Francois
   dare ye

      . . . 50 yrs seems like a compilation of the other 49. Summers as usual
      con me by their profanities. Tease tease. Jeezus! Claudia, now that
      you're 30, does the Night hold any terror? And the mirror—does it scare
      you? It can still do it to me, tho mostly it's a bemusement and a few more
      grey hairs.

—It almost seems that everyone we know went off to Mexico this past
winter/spring. We, Daphne and I, were certainly there: faced w/ the brute Sun I
was mostly mute or scoured sometimes both at once. No matter, the Nahual spoke,
I thot, thru me, forcibly.   Daphne is still into it   she spins it out into a novella. Ah
those heapt mouldering Stones those oracular bones—How they VEX'd us with
their undecipherable MYSTERIUMS. Conundrums and Coruscations . . . till the
last stone breaks Silence

                (Tepees
                certainly those used
                by Plains Indians
                posit *Space* the 4 quarters
                of the Wind as
                an act of Divination.
                and Time to them
                was a windless summer day
                or so it seems at
                this moment
                          etc.)

   —All impingements occur
on the epidermic plane. Nomads carry
Space/Time inside them. The tick-
in' Clock is a remorseless chatter . . .

More to say when I'm in touch again.

July 15th, '76

Dear Richard and Vicki

    Ah! Watchin' the Olympians here in Vancouver beside
a Pacific Ocean the Greeks who invented the Games couldn't
have lain beside tells me again a finely made piece of
machinery the human body can be . All that stamina—
intelligence vis an animal's kinetics for the sake of an
absolute moment of the sheerest despair or exultation—does
turn me on . The once fleet-foot'd athlete I thot I cld
be hangs on watching them do it on television, o breath-
lessly . Meanwhile I'm favouring my right foot the swollen
one with five stitches lacing up the incision from which a
3/8th inch piece of a steel pin got extracted . I won't say
how it all happened 'cause it's all quite silly—I call
it my St Sebastian act . Talk abt a hot-foot or being gimpy .
I can see how even a limp might change a man like me .
Daphne's off to Penang Malaysia till the middle of August .
I'm headin' for Yellowknife N.W.T. for a week . Kit is with
his real father . That leaves Coopey and I to bug each
other and the O limp foot itchin' to their extraordinary
feats . Now that we're headin' into the last half of the
ho hum '70s and we earthlings who have imagined a horde of
bio-blobs called Martians have hurled ourselves aloft—it's high
time we dreamt of new conquests like the interstellar
spaces within . And it does appear to be a very real sort of
possibility that I shall be in Monreale this fall or
winter . Thanx to the beneficence of our Kultural Medici—
not even Gulliver had a better trip . Letters get written by
fools but God can make an Anne Oakley or a Bliss
Carman .
              Ah Richard if thou be Gerty's husband I'm
              H.D.'s unmentionable gnomic lover

                      Mid-summer Love in the loft to
                      everyone of you

Sat/ July 17th/ '76

Dear Wilfred

O C a n a d a despite the fossil-fuel velocities remains WILDERNESS to those of us who are for whatever un-reason 'artists'—can't count on anything like RESPONDEZ! And that despite an absolute plethora of everything inc. printer's ink and steamy publications . These days the far Eastern Establishment's Kultural Trips seems to consist of   1/   endless 'gropes' viz the high-priced vice-commissions confrontations symposia and other forms of miasmic fantasies. 2/ The C.C.'s top visual arts officer not to mention Art Bank's are both Yankees—tho i know as well as anyone that in terms of corporate con jobs it's always hands across the border etc. 3/ The 'kultur dept' of multinational corps and their dividend-minded banking buddies are sending out coteries of bright as new minted coins men and women to scour the country and buy up yards of Art as tho it were gilt-edged and providential. (The Medici too had their own branch plant art factories.)   4/ The hobby house art galleries w/ their million dollar budgets and puny allocations for art their blatant hierarchies. 5/ The GROSS NATIONAL INFATUATION   'i' sometimes feel like one of the lazy penny-pinchin' big-time spenders hell bent for sweet depravities' sake etc . Havin' got this diabolism off my chest, i want to say that i received (anonymously?) a tatter'd copy of OUTWEST w/ 'Born in Moose Jaw Saskatchewan'— to wit, Wilfred, it pleasured me even as i felt embarrassed by your luvly salutations: it must be that i am nonetheless ASTONISHT and want to thank you.

>—art/   language as 'translucencies' surrounding our bodies/   meta-body, respite, and repository of all our thwarts etc.
>
> Sheila, Sheila, have you got yrself hookt again. . . ?
>
> better hookt than double-crosst

July 25/ 1976

Dear Suzanne Rivard Le Moyne

> I've had a number of invitations to go East
> this fall and winter and when I've got them coordinated
> (including yrs) I'll be in a better position to
> let you know 1/ whether or not I can make it on Oct. 25th,
> 26th or later. 2/ It might be during the spring
> semester. 3/ With or without a studio encounter, etc .
> Otherwise, you can count on me to come to Ottawa U—
> so keep in touch .
>
>> Give my regards to Ken Lochhead
>> and Pierre Elliot Trudeau

p/s viz Can/Art: My *Transcanadaletters* ought to be required reading for yr art/ history students 'cause it purports to be abt one artist's PROMPTINGS . (If you haven't got a copy of it, tell me and I'll have one sent.)

July 26th, '76

Dear Luke Rombout

    Apropos S t o n e d g l o v e s : I'm
of course pleasured that the V.A.G. has acquired them for
its collection . Almost abandoned   I can imagine
them smiling behind their tatter'd palms and waving to
each other . Tell 'em for me I'll be by to see them
the very next time they're hung .

                For the records I'm
enclosing the poster/s and catalogue/s from the 2 occasions
they got shown all together outside of Canada . I'm also
enclosing the N.G.'s original xerox copy of the show's
Canadian itinerary together with the reviews the show got .
SG's Canadian catalogue is the book of pomes by that name
printed by Coach House Press, Toronto . There's probably
copies floating abt in Canadian Bookstores thru-out the
country . I recently got the last 3 copies they had in
Vancouver at a mere $3.00 per copy . And as you probably
know it was lovely Danielle Corbeil who organized the show
and catalogue for the N.G. Last but not least a considerable
number of my *Transcanadaletters* have to do with SGs .

        . . . I speak for *ol'* friend
        Glove who sends his tatter'd blessings

p/s goin' up to Yellowknife NWT late July/early August for
of all things a mid-summer Northern Arts Celebration .

July 28th, '76

Dear Greg
(Apropos the Couchiching Conference on
the State of the Arts in Canada July 1976:

—Despite yr recommendation and my good faith I won't be there to join you, let alone the numerous Others. That is, between my answering 'Yes' and their receiving sd letter someone on the conference committee took it upon himself to contact another person etc. If it had been another artist in my stead I wld not have minded but the fact he's a gallery dealer pisst me off. I mean, given the topic for that Thursday morning, I can't imagine his take on it unless it's as the artist's ol' nemesis, Mr. Middleman. I am thinking abt the need for the artist's voice on such occasions without which the whole process will be another great slither. Glad that you'll be there: someone has to 'speak quitely but carry a big stick' as Ad Reinhart sd .

The enclosed RESPONSE can 1/ be read on Thurs. morn. as my contribution; 2/ xerox'd and handed out that morning; 3/ both; 4/ to be perused by you and you only; 5/ disposed of at yr discretion; 6/ a combination of all. (—I've got it off my chest, etc.) (Need I add that it's a jaundiced but serious view from, like I say, the back pews of the Can/ Art Est.)

a minority view from the back pews of
the Canadian art establishment in vancouver bc 1976

despite the unprecedented moneys going into the arts the typical Canadian artist is as marginalized as ever.

remember the famous '30s cartoon of the hobo (artist) lying in a ditch looking up at a spiffy guy in a pin stripe suit

who is asking him what he's doing down there and his reply is where i've always been, buddy. to wit: the notion

that a benign poverty is better for an artist's raunchy soul than dow-jones or an art-bank. and how much of the tolled

millions spent by benevolent government agencies go to inflate the affluence of the interchangeable kultural brokers. that the

name of the kultural savant's money-for-the-good-of-the-arts game is the more there are of us the merrier the arts. all of which

adds up to less and less for the *artificers:* the so-called primary producers on whose backs the whole edifice called the visual

arts happens to be erected. our peculiar form of absentee patronage often seems to be the invisible branch of the welfare dept.

ah! the ubiquitous mythology of efficient administration. the princely sums we have to pay for our gross national deficits.

i wonder what John Galbraith has to say about the interlocking stratagems of multinational corporations and kultural institutions

which both in their own ways play a surfeit-of-commodities game. let's have a 10 year moratorium of all kultural commissions.

let's forgo our expensive habit of hiring academics-know-it-all and other recondite specialists to offer expensive panaceas.

let's not even sit across the bargaining table from each other. you can lead a horse to water but you can't make him drink unless it's

thirsty and as we all know: visual thirst in the last quarter of the 20th century is satisfied by a weekly sitcom on television.

i'd say let's pull the gold-plated plug out of the kultural-drain, dump a can of draino into it and let the wind pass through. the

so-called state of the arts in kanada today is the same as it was yesterday, perhaps even tomorrow. it's got to do with a simple

proposition, viz: does the thing on the wall turn you on? it takes love, or a reasonable facsimile thereof, to make a painting and

be able to see it for what it's worth clearly. despite the unprecedented moneys spent on the arts the average kanuck is kulturally

poor as a protestant church mouse. these words are betrothed to art first and foremost and bureaucratic levity not at all.

July 1976/ Vancouver BC

mid-summer, 1976

Frm the catalogue to Ann Kipling,
The Vancouver Art Gallery, October 2-31, '76

> Great Sea
> Sends me drifting.
> Moves me,
> Weed in the river I am.
> Great Nature
> Sends me drifting.
> Moves me,
> Moves my inward parts w. joy
>   (Eskimo)

MOTIONS: Concerning the Drawing/s of Ann Kipling

Given the corporate hype these days for le grande painting and the diminution of, its twin, drawing—I wish there was another word for what Ann Kipling does with ordinary lead pencils. Dozens of them, sharpened to an exact point and bundled according to their nuances before she heads off with a pack on her back across the neighbouring orchards up into the high country above Oyama (O Mountain, in Japanese). Or, how in mid-winter she sits down in front of a tethered goat and draws it, hair by hair, till the whole sheet of paper is filled with its frosty breath. Whether it's the whole sweep of mountains across the lake or the tree right in her own backyard doesn't matter as long as it compels her rapt attention. For Ann Kipling the daily ritual of drawing is an urgent act of drawing-out of the thing/s to hand an 'elemental commotion.' For her, drawing is 'entrancement.' She speaks of a 'point' in space—how it becomes the actual entrance into a drawing, how without the pointer the marks on the paper remain invisible. I think of how her weathered face has its correspondences with the mottled grass slope we sat upon. Like this Land's first artificers and certain Chinese painter/poets, she knows in her very bones that the daily act of drawing is a speechless but substantial 'dialogue' within the domain of all phenomena. It takes a wind-cloud-sea-air-land artist as Ann Kipling to put the wind in the tree's branches down on paper. It takes a woman-of-all-seasons with a keen eye and nimble fingers to breathe life into the least phenomena. Listen, listen to the wind. 'It was the wind that gave them life. It is the wind that comes out of our mouths now that gives us life. When it ceases to blow we die. In the skin at the tips of our fingers we can see the trail of the wind: it shows us where the wind blew when our ancestors were born' (Navajo). Ann Kipling's Drawing/s are a moving testament to the weather that is 'within' and all 'around' us. The haunted voices of the land have their own commotions. I wish that paint/s could bear again such intense scrutiny as her drawings propose.

Dear Victor-Levy Beaulieu

Between leaving Vancouver on July 29th for Yellowknife NWT via Kelowna Edmonton Hay River and returning via the same route in reverse) five days later: i read and re-read yr 'chicken-essay' concerning an American/ Quebecois named Jack Kerouac—remember him? 'i'/ 'we' converged upon Yellowknife for an art's fest called the 'general idea' tho of course each of us were, for whatever it's worth, entirely specific. we, that is Ann Szumigalski, Judith Merrill, Robert Kroetsch, Rudy Wiebe, Gladys Hindmarch, Garry Geddes, Susan Musgrave, and myself were there to read from our poetry/stories and yea 'dig' the ol' clear-bright northern hemisphere sunne and other tundra litanies. i wanta call it a gathering of a divers clan who only had their particular senses of a (Canadian) 'English' to make some sense out of their northland experiences. And, yes, we declaimed our poetry, some of it having to do with the native Dene/ Inuit Mythologies without a single actual native present. Languages are not holistic—they tend to be selective viz what gets carried across. And as you so well know translations are barely adequate. Nonetheless, we did it and i feel, at least for myself, that the breadth of that vast country alone measures our puny statures. Jack K. (i wrote a few yrs back) is no longer 'on the road'—he's chasing old angel midnight. i wanted then to say that i was doing that too, but of course it wld have been just another lie. i mean you can't lie in the face of eternal night if tomorrows still sit lightly on yr eye-lash. Or how else explain these words, the bent/ twisted accumulation of them? Levy, i have three daughters, mostly grown up and away frm home etc. Levy, i'm Jack's age (born in 1926) and have spent time (4 yrs) in Monreale. i've lived in Mexico, Kyoto, as well as all over Canada, including Nova Scotia. Levy, the NWTs are also a part of my own mythology as i spent 5 long war-years summers there between the ages of seventeen and twenty-one as a fish processor and all round tout. Levy, i'm telling you these things because they're a part of why i read yr Kerouac. Levy, we've all got a monkey on our backs. We're all bedevilled. Allen Ginsberg and i spent a memorable afternoon high up on the top of the Tokyo tower in summer 1963. We had come via train frm Kyoto where Gary Snyder saw us off. Levy, frm that height atop that tower, we could see the grey abysmal city stretch out in all directions as far as the eye could see etc. We felt nonetheless a momentary elation, even exultation—percht as we were high above a seething fossil-fueled fulminating dragon. Levy, it's the price we all have to pay for the sweet soul's desolations. Or else it's that fearsome God without a trace of favoritism that can (equally) devour us, spit us out into black oblivion, but, but do we, Levy, really have a choice?

Mother, mother Memere, mother tongue, everyone's got a mother and a tongue. Put 'em together and you've got the speech each one, one by one by one, has been given. Long before we come to know the language-babble mother teaches each one how to untie their tongues. i, for instance, learned, by osmotic repetition, mother's tongue at home and a ghetto english on our neighbourhood streets. Japanese and Canadian-english if you please. i am in that sense different from both Jack and you—and representative of the west coast as you two are easterners.

For you see, Levy, that the history of the west coast, that is, the unwritten history of the west coast, the history whc at this very moment is being enacted, is the whole flow of, if you will, Asian culture from the time of the last glaciation forwards, and the fact that this province happens to be B.C. much more than A.D. is its own proof. Whereas you, Levy, and almost everyone else east of Winnipeg, is part of the European flow and the Atlantic myth and cultures. All of which leads me to this thot that the wasp is your true protagonist and it cannot be otherwise. As for my children who are caucasian half-breeds to Asian metis, their protagonists will simply be another human being irrespective of their colour.

Dear Terry

—Back and all that. This is simply to say how much I enjoyed being in Yellowknife with you (despite the small animosities, etc.)   and the Others . This is to say at least that much—the rest of it—the appetite for sun and poetry's convivialities are best unsaid .   I can't of course speak for the Others but for myself let me say that I can't imagine how it could have been better. I can't imagine that . There are the countless places we visit for long or short periods and never return to and there are places we have visited that for whatever reason we have to re-turn to at least once and Yellowknife meant that to me. Thank you for facilitating my visitation. Thank you for the re-kindling of my true North strong and free etc. And YES please thank all of the other women who had a hand in it as well as the others who were in their way equally numinous, equal even to the natives we all thot to be blessed by .

> pleeze thank yr husband Bill for
> the plane air ride without whc my portion of
> the trip wld not have been accomplisht.
> tell him that i did find my Gros Cap and that
> alone is to me just an astonishment thru
> and thru .
>   everyone's got their North South
> East and West: every one inc. you.
>
> see you ALL in my super 8 movie. in it
> you'll see all-of-us grinning back at you,
> profusely.

thurs august 5th, '76
midnight

dearest Daphne

Kit's up in Robt's Creek   Jan who had gone up with them sd he's bored and wants to come home and be just be with his mommy   i've started to fix up our bedroom—won't tell you what i'm into but think it will please you   and phase three of SPOTA's project has begun with a vengeance   between the time i left for Yellowknife and got back they've trencht the vacant lot across the alley and have already put the foundations floor and walls up   and the big two-storey clapboard next to the one on the other side of the church has been torn down and the ground trencht   the vacant lot across frm Benny's   is heapt with lumber and a 'johnny-on-the-spot' fiberglas portable toilet   with all the racket going on all around you couldn't have done any work anyhow so you might as well enjoy Penang whc almost sounds like a doppleganger   or Miss Daphne Buckle's fairy godmother's crenulated hauntings   yr mother sits in a photographic alembic behind me   she listens to everything on CBC and knows what's going on in Malaysia   o my own mother can't be deceived either   and as far as fathers go—i speak for myself   they all 'ave a bit of the fool in them   penned caged routine-ridden driven scrivened or whatever we all need a woman to abide our fool-hearted propensities etc   yr pa likewise   i stared at my own father's visage on mother's dining area wall and could only hear my own heart's stammerings   a man of few words we had even less to say now that he's dead and i'm as they say going   and i feel i have already had my too too brief summer   had it in Yellowknife   already the scents of fall are in the air and your green peas stand four-feet tall   and already the days are shorter the nights grow longer and sunshine dwindles   autumn must be the dwarf's prime season   or is it my own time of life?   as you have come into summer   a crystalline Yellowknife summer like the one i've just come back frm   was i up there was i as a twenty-year-old lad up there—only the northland's vast silences and that brilliant sun my body remembers tell me yes yes yes you were there you saw Gros Cap and told the pilot where to circle the skeletal remains of an old fishing camp   too bad we couldn't have landed on water but there were others along who had their own thots and so we circle-dippt a wing and passed on and around back towards Yellowknife   i thank Bill Padgham for that   i who had spent so much of his time up there on land and water thot that the means of locomotion defines our knowledge of the elements and so it was that even as we flew high up above that rock and water immensity i could imagine my self laved by water best Daphne my small tree my water maiden we're very much united despite the awesome distances   i mean what's love all abt if it ain't a telegram

September 11th, '76

dear Dave S.

    'like' why not—
anyone who's been at it as long as you ought to
get a C.C. with or without my
recommendations . i've had my share of 'em tho
i can't say it's helped much viz
productivity etc . i mean how the ubiquities continue
to tease 'will' etc . and what's happened to
yr/ our/ Canadian *sculpture*? you'd think in a land
with the breadth ours *has* there wld be room for
acres of it, etc . mine haven't been uncrated for years !
nobody wants 'em even as the ol' wilderness en-
crouches on 'em and threatens to swallow them up . the
Prairies seem today to be the only place it can
happen . Richard T. is painting again and doing extraordinary things with air-brush and camera . he's
almost given up sculpture, too . Chris H.
got his shit together and is among the last of the
original 60s 'heads' left with whom i can still toke up .
—be in Montreal this winter for sure . send on
yr forms and i'll attend .

Sept. 12th '76

dear G e r r y

    . . . got yr letters and meant to say
sooner than yesterday that yr on the right track
that i do like yr selections despite my
apprehensions viz contexts etc. and the recording
of 'em ain't no problem as i'll be around
till Xmas . i want to know when the recording will occur
several days in advance so that i can have
previous takes on them etc . the rest is yr biz and
the C.B.C.s . i'll be in Toronto late Oct. for
a reading at Glendon : let's get together then . Other
wise i'm back at U.B.C. feeling like a tawdry pro
with nothing to say . etc .

                        throw another brick my way

                        if you need to

dear Yves Trudeau:

> despite, despite the politics, the inevitable chaos in higher education these days and my being caught up in its thraldoms at the U. of Q. i do want to thank you again for inviting me to be a resident artist. to be back in la belle Monreale and seeing a number of dear friends in itself was heartfelt. long live the myriad strands of kultur! say 'Hi' to Jacques de Tonnancour. tell him his impaled butterflies and horned beetles stalk an imaginary paradiso in my winter reveries. please pass on the note to Joan.

dear Joan:

    i tried to get in touch with you to say 'hullo' and 'goodbye' but try as i might i couldn't connect with you. no matter, i just want to say i had a salutary time. give my regards to Jacques and Fiore and his lively graduate students who treated me so royally down on Notre Dame Street. it's finally what i would call the epiphanies of art that keep all of us enthralled. and, furthermore, goad us on to excel ourselves. these days i don't really have anything else to toll. tell it like it is .

                        yours,   indubitably,

dear Barry:

this won't save your neck but it is a whole-hearted response to your predicament. let the enclosed letter speak for 'me' if not of me, which i'll save for another perhaps less fraught occasion. where i am and what i'm mostly into has no public face of any political importance. the artist i be has gone to bed in recent years, mumbling, fuck History.   anyhow, Barry and Joy, the trammels of this our post-modern world don't bear down on the shoulders of a Saskatchewan-born boy's sense of a vast unmitigated space. nor, i would hazard to guess, has our economic malaise got much to do with peering down Alice's rabbit hole.

take care of the Ps and Qs and let the preposterous educational emendations fake a non-taxable plenitude .

it's nice to see how you guys and gals can and do survive in the northern hinterlands. O Pioneers!   i know i would have probably burned-out years ago. O the luvliness of the Skeena River's serpentine Hauntings!   i wunder if i'll ever follow its salmon down to the ocean again. . . .

dear Brian:

   here's a copy of my response to Barry's plight. how to be just an ordinary guy, even a downright redneck and still keep all the channels, not to mention the network, open to an utterly local vernacular goes right on being a full-time job in a small town like Prince George. as for our sidelong glances at each other whenever our paths happen to cross, let's just say that friendship (as i know it) is almost always preordained. 'aggressive transport,' that forlorn male ego humping the old switch backroads, not quite drunk, not quite out of control, a veritable meatball fused to a crest-fallen frontier romanticism. i mean, what do ya do when you get the message and your big prick droops? 'i' hate to say this, but i too am a succubus of both dialectical materialism and Darwinian evolution. i too have worshpt at the altars of an insatiable democratic polis. count me among the unbereaved ones. fuck the tallow quantification machines. ream me out.

>   pedagogy has bitten the dust, again
>   long live all the un-copyrightable things in the world
>   i'd like to live till the dawn of a new
>   literacy, one rooted in a non-ideological world class
>   consciousness: ethnic superiority is
>   given the lie everyday through chinks in the media
>
>   Ah! the thraldoms of New Caledonia!
>   ignorance is an invisible best stalking the hallowed
>   corridors of pedagogy and power.

>   beware,
>   brother

Circa late 1976 / January 1977

Dear Dennis Reid:

got yr message re: the big Canadian Painting Show to be held in Nippon. i hadn't planned on going there till next summer when i ought to get a sabbatical but when it comes to even a brief sojourn across the Pacific almost anybody alive could twist my arm. anyhow, i've asked the C.C. to forward 'short term grant papers.' need i add that without a small stipend to defray the costs it'll just turn out to be another pie-in-the-sky which all such occasions tend to be anyhow. kultural lip-service with all its subtle ideologies would (nonetheless) seem to be as efficacious (speaking of matters of conscienceness) as the tawdry rhetoric of detente.

it's harkening to think that i'm in the estimation of those who keep their eyes open wide a painter still. i mean i was never meant to be a household Tom Thomson, Margaret Atwood, or a David Suzuki, but it's true that i did have a reputation of sorts. it's been 6 years since my Retro at the V.A.G. and since then i've gone under ground: the post-modern kultural establishment's blandishments haven't got much to do with what i'm all about as a friable artist. as for T.T. and The Company He Keeps, it'll have to sit on the old back burner till i re-birth my Dirty Thirties and Atrocious Forties in the guise of a paradigmatic Kanadian Fable.

anyhow, it's apparent that you're on your way to becoming one of our eminent kultural ambassadors. why, the next thing i know you'll be putting up a Group of Seven Show in huge yak tents somewhere in outer Mongolia. and if i may say so, it'll serve you right, given your long black pigtails. these days our meeting in the foyer of the Tokyo museum of modern art is as likely as it would be in Toronto or Ottawa. let's look forward to it. . . .

yr unruly post-modern oriental

January 30th '77

Dear Louise Walters

apropos yr *Ex-patriate* show: hope the (ugh) title is
a provincial 'pun'; or an 'ironical' poke at the nomenclature of
CanArt Histories; or it's nothin' but another one of those
sentimental titles without wch nothin' wld get labelled not to
mention, after all, *clichés*
are an artist's best friend.
wch thought has something to do with even my contribution to
yr show. (more abt this later.

. . . don't know 'who' will be in the show but 'those' you mention'd
earlier—tho i take it frm the funny title for the show that
it has to do with those of us (artists) (in the Tommy Douglas
Era) who had something (special?) to do with Saskatchewan Art then.
and Others?   for 'those' of us who intersected 20 or more yrs ago
were once upon a time. etc.   3 C H E E R S for that.

The SERIES   (9 of 126 folios)   is called the
            F o n t a i n e b l e a u
            D r e a m - M a c h i n e

            & comprises 18 collages 23 x 17 inches
            printed on offset by the Bau-Xi
            Gallery in Vancouver B.C. January 1977.

            thus you'll need 18 shts of plexi 23 x 17
            & affix 'em to the wall like you sd
            a mirror wld be. the exhibit will include
            the 'text' that complements each collage.

More later . . . & take care of the *NEG* pleez!

Feb. 20 '77

Dear Gwen Hoover:
    (Visual Arts Officer) C.C.
    —the enclosed brochure shld inform you abt
the Painters' Symposium, March 2nd & 3rd, in Kingston wch
I spoke to you abt on the telephone. And it seems
like an important occasion at this moment in the ongoing
History of Canadian Painting, one I want to lend
my voice to. *Hence* I'm asking the C.C. for 1 round-trip ticket
to Toronto and back, plus $50.00 to get me to Kingston
& back.
        You askt for a 'resume' of what I've been doing
and here it is: I've just abt completed an edition of 126 prints.
Each print is 23" x 17" and printed in 2 colours on offset.
These prints will comprise folios of 18 prints together with
a book of Texts with a repro of the print en-face. They
are titled the FONTAINEBLEU DREAM-MACHINE and will be released
thru the Bau-Xi Gallery early this summer. This project rep-
resents abt 4 to 5 months' work. There's other things in the works
wch won't come together till later this year. Previously
I was preoccupied with my 25 YEAR RETRO, the catalogue for it
plus a large book of letters titled the *transcanadaletters*—
and so it goes .
        A further letter concerning
        the 3rd Installment of my Senior Arts Grant
        will follow, shortly

—Let me hear from you at your earliest convenience
    yours truly,

early March 1977, Powell St., Vancouver

Dear Gerry

    this has got to be 'it,' i mean shit, a draft a year for a decade ought to be sufficient. what can i say? that it took all that time to see what it was all abt. i mean what my father & i were abt. what the trip was abt. what families are. & how to orchestrate the whole damned thing without leaning too hard on the form of the Japanese travel book a la *Oku-no Hosomichi* by Basho or my own favorite Issai's Year Book. it was also the problem of getting a Canadian-Japanese voice in there. & last but not least a homage to my father. & what he spawned, what, therefore, i also am.

    ok, throw the draft i left with you away. don't let it get in the way of your selecting. don't let it hang around to crap up the landscape. make your selection again after reading the last draft & let me know which pages you choose 'cause some mags want to use other parts of it. then pass the whole manuscript on to Stan & or Michael O. to see it thru a Coach House manuscript edition. or pass on a copy of the copy & keep the 1st copy for yourself. for what it's worth, the book i would like to see would include almost as many pages of photographs. or is it silver bromide glyphs? that's abt it.

    spring is upon us, almost. & as the days lengthen i feel the onus is on me to grow green. grow into ah another summer. do, do keep in touch.

early March, Powell St., Vancouver

Dear bp

    i've sent the final draft onto G.S. to make his selection from. you could ask him to pass it on to you to pass on to Stan for the C.H. manuscript editions. that is, if you have the time to get into it. if you do, you will find a number of inconsistencies like using both upper & lower case 'I's' not to mention uncapitalized nouns. i've left it that way 'cause i couldn't make up my mind & you could advise me on this. a part of me wants the formality of caps thru-out & a part of me doesn't. i want the casualness of lower case. so what do you think i ought to do about it? please advise Stan before it goes to press. i'll take your word for what suits the occasion. p.s. your 'selected' gives me a few clues but i can't quite apply them. or rather i can't simply carry 'em over. language is a monster. a beast of (karmic) burden. heroes are made of clay. i like the music in you. it ofttimes feels that my own efforts at singing have too much phlegm in them, their vocals. the issue, the issue seems to be how we are, despite ourselves, estranged from the dominance of the capitalist ideology. the issue is how we use the very 'language' of mundane views to shape a true body of knowledge. the issue continues to be how we reify ourselves by throwing ourselves into the flux of it & sink or swim. nothing quite as monstrous as ECO-NOMICKS with its fettered predilections, its WHAMMY.

    dear bp, keep truckin'

Tues. Mar. 8, '77 midnight

Dear Louise

    got final Draft of Frames finisht abt 3am Sunday March 6th after nearly 4 months of an intense preoccupation with the un-ravelling of its coruscations, etc. Monday noon got 'em XEROX'd at U.B.C. then mounted them and sent them on to you. WHEW!—there were many times when I wanted to abandon them, etc.
    the F o n t a i n e b l e a u   D r e a m   M a c h i n e
_____

18   F r a m e s   from   A   B o o k   of   R h e t o r i c k

its true-blue Title.

it's a Weaving together a Shuttling back & forth of Divers Stories a 'collaging' if you want & part of the weaving together has to do with How almost all of our Stories/   our Histories/   our Hoary Tales are woven right/lie or wrong/lie into the Cloth of our Language, our

    D r e a m M a c h i n e s   (then
                                    Pictures/ Words: *Collage*
                                    of
                                                even   a re-taking of
                                                Art History . its awesome
                                                ofttimes comic verities

        say hullo to Earnie L. for me

M 10th '77

Dear Mariko
    a
    r
    c
Hare wch i ain't seen in yrs   nonetheless
comes to mind today 1st day in M. with ah luvly
'caress' in the air following a week of belated winter's rain. —i've finally finisht the
F o n t a i n e b l e a u   D r e a m   M a c h i n e
_____

18 F r a m e s from A B o o k o f R h e t o r i c k
after more than 4 months of . . . of what? what
was it if not a form of insanity, a lustin' after the
Husk of a Dream viz the Language? etc. anyhow it's
in the hands of the Coach House Press People (Toronto)
and out of my own. like gettin' a huge fucken Octo-
pus with too many tentacles off my back. tho wasted, i
do feel lighter. that ol' Spring Hare again.

Daphne is in Toronto & havin' a great time. Kit's with
his pa Allen. & Coopey & i abide each other as we
will. meanwhile yr Grandma is comin' this weekend &
Maurice Joslin is stayin' by while he looks for a place
for himself, etc. have you written to Jan? she needs
some help viz a job. at this point if it can't be tree
planting, it cld be anything. any green stuff at all.

say 'Hi' to Bob & Others & do stay by awhile when you
do come into town.
        . . . already you're All out in the world
        & that's 'where' we'll meet each other
        for Seasons still to come

        love

                    Kenneth
dear Stan/ & Gist

    here it is 'for what it's worth' as they say:

    the   F o n t a i n e b l e a u   D r e a m   M a c h i n e
    ―――――――――――――――――――――――――――――――――
    18 F r a m e s   from   A B o o k of R h e t o r i c k

    whc: began 1/2 a yr ago as simple collages
    then became off-set lithos (27 x 17) done on Bau-Xi Press
    in an edition of 126 prints of whc 26 are signed etc.
    & any publication of the F.D.M. will have to include 126
    copies wch wld accompany the folios as a text.
    the book 'to be' is already a part of a process, and yr
    consideration of the mss. ought to include that fact. so
    it's like 500 copies/ plus 126 of which 100 are the same
    as the 500 excepting the signature bit. & 26 cld have, say,
    a different cover plus signature bit, etc.
    •

    have 2 1/4 x 2 1/4 negs for all 19 prints   (incl. cover
    & the layout wld interface print w/ texts whc i call Frames.
    or you cld use the 'real' collages if photo-process
    used can make use of them. wch ever
    •

    . . . it's a Weaving together/Shuttling back and forth of
    Divers Stories   a collaging if you will & a part of
    the Weaving has to do with how the fucken stories were woven
    right/ly or wrong/lie into the Cloth of our Language,
    our Rhetorick
                    D r e a m M a c h i n e s   (then
    even the 'bad mouthing' goin' on daily in the BC Legislature

March 27 '77

dEAR G e r r y
    e   r
    r   r
    r   e
    y r r e g
    o
    u
put a wind into Anthony.
hearing Japanese on CBC is in itself
almost poetry. our flesh bears
the 'sounds' as well as the 'colours' of
more than a given language.
tho i keep being pleasured by the company i keep
viz the english i'm apparelled in
i felt an actual loss at how little i have
surrounded myself with the language
i learned at my mother's knees.   etc.
'we'/Japanese.

                'you'd think the years

                would change some first sense

                of whatever it is—

                but it comes again and again.'

                sez B. Creeley)

keep in touch
ok?

dear Penny

      Thanks for the belated review of my
      Gig at A Space fall '73 or thereabts .   It was
      a *smoke-screen* or a *fire* .   No matter
      all those charred and embered sheets of paper
      don't have anything on them that ain't in
      mind's midden-heap .   One way or another *the stuff-*
      ings conglomerate   :   Fate must have something
      to do with it   .   And the same with a collective
      such as the Parti Quebecois   .   i mean their
      fates .   The bonfire they've lit under
      our constitution   .   From a distance 3000 miles west
      of French Canada the News of their machinations
      abhors the vacuity of our indolences.

      be into Toronto last week of May for more of
      the same

                          how's Ward's Island
                          is it above the water level
                          have the birds returned

                          remember

Dear Rosy

    loveliest & most unflappable of secretaries: considering the countless letters you have written for all of us, considering the fact that 'they' were on everybody's behalf but your own, i have decided to sit down and write a letter just for you. moreover, it won't mean anything to another member of the faculty beyond the fact of itself. if i say that i'll miss your morning smile i'll be accused of sentimentalism but who gives a shit in the face of all the other grit.

    years ago, when i was already a middle-aged fool and you were just another graduate student, i never once thot that i would be around to watch your leave-taking. i never thot i would see myself growing older in your daily surmise. if, at the turn of the century (i was going to say 'monster' century), your children decide to take up the lifetime study of art . . . i'll probably not be around to initiate them. ah, the labyrinths of time: how it scours all of our faces thoroughly. tho i would add that your wide-eyed presence had a wee part in keeping my spirit young. penticton . . . yes, i remember penticton. i fell in love there years ago and spent the summer sleeping in the middle of an orchard. my wee book, *nevertheless these eyes*, had its genesis there. in naramata. locals there have told me that it's a great place to raise a havoc of children.

    have you heard the story about the fabled secretary who was found buried under a veritable mountain of papers? when they got around to unearthing her, they found she had turned into papyrus. from the top of her head to the tip of her big toe she was inscribed with an ancient hieroglyph the authorities say pertain to a hermetic tally sheet. along with 'the world's oldest profession,' the papyrus tally sheet she turned into bespeaks of an equally ancient diversion.

    but to get back to all the letters you've typed up, addressed, stamped & posted. all those, by now inconsequential, ofttimes surrogate, letters we've embellished. not to mention all the reams of tally sheets, the assorted memos, together with the ubiquitous ring of keys, etc. what's going to become of them when they no longer pass through your agile hands? do you think they'll band together and go on strike for higher pay and longer holidays because they, in their pragmatic hearts, 'whoever' takes over from you, will change the whole demeanour of the fine arts department? why, just the other night i found myself sitting bolt upright in my bed after i had had a fiber-optics kinda nightmare in which your erstwhile successor turned out to be a parsimonious IBM computer. now, i don't know where this flurry of mad-cap ideas are coming from, but it's clear to me they point towards an unacknowledged anxiety about the whole future of free enterprise pedagogy.

    take a long lunch-break. have afternoon cat nap. watch the dawn break over okanagan lake. i'll give you a buzz when i'm passing thru. now, now that the great tall clock tower chimed in another half-hour and it's four thirty, i think i'll head home. thanks once again.

Fri. Sept. 11th, 9 pm

Dear Gladys

since we were there in Nanaimo I've been editing all the super 8 footage plus 35mm slides. how the owl-ish act-ivity of editing perplexes me even as it enthralls, etc. anyhow, sometime this winter I'll have a 'home-movie' together & you'll have to come over and stay with us and we shall have, as they say, a pre-viewing. or, if that's impossible, I'll bring it over to Nanaimo and give you a screening. but, more importantly, I've really left 'painting' behind and for the 1st time in years have some clear sense of what I must do for the next few years etc. or, as the oracle sd, '. . . let's wait and see, shall we?' this coming year is my Sabbatical and I of course mean to make the most of it, though I know how the best intentions of us mortals can go astray, etc. I mean I do have objectives of sorts and do intend to follow 'em through. Daphne is as busy as ever with the Histories of our neighbourhood, *Periodics*, Kit & family. Kit thrives, though we do have some concern for his actual size—he more than makes up for it by his acumen cum ebullience. well, here it is mid-Sept, and I'm wondering if we're goin' to have any autumn (Indian Summer), and if not, then I'm willing to settle into the grey un-ease of winter with its panoply rain giving clouds etc. this letter is simply an invitation to you to write if you feel like it. I mean, Gladys, that we should keep in touch. we owe it to each other.

        (The *Canadian Forum*/vol. IVII, no. 64, Sept. '77
        issue may interest you . . . it did me in w.
        its ofttimes grim prognostications.)

Oct. 1st '77

Dear Kazuko/ Isamu

    This is to say I am definitely coming to India
at the end of December/ early January and I want to do lots
of travelling with both of you. I mean I can't imagine
better travelling companions and am counting on meeting up
with the two of you. So—keep in touch, tell me where
I will be able to get hold of you. In other words, write,
won't you? Write from 'wherever' you happen to be and
send me directions. Like I said, I'm counting on you. I
don't of course know yet, but I am planning to stop-over in
Nihon first and fly on from there. Take care of yourselves
and write me c/o 648 Keefer Street, Vancouver B.C.

                      yours truly,

Oct. 3rd '77

D(ear D(avid/ S(tan or

    How's the *Fontainebleau Dream Machine* comin'?
    Is it, as they say, in the works, or
    merely moribund . . . ?
                   —If there's anything I kin do to
    hasten its birthday, do let me know. Like one's
    children, one worries abt a book tho there's really nothing
    one can do.   Tellin' either abt the birds and bees
    hasn't a pinch of salt to do with the Confabulations, etc.
    Didja watch the big teley production of the crazed
    Life of J. Harvey Oswald—the wafer thin line of demarcation
    between the original scenario and the teley reproduction
    must surely posit what we have all along suspected—as the
    overlapping/s of life and art, etc. Will we ever know who killed
    President John (F) Kennedy?

        Sarah—did Naropa grab you?
        David—you need the C.C. like a hole in yr head.
        yrs till the C.H. becomes M. McLuhan's publisher

Oct. 3rd '77

Dear Phyllis

—here's the G.R.B. i unintentionally took:
think of the interval i have had the book as, say, an extended
stop-over in Katmandu or Calcutta—now you can
get on the train again if you haven't already finisht
the trip by borrowing the book frm the store.
t'was a lovely visit—lovely to see you with yr wit intact.
don't know if i'll ever write a sestina—don't in fact
know the rules governing the composition of one—but if i do
yrs would have to be some kind of measure. the enclosed
Vanguard shld inform you as to the other things i've been up
to besides looking for a piece of sod i can call my own—
the futility of that act.

ah! i begin to 'see' how being 50ish is in these conservative
(dullard's) '70s   can only lead to more bureaucrats
and entertainments. hopefully i have a few loud GROWLS left in for the
Orwellian '80s. (Sung Dynasty Civil Savant Poets never had it better than us.)
will Willie Vander Zalm please stand up and be counted among the louts?

          Michael O. reads here mid-November. how
          all of us gettin' together?

          your friendly quasi
          oriental fiend

October 4th '77

—Walking thru the maze at the Lougheed Drive-in Swap Meet amazed at how the 'leavings' of all of our lives go on having a life of their own as if to spite us for disowning them. Everything imaginable that has accumulated in a hundred thousand garages, attics, basements and warehouses—everything you thought you would never use again but couldn't bring yourself to throw out—everything, including the hundreds of crumpled dollar bills and pocketfull of loose change, changing hands again and yet a-gain. Hail the tarnisht Edwardian Silver Tea Set with a broken handle. Hail the fluted porcelain tea cup without its saucer. Hail the new-minted Silver Dollars. The Nazi Medallions and rusty carburetors. The cast-iron Pincers, the Maul, the socket Wrench Sets, the Bits and Pieces of our Electronics. The cardboard cartons full of waiting-to-be-reread Books by a 1000 unheralded authors: The Impossible Logistics of a Billion Artifacts and we their makers taking it all in under this brief October sun.

—Got five pounds of ripe greengage plums for a mere dollar. Got a two-bit coat hanger to jimmy the truck door open with. When I asked the hard-boiled-looking one for a coat hanger, she said '—Yeah, and what didja do with the fucken dress on it?'—I couldn't explain how I had lockt my keys into the truck so I lied to her and said, '. . . Uh I need it to hang a coat on that I bought over there,' pointing into the crowded thoroughfare. Kurt Weill's September Song and ripe purple plums on my tongue driving along the Lougheed Highway, home.

Oct. 4th '77

My Dear Hugh:

    I imagined u doin' yr 100 push-ups after hoisting an un-
imaginably heavy bar bell high over yr head—while the
shrill Voice of Separatism echoes down Sherbrooke Street
past Westmount City Hall—right on cut thru N.D.G. to
Montreal West and hence into the suburbs, etc. Yeah—I kin
almost see u grittin' yr teeth while crackin' yr knuckles
while Ideology makes us artists anarchistic again.

    Richard Halliday on Thur—he sd that the Museum Art School
was definitely finisht for good. And the last time I was in
Montreale I couldn't get into the Hermitage Show 'cause the line
was a block long and I thot to myself I won't stand in line
'cause even if I did get in I couldn't see a thing because of
the Throngs . . . It would have been neat to greet Matisse. And hail
a Constructivist, a Russian Molinari, for instance. Met Moli at
his retrospective here—his unflappable arrogance was a refreshing
divertimento. And Louis Dudek read here. I, for old angst's
sake, attended and tho I found myself, almost despite myself, a
little embarrasst by his homilies, we later had a good chat.

    The enclosed VANGUARD should disclose 'something' of what
I've been about.

                    This wee note announces the small fact that
                    your once upon a time steadfast friend is your Pacific
                    coast friend, yet. Say 'hullo' to yr mother for
                    me.—It's the Juice of our CHROMATIC ANTICS I keep
                    talkin' abt.

Oct. 4th '77

Dear Sheila/ Wilfred
    Sheila

autumn upon us. blah. and parimpsest.
the peregrinations.
            we're both hard at it:
            both brim-filled with the work of our *days*.
            astonisht by the remorseless
            succession of them here on the verge of
            another rain forest winter.

    the enclosed *Vanguard* shld brief you on
    my doings.
            (Sheila—do yu think R.Turner's Mother wld
    continue to wonder abt her Son?
    _
    Daphne asks: whether either or both of you have
    any prose pieces for her magazine *Periodics*?
    _

            a seldom met nonetheless old friend
            sd 'shit the '70s is like a 10 yr
            hiatus.' adding, 'it's mostly nostalgia
            in other words bullshit.'

  INDIA—on my mind
time (again) to look around to see
what I can find
Finders / Keepers / Losers / Weepers

Oct. 7th '77

Dear Dennis

apropos the inexorable passing-of-time: yes, it does seem to go 'faster' than before, almost a rushing past. now—whether or not it keeps on going faster till it leaves one, as it were, 'breath-less' at the end—i at this moment don't of course know as i do know in my bones that my body does seem to move somewhat slower than when i was, say, thirty two and i did have the thought that i really could move faster than most men moved, moving as most men do in parallel grooves despite their particular 'bents' or whether or not they have let themselves go because the metaphoric 'brink of consciousness' is where all the grooves end. i for one can't speak of or for those other grooves in the so-called other worlds beyond this rotund one i've been given to enliven as best i can.

      (glad you askt me—.

speaking of Time's passages, i'm reminded of one of our intermittent preoccupations—our good friend T. T. of whom it could be said that he persists in our everyday conscience and that small fact acts as a brake on time. through his work he has enter'd a timeless continuum i would name the ghost of history, our ubiquitous monitor of what seems ofttimes to be sheer madness, if not folly. fee-fi-fo-fum—'where' but from within our very psyches do the legendary ones step forth from? to wit, watching a Donald Sutherland playing Norman Bethune on CBC proposes something about us as erstwhile Canucks that the true blue Indian natives among us couldn't really give a shit about.

—if i ever get to Ottawa again (given the fact i've only been there about a dozen times in my life) i'll surely stay with you, despite the fact that i do seem to have less time for kids no matter their gentleness. my own 3 daughters have often said—'what do you really know about us you've hardly seen us and now we're almost grown-ups, etc.' come to think about it, i seem to have not had the time to see myself as i really am. Harold Town comin' to town to talk up a storm about his and D. S.'s T. T. . . . i'll be there to lend an alert ear.

      enclosed *VANGUARD* shows what i am up to
      besides photography

Oct. 18 '77

Dear Editor/s
    at McClelland & Stewart

Re: the Silcox/ Town Book on Tom Thomson.

Could someone who has been interested in the Group of 7 cum T. T. for a good many years—/ someone who counts himself their heir—/ who can't afford the $30.00 be given a review copy? For what it's worth, I have also been involved in T.T. at least since the early '70s (to wit, my letters to the editor of *artscanada* about the 7) & I want all those luvly colour repros to hang more of my prose on. Their text—I take to simply be the latest installment of an ongoing work-in-progress, to which I will add my own chapters.

So much has been written about our hero that it all begins to sound like a collective mythos everyone has had a hand in the shaping of. No matter—

                Ask John Newlove whether I ought to have one.
                              Yrs truly,

Dear G.G.

    T.B. and I have been working like minimum-wage slaves
viz 356 Powell Street. Our 'place' has been renamed
'4 x 5 Studio.' Mick came by one afternoon when
we were naming and helped us make up our minds. Otherwise, it's been 'clear mountain' among other names.

    Al gave a moving concert at UBC/ Michael de Courcy got
it together for him. Distill'd passion, someone
called it. Abt the only comment I heard otherwise from
several quarters was that he was altogether too
too cool. Madness and frenzy viz the ebullient '60s
misst. Like Barnum sd, 'You can't make everyone happy 'cause
there ain't enough freaks in the world.'

    Yesterday, a false SPRING DAY with that suppliant balm
in the air. Everyone took something off. Today
another drench—this time with vengeance. Tell whom-
ever that Daphne and I'll be in Toronto cum mid-
April.

> Now they're goin' to be hauling massive
> iceberg up to Saudi Arabia from the South Pole
> and one short extraordinarily robust son
> of the Rising Sun is gonna dog sled his way
> all by himself to the North Pole. Mean-
> while the S.S. (satellite shit) we sent up
> keeps shitting on us.

                  What news?

Dear Phyllis

    Fra Lip-o Lipi the luvly precursor to-
gether with Fra Angelico and Giotto of the High
Renaissance comes to mind for no reason at
all (or so it seems) except to chime yr name.
I've had nothin' but HURRAHS for the F.D.M. but then
they've come from mostly dear friends.   Otherwise
it might just as well 'lie in the folded slit'
under a Canuck's tongue. No matter, it sez
more than I had thot to say and less than I wanted.
For whatever . . . it sez that 50 yrs is itself
but a surmise. How are you? I mean that and more
of course. Didja ever see Irv Layton on t.v?
He comes on like a sawed-off light-heavy weight old
testament prophet who has shadow-boxed with
his own self far too long.   Gross is I suppose also
a place to be: etc.

Dear Nancy Ryley and Peter Mellen

'The Passionate Canadians'—BAH! They bored me stiff as, say, any Canuck feels when the word 'passion' gets mentioned . You've pusht the well-known facts as far as they can go without once breaking the mythos/ mould is abt as far as I can go to comment on the show. As for the words you've put into Harry Adaskin's mouth or, for that matter, A. Y.'s, Harris's, or Thomson's—they come out sounding like a simpleton's art history cum northern romance. Their pompous mouthings made me wince. After the ugh! un-passionate Canadians, there'll be no further need for such aggrandizements to prove we're hardly Canucks, even French-Canadians. The notion is that 'if you don't recreate them, you lose the callit credibility of a myth.' Why doncha ask the young buck from southern Italy or a prairie-born Indian not to mention the Georgia Street kung-fu expert where can we go from here? Rubric: don't let the old-fashioned narrative with a cast of fictive characters con your language into platitudes.

p/s Didcha ever see Jose Ferrer on his knees playing Toulouse Lautrec in Technicolour? Or, earlier, Charles Laughton playing the immortal Rembrandt? How abt Andrew Wyeth playing illustrious father N.C.? I mean the aforementioned mythos/ mould—How to S-M-A-S-H it to let the 'ongoing' in.

Yours,
for an improved tranquillizer

p/s—And a further thot frm the horse's mouth, a painter's life ain't more exciting than anyone else's—the real events all go on in his head and into his canvases. Get in behind your eyes and see thru them.

Bingo died in Spain. as far as i know he
never read Lorca or talked to Velasquez's dwarfs
in the Prado. he died on the 18th   green
with his toupee intact. Bob Hope, Dorothy Lamour
and Rudolph the red nose reindeer were
among a handful of guests at his Hollywood funeral.
imagine an irish-americun lad from the mid-west
singin' his lachrymose heart out with some
of the ol' blarney of a Barry Fitzgerald and
you've got an authentic slice of Hollywood
folklore. meanwhile, ol' blue eyes keeps his chin
tucked in as all the accolades smother his
velvet purr. somewhere just below the heights of
Mount Olympus and its pantheon of gods i'd
place the whole roster of Hollywood stars who danced
kicked, fucked, sang, laughed, and made love
all through my feverish adolescence. ah! even today
they can raise an occasional hair by their
adroit re-enactments on cabala-vision. someone sd
Bingo's hitchin' a ride to Mandalay. star of wonder
star of Saturday nights. which of all the stars
will i let woo me tonight? hullo, Dolly Parton. how
are you, honey-child? there i go, again . . .

A Brief Letter to the Publisher of A Short Sad Book

Dear Mr. Siegler and Associates:

My name is Samuel Chan. Assoc. Prof. Chan to my students and associates. My father who played Charlie Chan's obedient son left Hollywood (alias U.S.A.) when Warner Oland's credibility ran away with him. I won't speak of his cleft palate or his lifelong opium habit . . . this being a short sad letter. It was during those awful days when the Japanese were laying siege to China that my father whose name was Samuel became a Canadian. If I seem to be rambling, it's because I feel that some sort of personalism will help to establish my true sympathies. I attended Strathcona School and learned my A.B.C.s on Hastings Street. Later I went to U.B.C. at my father's behest because he wanted more than an inscrutable Chinese detective for his children's legacy. It may be of some interest to you that I was in Mr. Bowering's class which met twice a week with the renowned oriental scholar Dr. Kato who lectured us on Buddhist Metaphysics.—So you see that I have my own, however peculiar, qualifications to address his *Short Sad Book*. To make a long letter short, I recently received his book by post here, in Hong Kong, where I am the headmaster of a private girls school. Imagine my pleasure when I fell into Mr. Bowering's adroit words! And the very deep pleasure of the pleasure he felt manhandling the Canadian Mosaic. I read the book in a single sitting and immediately fell into my memories of laying about on the cropped grass at U.B.C. trying to get a handle, as it were, on Canadian esoterica. Even then Mr. Bowering seemed to be on his way. Please convey to him my deep pleasure. For what it is worth, you could mention to him that my class of 16 year olds unanimously thought it was the best fairy-tale they had ever heard about canada. (Forgive me for not Capitalizing the 'c' but we orientals don't have a sign for them.) Further, that several of them would like to have his autograph and have opted to immigrate to Canada upon graduation.

This is a much longer letter than I intended.

Please tell Mr. Bowering that I once kissed the hem of Miss Claire Trevor's lacey petticoat. For some reason I am sure he would approve.

Dear Kyoko

whata pleasure to hear frm you.
i spent a long afternoon going through the Kuniyoshi
catalogue. in the early '50s i thought
seriously abt going to the Art Students League in N.Y.
to study with him but we were too poor for
me to do that. Yasuo, you and i make 3 generations
who have at least 2 things in common: 1/our
love of/for art. 2/ a common tho utterly particular
Japanese heritage.   everything else abt all 3
of us seems to be quite different.
i don't know when i shall get to Japan again but
the next time i shall visit you in Sendai.

thank you for remembering me, tho i am a bit embarrassed by
the fact that i did so little for you in Banff.

yrs sincerely

Dear Penny
        To fill in the silences with—*this*.
        Remember Richard Turner? Otherwise, everything is,
as they say, in the works, including self.
'What works' and 'what doesn't' and what's the limits
of 'grace' continues to plague. How about you?
Daphne is, as usual, up to her neck in you-name-it and
she's there going full tilt. So's Kit who is
gettin' his Halloween costume on and can hardly wait
for Tricks and Treats. . . . I haven't had my fill
either. Which thoughts turn into a peanut butter cookie
Daphne has just brought down, sayin' 'there won't be
any left,' etc.
                        Harold Town and his side-kick David
                        Silcox here to flog Tom Thomson. Who woulda
                        thot T/T would become such an industry?

        How's Ward's
        Island—
        are its denizens
        thwarted?

        Cheers
                        Roy/ Daphne
                        send Halloween Greetings

Some thoughts concerning
the proposed 2nd B.C. Almanac
for Lorraine Monk &
the N.F.B. Still Division

At least since the 1st B.C. Almanac (h) (1970), the art of photography, by which i mean both the original print & its varied forms and the host of reproductions in the form of occasional prints as they occur in sundry magazines, plus the Photo Book viz Aperture and the N.F.B.'s own photo books, have come in to their own, at least in terms of sheer quantity. Not to mention of course the proliferation of photographic exhibitions everywhere. Ah! the ubiquitous eye of the camera—how it pries into everything.

Anyhow, it is our belief that the 1st B.C. Almanac (h) needs to be followed up with another in 1978. It is our belief that changes have occurred in the momentum of B.C. —the lower mainland in particular—and that it is the business of those of us who take pictures to see if we can probe the changes and make them apparent in our pictures. It is this *probing* that we want to do thru the sponsorship of the N.F.B.

Ok then, here's a few ideas as to the form of the B.C. Almanac:
1/ We still like the idea/s of a series of books plus a serious exhibition.
2/ Both book/s and exhibition ought to be viz image/s & process—innovative. There should be no need to stress that what continues to be commercially feasible is, in the matter of innovation, not our cup of tea.

We would prefer to do our probing in *colour* this time instead of black & white (in so far as it's affordable). We have thought abt using or through the media facilities of the N.F.B. having access to a colour Xerox machine to do a limited edition of colour books derived frm slides. The exhibition could also be done through the xerox process. Or—and this is also a serious possibility—that we work with the new CIBACHROME process and put both book/s & exhibition together that way.

We want to do our various probes in colour. Colour xerox, say, if possible. Beginning with slides we would—if it is possible—rent or lease a colour Xerox machine and process all of our own images, then correlate and have them bound into small format books. By as many artists/photographers as we can afford. The exhibition could be made up of colour Xerox images—sufficient numbers of them to make up whole walls. Or the exhibition's images could be done in CIBACHROME: a simple colour process that many photographers are already into.

As it was with the 1st so it ought to be with the 2nd Almanac: by which we mean 1/ small photo books by several photographers using either colour Xerox or /& cibachrome. Their images to be a probe into the urban/rural landscape of whatever is of deep interest to each of them. It has to be image/s of B.C. now. 2/ Investigating photography rather than the isolate image proposes a line of preferences. 3/ The participants can but need not include those who were among previous participants. So that our first job would be to find out who is doing what and gathering together a group of photographers then to outline a plan (the working idea of B.C. Almanac).

                                                    c/o de Courcy/ Kiyooka
                                                    October 20 '77

Dear Lorraine Monk

   Apropos Michael's phone-call all abt:

   A brand new *Now* edition of B/C Almanac   or callit what we have been calling it the
   B. C. Hand Book simply. Our Notion is that we think the time has come to take another look at ourselves & where we stand—together with the distances we have all covered
   since the late '60s / early '70s. In other words we think it's time to do something abt the
   ambiences we've all lived tru and how they inflect our pictures of, at least, ourselves .
                          —Here's some of the Notions we've knockt abt:

   1/   Like its illustrious predecessor, the new edition should comprise as many artists/
          photographers as *the budget* enables—allowing for the ubiquitous fact of our
          gross national inflation which will affect every aspect of the overall costs .

   2/   That we be given complete autonomy in the overall organization of the *B. C.
          Hand Book* which (initially) would consist in getting in touch with as many pho-
          tographers & their works as possible. Then after we have made our choices we
          would get together with them and work out the actual format together. We would
          be the go/ between with the printers/binders etc.

   3/   Speaking of format/s, we're excited by the possibility of using both black & white
          and colour. That each page be printed 'loose leaf' fashion and tippt into a spe-
          cially designed 3 ring binder. We like the notion of each photographer's book/s
          and/or photos being interchangeable. There should be room for other people's
          pics also. (The above is simply one of the formats we've talkt abt—it's the one we
          like best at this moment.)

   4/   Concomitantly, there ought to be (as before) a large scale Exhibition comprising
          all of the book/s plus relevant 'other' info. Or it could be a context onto itself, an
          exhibition made up of wholly different processes/ideas/images that are rooted in
          the same sources—a whole series of Cibachrome walls for instance.

          Our deadline wld be next September for both the book/s and show (assuming, of
          course, we can begin soon).

   5/   Try mouthing *B. C. Hand Book* and 'be' while you 'see' it make sense. Again,
          we like the sound/sense of it—it's our favourite at this very moment.

Over the telephone this a.m. (Oct. 15th) Michael sez he's been thinking abt the Proposal all weekend. —How what we seem to be agreed on is a kind of photo journal but definitely not the old hype, the Time/ Life/ Look magazine sort of television's equivalents, the dramatic heavies. None of that stuff. Rather it's the plain, unadorned photos that can speak to Anybody abt their own real lives as they live them. Something like that. Something simply underfoot or looking up—in the ambient air. We've been talking abt all of these things and it occurred to us that 'journals,' 'notebooks,' 'serials,' 'diaries,' or 'log books' are formats which can hold both the intimate idea/image together with the broadest words/ vistas and that these formats propose an equivalent of what we want to see. There ought to be space enough for the timely photo & the words attendant on their taking or afterwards.

We have both had many occasions to go thru the 1st B. C. Almanac (h) and, even as we both have our reservations abt some aspect or other, we feel it's a telling document of its time and place. Now, whatever form the 2nd one takes, it ought to be at least as relevant in, say, 1984.

.

Meanwhile, we intend to go on talking it up and assuming a 50/50 chance.—We shall look into all of the different aspects inc. 'costs' and 'processes.' How abt 1/ meeting with us abt it? 2/ or, if that's unnecessary, phoning us when you have a decision. 3/ Be 'challenged' by us who are out west.

Yours —

Michael de Courcy   Roy Kiyooka

Feb. 1st '78

(Artist in Residence, U. of M.)

Dear Michael:

—April 17/'78   Ok, in fact, perfecto.   Didja see
the . . . Anniversary Issue of *Saturday Night* with all of
those ads from past issues? Well there was one ad
advertising JAP CIGARS yet! Talk abt yr Turkish
blends and all that kinda exoticism   .   I thot only the Nips
did that kinda thing viz Ghana Black Chocolate Bars   .   Anyhow
I'm going to the Investiture for the Order of Canada and
Ottawa is paying my way so you're off the hook that way. I'll
take the $125.00 plus meals and accommodation for a one
(long) day workshop by wch i mean a morning afternoon and
evening session with not more than 12 people. If it has to
run over into 2 days (say with another group) then it's
another $125.00 for that occasion. Apropos size/s of
group/s—7 or 8 is ideal with 12 to 15 maximum. Larger than
that and it becomes a lecture or a talking-to wch I don't want
to have to do.

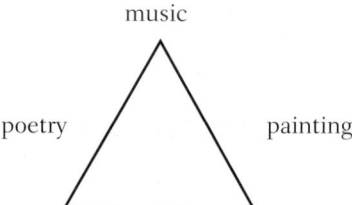

: A Triad corresponding to EARS/ MOUTH/ EYES
their intricate Interface as the Theme for the WORKSHOP.

Keep me informed.
                         Sincerely,

Feb. 7th '78

Dear Geoffrey:

Apropos my phone call last year: Michael and I are applying for a *short term grant* to help us get the B.C. Hand Book together. We've been having weekly sessions with varied photographers with the intent of making a survey of what's available to us for the book and exhibition. Concomitantly, we have been researching what is possible viz 'costs,' 'design,' 'production,' and 'format.' The application covers the period thru till April 31st when we will be on the N.F.B. payroll.

Apropos our phone call: As participants won't be chosen until this survey and research have been completed (April), there won't be any short-term grant applications from them till then or a little later, but do anticipate the possibility.

We're both excited by what the prospects are and hopefully we'll come up with something worth looking at!

(Chinese New Year, the year of the horse)
2.10 AM
         yours sincerely

         (for Michael de Courcy and I)

Feb. 7th '78

Dear George :

    Apropos 'arts one' and all those alternatives
I'm going to stick with the B.F.A. O I've thot
abt it (have in fact be askt several times) and again
and yet again I have finally sd 'no' —as I do
once again. Bed-rock proves to be I'm much more interested
in the specifics of callit 'art' as against the
liberal approach wch has become more than ever platitudinous.
    Viz intellecto/   cum knowledge.
Anyhow, cld you inform the 'arts one' people of my decision?
And do let us get together soon.

        yrs sincerely,

        Roy K. Kiyooka B.F.A.

It's the year of the Horse and
I'm feeling like a drencht unicorn w. hoof and mouth
disease. Given the fact of a dreary Feb.
I is Ok and then some.

Feb. 12th '78

Richard: where, where shall we start—

    or rather 'where' shall i begin to acknowledge
    the 2 of you and all the luvly moments
    we shared together.   Your wedding was one of
    the late '60s highlights.   Wonder . . . what's
    happened to Jill?   For that matter, i wonder what's
    become of that R.S.phd. and Quebecois
    politics during the heyday of Bourassa, not to mention
    Eric Kierans.   Inexorably . . . *time*, as they say, passes,
    indeed 'surpasses' our comprehension.   Need i add that what's happening there
    ofttimes seems like the carryings on of one of
    them there foreign countries an
    N.A. Ethiopia or is it Belfast.   No matter that
    we're flanks of the same piece of sod.
    (3000 miles and a formidable mountain range apart is
    a metaphor for the breadth of time/space
    this letter comes to you across.)   Where, where
    shall these words lead me—if not to
    your door-step anytime i'm in Montreale? Headin'
    into my 52nd yr.   i've got much to be,
    as they say, thankful for.

Vicki: we must connive (if it's necessary)
    to do another performance together.
                      Daphne sends her love

              luv

Feb. 21st '78

Dear Luke:

Apropos of Michael and I and Jo-Anne and our hasty meeting viz the N.F.B. sponsored B.C. Hand Book and the V.A.G.'s photograph show: the 'issues' of our collaborating with you also bear further exploration. Lorraine Monk has already said that the N.F.B. (Stills Division) didn't really mind if the 'exhibition' of the H.B. happened in Vancouver 1st, then Ottawa and/ or elsewhere. The Book was the 1st priority. *We can go on from there.* Michael conveyed the substance of Jo-Anne's message viz the V.A.G.'s solution for their own Photo Show. We both feel that you're about to shortchange yourself . . . etc. even as we recognize that it's none of our biz.

Would the 2 of U like to get together and
talk the whole matter thru?

                              For the B.C. Hand Book
                              yours sincerely,

Dear Martha Hayes

> Michael de Courcy in conversation with Lorraine Monk last week viz How We Stood With the N.F.B. re The B.C. Hand Book and other matters subsequently told me that you had taken over and that we would have to write you a detailed letter outlining our project involving a comprehensive take on 'the Lower Mainland of South Western Canada' with the emphasis on Vancouver where all 13 Camera Artists do hail from and other more measurable matters such as a List of the C.A.'s., together with Costs of Publication, Format, Exhibition Details, and a Progress Report of What's (as it were) Been All Along Happening so that you can take up the so called threads and get us going even as we are already off to a fast start viz the 1st Gathering of all 13 Participants and Ice Scream last Sunday afternoon and the enthusiasm that got generated viz that old homily 'the right idea at the appropriate moment' etc. All of which proposes the possibility of a unique take on the range of photography cum image which for C.A.'s. like us is really what it's all about. I mean the energy that William Blake spoke so truthfully abt when he sd 'Energy is the only life. . . . Energy / is Eternal Delight.' Speaking for both of us, I am packing as much info into even this intro as possible for yr edification and not the least your puzzlement and delight. We—Mike and I—speaking for the other 11—give you our unqualified assurance of carrying out this unique venture with as much aplomb and gusto, not to mention a knife and a camera as any comparable group of whatever vocation you care to name, including the rank and file union worker or the board of directors of a multinational corporation an EXXON or a Mitsubishi. And while we're into politics, I wanta say that Joe Clark saying that he stood to Pierre Trudeau as a western frontiersman stands to a Wall Street Dude was one of the most notable utterances I've heard lately. Which trifle brings up the theme of this letter and the following detailed proposal and progress report:
>
> > (See file on B.C. Hand Book or Lorraine Monk viz our Correspondence plus long-distance phone calls. Then, refer to the Press Release of our project and note the details carefully.)
>
> We are enclosing xeroxes just in case of unnecessary delay or confusion. What follows purports to tell abt what has been happening in/ between times. In and thru these several months—we've held a few guidelines like How the task to hand is to show forth our vision of Beautiful B.C. without all of the tourist claptrap so that that vision can then stand up beside the sentimentalities of the other and that we do have a polis of which we are the watchers as much as we are ordinary citizens like everyman also is. That we are inclined even biased towards camera artists rather than, say, trad-type silver printers or so called documentaries and agility, if not always inventiveness, both behind the camera and in the darkroom is part and parcel of the challenge and that both camera and enlarger together with the chemistry and papers are nothing but the

post-industrial mode of ordinary tools like lead pencils or satellites and that we had as it were an obligation to look intently at the very ground under our feet and see the wonderment of the bewildering multifoliated world anew.

We approve of that luvly old homily that sez there's nothing new under the sun but the constant renewal of all intransigent things as they are come upon. Or words to that effect. Hopefully this insistence upon our seriousness doesn't lead you on. I mean we also want 'wit' and the clarity of 'geometry' not to mention the awesome breadth of the heave and heft of the sea and its attendant ofttimes breath-taking silences. And in and thru our many many meetings we have held onto the notion of a collective but nonetheless singular undertaking in which all decisions thru-out the collaboration wld be made by the participants and that even the very format and the subsequent exhibition wld be shaped that way. For ourselves, we want to push this possibility of an idiosyncratic collective vision as far as we can. At this moment, for instance, even the name of the book is as it were up for grabs. Someone sd they thot it dull and suggested offhandedly Vancouver Corrosives and we talkt a bit abt that and so it goes on. We see ourselves as simply being among the active participants together with the task of being caretakers, sorters and hopefully catalysts. The enclosed list shld inform you abt those we had the occasion to meet and look at their works and those we have gathered together to work along with. We held open house every Thursday for abt 6 weeks and saw a lot of stuff for which we were and continue to be thankful for—it enabled us to have further confirmation of our parameters etc. If our 1st gathering means anything it must surely mean that our choices will prove to be exciting. We do want no diminishment of the personal together with the putting of that singularity into a larger collective vision. Dear Martha, even as I am typing this I am re-inventing the gist of many hours of intense conversation and so it must be that the B.C. Hand Book or whatever it will get named must itself be at all points a tension. As for the photographs we will take during April May and June, they will have their occasion to speak in and thru themselves when that time comes. Tomorrow is the 1st day of Spring and here it's heralded by the pink blossoms of cherry trees thruout the city as much as by, say, the added spring in everyone's step as they leave off the shells of their winter clothing and the long night's shadow falling across the peaks of the lions.

For The Gathering of 14 Camera Artists on Sunday April 2nd '78:
_____

3 Takes on a Working Script for the (new) B.C. Almanac. The Intent of these working scripts—to provoke all of us towards whatever clarity we can get a handle on for the sake of the book .

1st Take Begin with a map of the city. Locate your house (domicile) (room/s) (abode) (residence/s) on it. Mark off your neighbourhood together with your typical movements in and thru it. Note the movements from your house thruout the neighbourhood, outwards. Their directions and where these movements lead to. Think about all of these movements on your map as 'points-of-interest' along which you can focus in on a cup, a face, or a tree in the landscape, as you happen upon them. As you make it all up at home or in the street. As you attend to the negs in your darkroom. Etc.

> The Body, equally an abode. The whole or parts of it a domicile. Its meridians focused in on. The Body itself as a Landscape with all of its variegated textures, probed. Etc.

2nd Take Each of the 14 Camera Artists to photograph 15 Aspects of The City and its Landscape   viz

5 Elements	5 Senses	5 Organs
Ether	Sight	Eyes
Fire	Hearing	Ears
Air	Touch	Hands
Water	Taste	Mouth
Earth	Smell	Nose

3rd Take Each of the 14 Camera Artists to photograph 15 Others. Hence a profile (portrait) of 225 or more people. In other words, an almanac of faces, features, expressions, etc.

•

Further: That we all get together on Sunday April 29th at 2pm to have a first look at whatever photos have been taken and to renew our terms of reference to each other and the book and exhibition. That we keep in touch with each other individually as the need to do so arises.

for 1 4 C a m e r a s
_____

                            (from now on . . .
              —let the eye do the *talking* . let all
              the talking we do lead to a slender-stemmed *flower*
              water to step into the aperture-of-light   to
              delight *the tides* of our *eyes* and *tongues*

                     breath and image of/ abt the pacific littoral

Paul Blackburn

        BRING a leaf to me
        just a leaf just a
        spring leaf, an
        april leaf
        just
              come

        Blue sky
        never mind
        Spring rain
        never mind
        Reach up and
        take a leaf and
            come
        just come

Francis Ponge
'The relationship between man and object is not at all limited to possession or use. No, that would be too simple. It's much worse.'
'Objects are outside the soul, of course; and yet, they are also ballast in our heads. The relationship is thus in the accusative.'

Frank Meadow Sutcliffe
'It seems to me that the long and short of natural photography is that, as everyone sees differently, so some like to make their photographs sharp everywhere, others just the opposite. Living in this age of freedom, I do not consider myself bound by any rules . . . Some people . . . can see nothing and care for nothing in a photograph but the detail . . . They take out a pocket microscope, and, placing the eye to one end and the photograph at the other, exclaim either "How beautifully sharp!" or "Why, it isn't sharp at all!" Such people do not think it right to take photographs except when the air is clear, and look upon the photographer as a fool if he sets up his camera when nature is veiled with fog, or blurred with rain, or almost lost in the shades of evening. . . .'

Wynn Bullock
'. . . Every speck of matter, every idea, is a space-time event. We cannot experience anything or

conceive of anything that exists outside of space-time. Just as experience precedes all awareness and creative expression, the visual language of our photographs should ever more strongly express the fourth-dimensional structure of the real world.'

water/ words

>What is it to see?

>A dart more acute than the tongue
>the course from one excess to another
>from the most profound to the most acute
>from the most somber to the most pure

>a bird of prey

>> Philippe Jaccottet

From the 1870s, the comment of a visitor to the factory of the inventor:
'M. Carpentier can be proud of his work; he has realized his dream: to produce a camera of extreme simplicity and irreproachable construction, to obtain images of a sharpness and definition such that the final enlargement may furnish perfect results to give the scientist a powerful working tool, the amateur a faithful travelling companion with which he can keep forever charming souvenirs of the countries he has travelled through, to furnish to all a means of fixing fleeting images which, up to now, have been preserved by thought alone.'

.

Brassai
'I make no comments with my camera. My camera sees all different kinds of people and with impartiality fixes them on the negative. Here they are the Apaches, the male and female homosexuals, the eccentrics. Whatever I see and I feel about people, the camera sees . . .'

'To keep from going stale, you must forget your professional outlook and rediscover the virginal eye of the amateur. Do not lose that eye; do not lose your own self. The great Japanese artists changed their names and their status ten or twenty times in their ceaseless efforts to renew themselves. It is not right that the originality of that first vision should become a trick of the trade, a formula a thousand times repeated.'

.

Tristan Tzara   (especially for Michael   his photographic prints)
'A form plucked from a newspaper and introduced in a drawing or picture incorporates a morsel of everyday reality into another reality constructed by the spirit. The contrast between materials which the eye is capable of transposing almost into a tactile sensation, gives a new dimension to the picture in which the object's weight, set down with mathematical precision by symbols, volume and density, its very taste on the tongue, its consistency, brings before us a unique reality in a world created by the force of the spirit and the dream.'

.

Ben Shahn
'Now, my knowledge of photography was terribly limited. I thought I could ask Walker Evans to show me what to do, and he had made a kind of indefinite promise. One day when he was going off to the Caribbean and I was helping him into his taxi, I said, "Walker, remember your promise to show me how to photograph?" He said, "Well, it's very easy, Ben. F-9 on the sunny side of the street. F-4.5 on the shady side of the street. For 1/20th of a second hold your camera steady." And that was all. This was the only lesson I ever had.'

Henri Cartier-Bresson
'You have to forget yourself. You have to be yourself and you have to forget yourself so that the image comes much stronger—what you want and what you see—if you get involved completely in what you are doing. And not thinking. Ideas are very dangerous. You must think all the time, but when you photograph, you aren't trying to push a point or prove something. You don't prove anything. It comes by itself.'

Jack Welpott
'. . . I would look at every aspect of you—the light on your cheekbone, the way your finger is curled up against your cheek, the lines on your forehead. Maybe when you were a child your mother stared at you with that intensity, but you've probably never been looked at like that since.'

Alfred Stieglitz
'I am the moment. I am the moment with all of me and anyone is free to be the moment with me. I want nothing but anyone. I have no theory about what a moment should bring. I am not attempting to be in more than one place at a time. I am merely the moment with all of me.'

Wynn Bullock
'The camera is not only an extension of the eye but the brain. . . .'
'Instead of using the camera only to reproduce objects, I want to use it to make what is invisible to the eye—visible.'
'To make a photograph of the human body express something more than mere physical nakedness or suggestive sex, one has to look for qualities that make the human body a natural and beautiful part of nature. The nakedness of a body is as natural as the nakedness of a tree. . . .'
'The qualities of the form of the figure, the qualities of the woman, if she be a woman, these are the things I search for and try to relate to a natural environment that has qualities of light and forms that make the figure and the background one in meaning. . . .'

Harry Callahan
'. . . I am interested in relating the problems that affect me to some set of values that I am try-

ing to discover and establish as being my life. I want to discover and establish them through photography. . . .'

'The photographs that excite me are photographs that say something in a new manner; not for the sake of being different, but ones that are different because the individual is different and the individual expresses himself . . .'

'I wish that more people felt that photography was an adventure the same as life itself and felt that their individual feelings were worth expressing.'

.

Gary M. Dault
'The truly advance-guard photograph now exists in all of our minds only as a perpetual possibility.'

.

Robert Cummings
'Our split-second sensory gaps are well-travelled thorough-fares for the traffic in illusion.'

.

Susan Sontag
'I came to realize that I wasn't writing about photography so much as I was writing about modernity, about the way we are now. The subject of photography is a form of access to contemporary ways of feeling and thinking. And writing about photography is like writing about the world.'

'The powers of photography have in effect de-Platonized our understanding of reality, making it less and less plausible to reflect upon our experience according to the distinction between images and things, between copies and originals. It suited Plato's derogatory attitude toward images to liken them to shadows—transitory, minimally informative, immaterial, impotent co-presences of the real things that cast them.'

.

water/ words

>
> the rivers of afternoon
> flowing about you as you
> move   .   stop, standing
> afterward in my bathroom
> naked among the young plants
> in the green light singing
> softly to yourself
>
>   Paul Blackburn

March 3rd, '79

Dear David & Sarah:

these days . . . things like *the movie you must see* keep whizzin' by me. like by the time i've got time to attend it's moved on to another town. but there's a difference which is that—i seem not to care to have missed it 'cause there'll be another act in town, etc. . . . the last movie that brought me to my knees (so to speak) was a jap movie titled *The Island* abt a family who lived on a small island & had to go get their water daily from the mainland via boat & get it a bucket at a time up the hill to their home & garden & the gravity of earth-born rituals, etc. . . . almost fondly, i remember bawlin' my fool head off. to wit—whatever t/v's hype happens to be abt . . . i ain't ever been brought to my knees viz the artifices of the melodrama on all 26 channels.

14 March '79

His Excellency the Governor General of Canada, Mr. Ed Schreyer
Rideau Hall
OTTAWA

Dear Mr. Schreyer

I am writing on behalf of 13 Cameras (Vancouver, B.C.) to ask if you would do us the honour of opening our exhibition on 3 May at the Stills Division, National Film Board of Canada gallery, Ottawa.

13 Cameras have been collaborating for the past year and a half on two large, inter-related photographic projects:

>   1)   the publication, co-incidental with the exhibition, of a 250-page photo-book titled, we think aptly, '13 Cameras, Vancouver, B.C., 1979'—a massive 'waking,' 'walking,' silver-bromide 'dream' of, we'd like to think, 13 typical Canucks.

>   2)   the exhibition itself—221 photographic pages (17 pages by each of the 13 Cameras).

The enclosed poster for our exhibition at the Vancouver Art Gallery, plus the article in *Vanguard* magazine, covering the show and the politics of collaboration, will further inform you of our brand of Canadian (West Coast) presences. Further information is available through me—hence us—and through the agencies of the National Film Board.

We would be greatly honoured if you would agree to open our exhibition, and we shall look forward to your reply. May you be capable of affirming the bequest of 'those who wish for a better country.'

Yours sincerely

Roy K. Kiyooka
O.C. for 13 Cameras
encs.

dear Martha:

>my 16 page sequence (& they are that, that is, they posit
a photo-narrative) is provisionally titled Auguries of a
Parking Meter Marking Time for a Thin Dime. it's abt a
neighbourhood & its divers manifestations/ it's also abt
'time,' the timeliness of images, of all our images, amongst
all images, in time. tho' ostensibly a part of this book—
it's also a small part of a much larger narrative, a photo/
novel i'm in the act of putting together. further, there's
an ongoing narrative (words) running across the top &
the bottom of the page which will be both accompaniment &
its own telling. 'these' words are being written, even now.

March 21st '79
356 Powell Street / 4x5 Studio
Vancouver, B.C.

Dear Martha Langford,

Here, for what it's worth, *my intro of sorts to the book, 13 Cameras/ Vancouver*. It's what got sorted out of 40 pages of notes & other digressions, etc. Being, among other things, the oldest member of the 13 (like 30 yrs older than Paul Wong, the youngest of us), plus the fact of my being one of the 3 original members of the original Almanac to be a part of this one, plus or minus the fact that I'm the only one who seems to think of himself as (also) a writer, & you know why I got the job.

The other (xerox'd) page consists of a list-of-titles to each photo, or set of photos, as they occur in the book: More as tex(t)ure, or the sound of—it must be—our very 'nouns,' & 'verbs' as aural equivalents & a kind of aggregate poetry, tho its pretext was a table of contents.

At this moment in time (Ides of March) our book is in the hands of Brock/Webber, our printer, and abt our only angst is will they get it printed for us in time to take copies with us to Ottawa & other points East, plus, *what can we do next—* given how we seem to have sorted out a lot of the hang-ups & could really do something ambitious?

We're all planning on being there for the opening. We're all looking forward to Ottawa & the push into high summer. We'll all looking forward to the next photograph of . . .

Roy K. Kiyooka,
for *13 Cameras/ Vancouver*

Stalking a Silver-image:
An Introduction, of sorts, to
13 Cameras/ Vancouver

'You can only see what you are ready to see—what mirrors your mind at that particular time.' Hitching a midnight ride on the old B.C. Almanac image-bus a hundred & fifty thousand, turnabout, miles & a laid-back decade later—I or, rather, the small 'i' my sightings seem to have become, sees 'us,' all-of-us & then some, as obdurate as the intransigent things we found ourselves standing among as the cameras we held in our hands 'then' beheld us, naked, most naked in a green wilderness filled with valences of silver hallucinogenic light, like, they say, 'younger than yesterday, etc.' Hitchin' a belated 60's smile up, on top of a typical 70's fossil fuel frown, telephoned Michael: We instantly agreed it was time to have another look at our fair city with all its intricate ties to all of our lives & the cadences of light. *The active eye* recording the sights & sounds of Vancouver during a fusillade of seasons. The daily beneficences of Light as it evokes a flying cup, a tree or a face in the landscape, etc. Or how the round of the seasons and all diurnal creatures 'inter- sect' at all points on the grid of a city, with the geometric & cacophonous Urban: the Clutter, Curvature & Colours of this interface . . . a jostling of 9x12 glossies for the eye's own tides. *Talking, talking, incessantly*, week after week, sitting among our divers photographs, the ones we keep bringing to the meetings for each other's perusal, talking abt images & processes, the plastic print-paper take-over, the acuity of lenses, talking abt the host of intractable things in their seasons, the politics of govt. grants with our animosities oftimes flaring . . . while our altogether mute photographs lie, cheek to jowl, androgynously, sun-struck. Talking out of the inimitably 'personal' & the agglutinously 'collective,' we found our idiosyncratic-visors falling from our eyes as our photographs aligned themselves along an axis of their own mutabilities, 'in which things explain each other, not themselves.' 13 salutatory encounters with the cadences of light during a round of seasons on the Pacific Littoral. *Mutualities* which include the very next pair of eyes bringing their own store-of-sightings to the book & thereby claiming their share of a winding narrative .

    Roy K. Kiyooka, for *13 Cameras/ Vancouver*, Oct. '77/ April '79.

A Gist of Titles beginning with: April. reflected landscape. the end of the line from the top of the broken tower. the pinch. flyin' tools. voyages over the horizon, 1 to 6. for Susan/ Seasons after. this is no dream. in Springsun she. gave his ashes. to moving water. chair with figured carpet we are sisters. hair cut. pulse. 1000. Jeanette Reinhardt. Patti Smith. burning & dodging, 1 to 8. September. Landscapes, 1 to 6. Aleh Fitzgerald. In summer we. go through motions. picture needing that. heat on our backs. Penelope Houston. heads or tails. the sink. Night letter, Greetings from the Other Side, Dear Jim: last night I dove off the spillway of the Gatun Dam. I saw the Trickster again and he almost pulled me under but I regained my balance and ran away. See you soon, love Dale (D. 78). summer & smoke meat. Fabio Mauri 'without.' Fabio Mauri 'ideology and nature.' Landscapes, 7 to 10. We make for her. snow-capped pate. when in fall she. flies to Cold Mountain my Hometown. 13 Cameras, Vancouver Meetings. Vancouver B.C. T-Shirt open. the nightwatch. dodge dart. kick stool. realm of the pyromaniac, 'feast' realm of the pyromaniac, 'confidence.' the cup. the hookup. one step. two step. three step. four step. five step. six step. seven step. eight vancouver beauty spot. transparent still-life. eveready doll. nude with a towel. eveready light switch, nude with lamp. Tina. Annastacia McDonald, Ken Fletcher. leaving town. turn round, sitting down. tan lines, star sapphire finger. waterfront/ parking meter. double-take on. a blue mule. aesthetic decision. georgia medical dental. inside out. Wall. waterfront metronome. powell street plantmen. savants & a green sapling, social landscape, vancouver, 1, 2, 3. untitled, pants. Santa. Vancouver Neon Sweep. Chuck Biscuit. Susan Britton. She dreams a tidal wave. the green winter water. this time. throws us clear. Vancouver's famous. moving Lions. for no apparent reason, 3 times. landscape with water. reflected Vancouver landscape handheld. Jason Anna Koko. *plus a key-page & self-portrait* in alphabetical order by each of the 13 cameras .

Acknowledgements 13 Cameras wishes to thank all of the excellent *personages, place,* & wondrous *things* in their seasons, for their unstinting presences in the book. We thank The National Film Board (Stills Division), especially Ms Martha Langford its director Brock Webber Printing Co. our printers, & 4x5 Studio for their pat in the overall collaboration .

March 24th '79

Tom Gordon, Chairman, Dept. of Liberal Arts,
Ontario College of Art,
100 McCaul Street, Toronto M5T 1W1

Dear Mr. Gordon:

     David Young happens to be one of my young eastern connections, viz, one of the few young writers, editors, & teachers who keeps himself informed abt the goings-on in the literary world in Toronto, the rest of Canada, & the U.S.A., one of the few who help me keep in touch with 'writing' as the real news.
     As one of the editors of Coach House Press he has been instrumental in a number of publishing ventures which have added a dimension to our publishing world none of the big presses have had the audacity to deal with. I could go on but I think his c/v ought to speak for him. . . . For/Words Foundation is, of course, one of David's creations, one which has no parallel anywhere.

                                          Yours sincerely,
                                          Prof. Roy K. Kiyooka
                                          Fine Arts dept. at U.B.C.

March 24th '79

Dear David & Sarah:

JEEEEEEZ!—It's spring, again.
Like birds, flowers, green grass & clear blue skies
that kinda stuff . Otherwise, there's
nothin' to say except we're lookin' forward to both of you
comin' out in mid-May/ early June.
I'll be passin' thru on the way to & from Ottawa
viz the 13 Cameras show at N.F.B.
(opening date May 3rd). Lookin' for a place & an occasion
in Toronto for a publication/ book signing/ party.
Flight after the Ottawa opening . . .
Would/could Coach House sponsor such an affair for us?
& our 250 page 9x12 book of glossies?

Right now doin' a colour-xerox book with students
called 'US 5' wch consists of 6 pages by each of us @
50cents per page, makin' it a rare edition (edition of 30)
costin' $15.00 per book. WOW! Talk abt the ol' inflation &
the high cost of 'makin' it new.'

Sarah, the O/C medal is in me muthur's keeping.
It's where it belongs, like it made me feel too much like a
war veteran of the hallucinogenic '60s to keep it abt.
        Roy for Daphne
               too

March 25th '79

dear john & susan spend

    or it's susan & john viz my daughter kiyo
who reminded me that she played with jeremy on 5th avenue
way back in the early '60s. this is kiyo's 1st
venture away from home and it's impossible to spend about it
without reference to 'having to leave home, etc.' for the
sake of 'her own good,' etc. anyhow, kiyo comes to u
of her own will. she knows she has her parents'
whole-hearted approval, like, anything to get her movin',
we feel ought to be good for her. etc. & tho
she's always been given optimum freedom . . . she ought to be
held responsible, to both of u, for the sake of your own
peace, etc. i'll be in toronto early may & will certainly
give a call . . . . appalling, to see, the re-enactments
the fibrous coruscations of the friable human
etc.

                            met joe c. in Ottawa late spring '78
                            he was like my kid brother someone
                            that familiar . do you think he's
                            gonna topple pierre elliot mackenzie
                            king's heir/? afflatus   .

April 5th '78

concerning   *Bruce Parsons*: whom I have known since the early '60s when he happened to be in Regina and with whom I taught painting and other aspects of A R T at the Nova Scotia College of Art. I want simply to say that I thought he was intelligent, well organized, and altogether personable. Further, I cannot imagine him doing a bum job as he has always struck me as being conscientious.

> As I am not into
> systems, analysis or even art as
> Education I can't give you a
> systematic appraisal.
> Hope these words may be nonetheless
> useful for his cause .

Yours sincerely,
Professor R. K. Kiyooka
B. F. A. Fine Arts Dept. at U.B.C.

April 5th '78/ 2.30 am

Dear Maya

Daphne and I are both coming to Toronto, then onto Ottawa for the O.C. Ceremonies. We're looking forward to seeing you and others. Both of us have been working hard and hence look forward to this brief trip as an intensive holiday. Our aged pear tree in the backyard is blessed with white flowers. And, I suppose, I tend to measure its annual blossoming as tho it were myself thus festooned.

viz Kiyooka at the Annex on Sat. Night April 15th
I'll need the following equipment:

>   1 projector and screen
>   1 video deck and a teley set
>   1 portable cassette and
>   1 large bottle of hot sake

>>   get in touch with Coach House Press
>>   for copies of my new book *The*
>>   *Fountainebleau Dream Machine*. The enclosed
>>   books are for all of you to have.

sincerely,

April 9th '78

Dear Dennis

    Daphne and I will be in Ottawa on Wednesday April 19th for the investiture of the O.C. The occasion ends according to the program at 9:30pm—shall we get together afterwards and have a drink even exchange news from the several pews of C.A.? As usual we won't be in O.O. longer than the business at hand necessitates tho i might find the time to lay over for a few days. etc. More abt this later.

    Just spent 3 months putting a studio cum gallery together in the heart of Japtown. It's gonna be strictly a place for photography (mostly my own/ and selected others). It's been years since I last painted and dreamt of colours tho both keep re-occurring in my other work. With the 1st balmy days and the white blossoms on our pear tree I'm already thinking abt and looking forward to a dazzling summer of taking pictures.

                              I'll be in Toronto on the 15th
                              thru the 16th. In Oshawa for the 17th
                              perhaps 18th. c/o J. Murray
                              at the R. McL. A. G. Then Ottawa.
                              We could meet you at any of these
                              places.

                yours truly,

Dear Dennis

the callit true Canadien Artist cannot
be a pre-Raphaelite 'cause
He/ She doesn't (in 1977) believe in the Golden Gauge of
the re-birth   /it having been born many times
of Greek Platonic Classicism:
known among Teutonic Art Historians as
The European Renaissance. He
or She if Canadian eschews the old Europa's Bull
and White Swan Mythologies for
the sake of the Ground he stands upon
with its own Deities 'who'—
I would remind you—pre-date the Christian Era.
speaking for myself—'i' want a

'true' 'blue' Native Cosmology to imbue
the things i make.
>   How abt you,
>   Dennis Reid
>   spelled *reed* also)

>   ask Everyman abt it.   ask him
>   what he does when he's got itchy balls.
>   ask him abt the Truce he makes
>   with the pale moon light   then ask
>   him what words prevail against
>   water's treachery . . .

yours till
the Group of Seven ascend
into Heaven.   tho
Limbo I've been told is
also a place to
be
>   p/s   how's Ottawa?
>   the Civil Savant's Valhalla

. . . been intermittently
working on a reel of splices viz
WHO KILLED TOM THOMSON   or
(provisionally)   THE ALGONQUIN
ADVENTURES OF CANADA'S EXEMPLARY
FOLK/ ART HERO: Title sounds
puck-ish if not ironic—but I do
mean to be 'serious'   to wit—
could you send me the sum of the Litter
at your leisure concerning T/T to
help hang a Fable on? or, if that's
impossible, how abt a telling
book list abt T/T and the
other 'passionate Canadians' etc.?
somewhere in a forest of
mutilated words I'll find my own T/T and
let him say his worth

summer & smoke

fully clothed, she lies at the foot of the bed watching summer & smoke
while he with his own insistences sits on the red shag carpet loading his camera.
she might have found herself weeping with miss geraldine paige the heroine
if he hadn't un-dresst and walkt across her line of vision to sit beside the t.v.—
staring back at her. undisclosed at the foot of the bed she watched him put
a mask up to his face and holding it there with one hand asked her to press the shutter.
he repeated his act several times each time slumping further and further down
into the upholstered chair while she presst the shutter and went on watching summer
go up in smoke over the fraser river. the sequence ends with him lifting the mask
away from his implacable face staring across the breadth of the red shag carpet into
the darkness above the bed. fully clothed she went on watching summer and smoke while he
showered and slowly dressed. 'she' lies undisclosed in these words while 'he,' with
his preferences for the silent flicks, or rather his nakedness, lies inside of these
photographs/ Palimpsests of a summer afternoon in room 214, mission hotel.

Dear David & Sarah:

> looks like I'll be in Toronto on the 5th for a publishing party at *art metropole*. we're (13 Cameras) going on to Ottawa on the 2nd for our opening at the N.F.B. and driving down the morning of the 4th. probably won't be in Toronto long as some of us are planning to go on to either Monreale or New York on the 6th. (like I ain't been in N.Y. since '69 & it grabs my fancy goin' there to see Tim & Ann & Others including F.D. not to mention seeing Rousseau's Sleeping Gypsy at the Modern.) *otherwise,* it's more than spring here, it's almost summer—and given the lengthening days the accumulations of heat a couple of weeks at Long Beach in early June ought to be good for all of us Canucks who seem to voraciously work our arses off.

Dear Stan

        (Michael), (Ric), (bp), (David) Others

. . . I'd love to re-issue S T O N E D G L O V E S: it
would have to be (given the kinks) BRAND NEW. that is
the matter (photos) and (pomes) but re-invented.
I can't abide merely 'editing' anything. I'm more
into 'transformations' of everything, even my own words
so called. It's a TESTAMENT of sorts I want to re-avow.
Hence the thought herein proposed.

                                        otherwise
                                    it's . . . tic . . . toc . . .

        Don't let the quasi-archaic rhetorick piss u off
        I mean I thought it might be efficacious.

April 13th '78

Dear Martha Hayes:
    (Stills Division) N.F.B., Ottawa

I'm going to be in Ottawa on the 19th thru the 21st for the O.C. Investiture and other reasons. Will it be possible to get together with you concerning the B.C. Hand Book or more accurately a Vancouver Almanac? It's been six months since Michael and I spoke to Lorraine M. about doing another Almanac and we are anxious to draw up an agreement with you so that all-of-us can get on with the project. All of us being the 14 Camera Artists who are already well into the photography for their contribution to the book. I'll phone you Monday before noon to arrange a date .

    I'll be in Toronto for the 15th and 16th.
    You could get me thru the Coach House Press.
    Then I'll be in Oshawa for the 17th perhaps the
    18th at the Robert McLaughlin Gallery.
    I'm completely tied up on the 19th but
    can make it anytime on the 20th or the 21st.

—You will have heard from Michael in the meantime.

    Yours truly,

April 30th, 12 noon, '79

Dear George/ June:

. . . So we can keep in touch during the summer months, here's my provisional summer schedule, at least for May & the early part of June. I'm leaving Tuesday (that's tomorrow) noon for the opening of the 13 CAMERAS/ VANCOUVER exhibition at the N.F.B. on the evening of May 3rd. It promises to be a gala event, hooked, as it will be, into the energies of the forthcoming federal election. Then, we're all driving down to Toronto in rented cars for a publishing party at ART METROPOLE on Sat. afternoon & evening May 5th. After which we're going to take the RAPIDO on Sunday to Montreal for another p.p. at OPTICA on Monday May 7th. Tho I'm due to fly back to Vancouver from Toronto on May 11th, I'm thinking of going on down to New York (for the 1st time in a decade), if I can get my return flight changed without additional cost. If it happens, I won't be back till the 15th. Then (busy, busy!) I'll be heading for Saskatoon in the 3rd week of May for a Conference (on The Asian Voice in Canadian Society) and won't be back till the 1st of June 'cause I'm going to use the occasion to do some visiting with my old-time prairie friends. Following which, Daphne, Kit & I intend to go camping for a couple of weeks in the early part of June. Then, it's 'at home' for the rest of the summer with tons of work to get on with. (Whew! just writing out my summer itinerary makes me tired!)

> I'll phone the 'office' next week, before G.K. leaves for Venice to check things out. Otherwise, I'll be home for what's goin' to be left of my summer.
>
> Have a good summer, both of you.
>
> ~

13 CAMERAS

MARION PENNER BANCROFT, IAIN BAXTER, TAKI BLUESINGER, CHRIS DAHL, MICHAEL DE COURCY, CHRIS GALLAGHER, BARRIE JONES, ROY K. KIYOOKA, MARTHA MILLER, DALE PICKERING, DAVE RIMMER, KAZUMI TANAKA & PAUL WONG

> cordially invite you to attend
> a Publishing Reception for
>
> SUNDAY 2 – 5 PM   MAY 13, 1979
> PUMPS 40 E. Cordova, Vancouver

for Richard
mid-winter, '79
356 Powell Street
Vancouver, B.C.

thru photography i would capture the luminous flash, you & kate propose. he lookt intently at the words he had just written and thot they were, to say the least, pretentious. after all, he was an artist first & secondly a photographer. least of all a writer. (try again) thru photography i try to capture what i see with my everyday eyes. see, see how the two of them melt into each other. see how they become, inextricably, part of the other. double-exposed: the light bathing their skin sinks into their very flesh. his profile & her breast, together with a hank of her hair & a cigarette, all sculpted out of nothing but light. thru photography my own flesh yields up its dark night. 'it' too would sing of a momentary warmth. body to body. dust to dust. if lust has a focus other than a body, it could be my kind of photography.

midnight, May 13th '80

belatedly, for Kit's 11th birthday

. . . this house this small house we three live in
is made of paper, strewn paper, i sd as i looked around .
this cardboard house is strewn with lotsa paper i
thot as i looked down at the paper filling up with words.
this un-bored house is plastered with paper and words
without a beginning or an ending, i sang to myself
as row upon row of paper and words paper and wonder tilted
their pages their pulp & ink pages at my small feet.
. . . this house this small house the three of us and the
two pets happen to be living in is made of *paper
breath* and *little words*, this house simply is

Sept. 5th '80

Dear Gerry:

got all yr letters, including the postcard, been out of circulation, intentionally, this 'll be the 1st letter I've written, business or otherwise, in the past 6 months.

yes, you can use what you have previously used but do
consider (1) excerpts from my *Transcanada Letters*. if you don't have a copy or can't get a hold of one—I'll send one out, pronto. (2) I'm finishing up a small book titled *Backcountry Trip*: an account of travelling thru the back country of Honshu with my father in '69 when he was 80.

I'll get a chunk of it off to you within a week or so.

yes, my own preferences run to 'sequence of pomes' but it doesn't matter. let the overall format determine what where, when & how. say Hi to David Aylward.

I've got lotsa photographs, taken in Japan, plus lotsa other photos, taken in Vancouver and Canada. you could use some of these—as illustrations. or whatever. as for 'me' designing the anthology . . . I'd luv to but I think it's yr baby. I mean you shld want to see it thru, whole.

but, all that's later. meanwhile, send me a list of titles of the pomes you intend to include so far and I'll get to work on the *Backcountry*.

                                            keep writing, insisting
                                            & I promise to be dili-
                                            gent

yours

December 7th '80

Dear Kathleen Moore

I don't know what will come out of this letter concerning D.L. & R.K.'s collaboration on *The Unquiet Bed* because it's been 15 years since it happened. But reading D.L.'s commentary I feel a vague sort of unease viz the changes that occasion has undergone in time. I'm almost tempted to say 'we' seem to have become a fiction to each other.

Nonetheless, I believe we first met at a poetry reading by Jack Spicer, the San Francisco poet, at Warren Tallman's house in Vancouver during the early sixties (see CATERPILLAR 12, 'A Gathering of the Tribes,' 'Vancouver Lecture #1,' edited by Stan Persky). Since then we've met, however briefly, in Montreal, Toronto, Edmonton, Calgary & most recently at the Collingwood Poetry Festival. In all these meetings I don't ever recall talking to her about my experiences as a Japanese-Canadian. If we had talked about it, she would have known that I was born in Moose Jaw, Saskatchewan, and spent all my early years on the prairies. And, furthermore, she would have known that my family had not been evacuated from the West Coast, tho we did suffer a common humiliation viz the rampant racism. Apropos all of this, my one & only copy of *The Unquiet Bed* bears witness. To wit, the gold jacket's copy and the poem to Spicer.

A word about the Illustrations: they derive from a number of repros which I had gathered while reading the poems, tho I had no thot of their context. One day I simply took them to the English Dept. xerox machine and began arranging them right on the glass plate and copied them. I copied them over & over, rearranging the bits and pieces until I got a satisfactory print, one that I felt complemented the feelings I got from the poems. The intent was never to merely be illustrative. All the illustrations including the cover were made this way. It took an entire afternoon to accomplish. Incidentally, apart from the copy I have, I do not have any photographs of them. You will have to get in touch with Earl Toppings who edited the book and probably owns the xerox prints. Jeezus, they've probably turned into a mere ghost of themselves on his livingroom wall!

p.s. While sitting down to write this letter, I've gone thru the book, again. I still feel good about it. It's a handsome book. & furthermore, it enabled me to get into Dorothy's poems in a way I hadn't been able to before.

For what it's worth, I have over the years had something to do with at least 7 books of divers sorts & their illustrations. At least 3 of these were collaborations between the poet & myself as artist. The other 4 books proposed that I be both, given my visual/verbal predilections. The proposition is simply this: one wants a wholeness, one wants to belong to eyes, ears, & breath, utterly.

a foot-note
to the finite line both poets and painters walk
---

off the top of my head
Pat Lane, Joe Rosenblatt, P.K. Page, even Peg Atwood have
all made pictures for their poems   & pictures
that swallowed up their words.
I would venture to guess that some of us are ambidextrous.

nothing queer in all this if you dig the Chinese/Japanese
poet/painters, or their European counterparts.
William Blake engraved word & image onto copper plates with
the same stylus. Michelangelo wrote sonnets.
Jean Arp & Max Ernst fused both into their brand of surrealism.
in short, 'we' do do it some of the time, seriously.

taking all the old myths and smashing them to bits in order to
re-animate the charismatic hold they have on us is
simply part of an ongoing visual/verbal probe for guys like me.
take colours &/or words and reify them to reveal the
intricate clockwork of all phenomena at the heart of life, its,
ofttimes, opaque deliriums, sez it.

How, but thru a monstrous 'specialism,' the so-called authority
of erstwhile 'professionals' have we come to leave
breath out of images and *images* out of breath, anyhow?

1980-12-08
The University of British Columbia
Department of Fine Arts
Vancouver, B.C.

Mr. Yves Trudeau
Université du Québec à Montréal
Montréal, P.Q.

Dear Mr. Trudeau

Just the other day or, rather, just a few days before your letter arrived, I was telling someone at a party about my Monreale years (1965-69), and much to my own surprise I talked about those years with what could only have been called fervour. A heightened evocation of a passionate love affair, fondly remembered. I am speaking about my years as the head of the painting department at Sir George Williams University and my association with Yves Lanier and The Galerie du Siecle on Sherbrooke Street. Not to mention the friendships I had with Guido Molinari, Yves Gaucher, Ulysses Comtois, Hugh Leroy and other notables on the scene. The enclosed xerox from my book of letters ought to substantiate all this.

Anyhow, how would it be if I came to Monreale and the University of Quebec in Monreale either *March 1st to 7th* or *March 8th to 14th*? I'll let you know which of the two dates suits me best as soon as I get my schedule straightened out early in the new year. Meanwhile, I shall think about what I can do for your students. I hope that they will bear with me as I only speak English and Japanese.

I have included a copy of my retro show catalogue at the Vancouver Art Gallery. It will inform you of what I was up to till 1975. Since then it's been mostly poetry and photography, although I have not lost my interest in painting and sculpture. In fact, since I have stopped painting, I've been able to enjoy the work of others even better. At this time I feel that all the varied modes/media we have at the service of *perception* have an equivalent viability. I see myself engaged in a remorseless act of elucidation. How about you?

Yours sincerely

Roy Kiyooka
Professor
enc.

1980-12-08
The University of British Columbia
Department of Fine Arts
Vancouver, B.C.

Mr. Gerry Shikatani
Toronto, Ontario

Dear Gerry

As if to prepare me for my midwinter trip East, we've had 8 inches of snow and uncommon cold. Like they say, you could freeze your balls off. Anyhow, I'm going to be in Ottawa through December 14-19 for C.C. jury work and I'm thinking that we should get together for an afternoon to go over what is in the works. I'm flying out of Vancouver midnight Friday the 12th and will be arriving in Toronto at 7:30 am Saturday. What's your itinerary, and could you phone me and let me know? If it's clearly impossible, I shall leave all the material with someone at the Coach House for you to pick up.

Apropos your letter, if it's going to be strictly a Japanese/Canadian anthology, my portion of the book ought to consist of the following: 1) a selection from *Kyoto Airs*, as you suggest, though I will have to go through it to affirm your choices; 2) a section from *Backcountry Trip*—together with accompanying *photographs* which I am in the process of printing. The notion is simply this—that these two go together because they're both about call it my home away from home. Thus, the packet I'll leave for you at the Coach House will include 1) my choices from *Kyoto Airs*; 2) the section from *Backcountry Trip* with its photographs. Having said all this, the decision of what goes in will still be up to you. It's your book afterall.

As for selections from some of my other books, particularly N.T.E. & S.G., I do want to see them back in print, entire, but I don't see them in this context.

Two further thoughts: you might think of using a reproduction of one of my late sixties all blue ellipse paintings for the cover. I would prefer the use of photos-as-illustrations, rather than paintings, particularly if you want a 'now' book.

That's it. There's lots to do and do phone me.

Sincerely yours
Roy Kiyooka
Professor

Ottawa, December '80

richard & karen: a belated wedding picture

they had known each other for twenty five years but, to all intents & purposes, she was news to both of them. 'beauty & the beast' had occurred to him while he was taking their picture, but something in him told him it wasn't true. it didn't fit the occasion. she was certainly fair &, as far as he could tell, cultured to the tip of her well-groomed fingernails. years & years ago, he had given him the back of his hand & their friendship bore its scars. for it was his fierce sullenness he had to withdraw from, it was the darkness that kept breaking thru his irrepressible wit & not the image you see of him, that suggested the word 'beast.' they talkt abt their mutual friends and had lunch together. they spent an afternoon in his new (old) book store. he offered him any book that took his fancy. going thru the shelves of books he came upon a thick square book the size of an average human head squared, & flipping thru its pages he was amazed to see all the strange faces with all of their pimples, warts, scars & crevasses staring back at him. months later he sent him a small note asking for that book & packt up & sent them their very own wedding picture.

January 13th, '81 (already!
The Blue Mule Photo Gallery
356 Powell Street,
Vancouver B.C.

Dear Gerry & Ros

      Yours truly is gonna be in Toronto the Gook come the 1st squeaky week in February &, believe it or not, that's gotta be callit my deadline (luv that word—its dire prognostications) for getting a definitive script for your anthology to you. In udder worts, I'm gonna be delivering them in the 1st person singular. The enclosed b & w 4 x 5s are of 2 sorts & several places. 1st divers *snaps* of mainly the city of Kyoto & its surroundings—to savour with a cup of hot sake. 2nd those *snaps* that are a part of the *Backcountry Trip*. They're all numbered to correspond with similar numbers indicated within the open spaces of the text. Here's a toss: if the size of the book to be can be thickened, you could think of a section of 'these' & 'other's' like Tamio Wakayama's Japan photos as a purely visual complement. Have a good look at 'em & ask yourself if they can be useful. In a lota ways *snaps* are nothing if not humanly un-pretentiously useful.

Heading into my 55th year with uncommonly clear weather. It's beginning to feel like I am going to squeak out of my self containments after nearly 5 years. Perhaps it's time to travel Eastwards again in both directions. Anyhow, I keep pushing against the political encroachments we seem to be veering towards. Come what may, 55 has to be a double-digit year.

Ros baby you just squeaked thru & it's gonna be nip & tuck if you don't come up with the best you've got for the 2nd round. Dig it!

                                    see both of you in three weeks

January 13th, '81 (already!
The Blue Mule Photo Gallery
356 Powell Street, Vancouver B.C.

Dear Richard & Karen

Up to my ears in renovating my Powell St studio for 4 upcoming photo shows since Xmas & haven't got around to printing your wedding pictures, tho I did process the film and pulled a contact sheet which looks, as they say, promising. I'll get a set off to you in early February, if not sooner. Did I happen to leave a large envelope filled with assorted books at your place that morning? If I did it's ok 'cause one set of the books therein are for you & Karen & the other set is for Gerry Grey. Could you get them to her with my friable luv?

My 55th year comin' up this weekend. Ah, just discovered why, among a host of fancies, one middle-aged goat would commemorate both his prairie birth-place & the ending of Capricorn's crystalline season. Now, I've never been hot on numerical divination, but I must admit that a double 5 could make me change my mind if not my wisp of a life. Seems there is no way of telling what lies underfoot further on down the road even at double 55. Perhaps I'll become an old toad choking on the livid air down on the ol' mudflats. Aesop's FABLES/ Walt Disney & Mickey the Mouse/ not to mention all the two bit anthropomorphisms that continue ad nauseam to wash down the ol' Media Gulch. Who could ask for anything more.

Richard, you have a big thick square photo book of full faces, page on page of full faces in your shelves. want to sell it to me & if so just ship it out, pronto.

yours

March, '81

dear Mike

      sent WHEELS on to G. Shikatani who is to get together with bp abt it. you could get a hold of it from one of them. needless to say, i am more than a bit curious of your take on it. tho i laboured over it letter by letter & silence by silence for a decade, it long ago assumed its own shape, one which i have had to smash over & over again to find a portrait of my father, not to mention a portrait of a son. & the ongoing challenge was how to get everything that simply went on happening in one's life into the book as each draft got written. let's just say it took ten years to find what had long ago become a palimpsest. p.s. the title came towards the end & brought a necessary strand of the narrative into focus. hence the re-working of the 'beginning' & 'end.' well, i'm thru with the tyranny of words for awhile. spring's come & there are other things to attend to, like silent stills.

      ah! so that's what it's like being in love, we sd to ourselves. well, we've been thru it ourselves & we're not thru with it. not by a long shot. he thot. & she concurred. it was our pleasure to have simply been present to the two of you. lotsa luck. & yes do give me your views. your mundane news .

nothin' like a March sun to lighten the desiccated breath.

regards,

April 15th '81

Dear Peter:

      I too have had a back problem for many long years and know how awful it can be. The only way I have learned to handle it is by taking things easy. By which I mean a letting go of physical/mental tensions and carrying yourself with more ease. Medication, therapy, operations won't be of much use unless you learn to listen to your body's needs. Remember how I stressed the doubleness of drawing/meditation? Keep it in mind. Be kind to yourself and you'll find yourself walking upright without a kink to throw you off balance. Peter, it does have to do with *balance*. Going to school isn't worth a damn unless you're whole. Maybe you ought to take a year out to mend yourself!

                    yours sincerely,

We Asian North Americanos:
An unhistorical 'take' on growing up yellow in a white world

for Joy Kogawa & Tamio Wakayama
(read at The J.C/J.A. Symposium in Seattle, May 2nd, 1981)

Everytime I look at my face in a mirror I think of how it keeps on changing its features in English, tho English is not my mother tongue. Everytime I've been in an argument I've found the terms of my rationale in English pragmatism. Even my anger, not to mention my rage, has to all intents and purposes been shaped by all the gut-level obscenity I picked up away from my mother tongue. And everytime I have tried to express, it must be, affections, it comes out sounding halt. Which thot proposes that every unspecified emotion I've felt was enfolded in an unspoken Japanese dialect, one which my childhood ears alone remember. Furthermore, everytime I've broken into my own ofttimes unwelcome but salutory silences, I've been left with a tied tongue. All of which tells me that every time a word forms on the tip of my tongue, it bears the pulse of an English which is not my mother tongue. There's English 'English.' There's American 'English,' paging Dr. Hayakawa. Then, there's our kind of, callit, Canadian 'English,' not to mention all the other English-speaking folks in the rest of the world, regardless of their race, colour, or creed. For good or bad, it's the nearest thing we have to a universal lingua franca. Unless the ubiquitous computer with its fearsome but cold-blooded logistical games has already usurpt its primacy. Having said all this, I would simply add that none of the above has anything to do with what I can say in my mother tongue.

I am reminded of these grave matters when I go home to visit my mother. She and she alone reminds me of my Japanese self by talking to me in the very language she taught me before I even had the thot of *learning* anything. If there's one thing I can say with a degree of certainty, it's that she did not, could not, teach me to speak English. Let alone, read and write it. After more than half a century in Canada her English is, to say the least, rudimentary. Not that that ever prevented her from speaking her mind. So it is that I find myself going home to keep in touch with my mother tongue and, it must be, the ghost of my father's silences.

Everytime I've been in Japan I've been acutely aware of the fact that my own brand of Japanese is previous to both the 2nd WW and television. That in fact it's contemporaneous with that original wireless talking machine, the radio. My more candid Japanese friends tell me that I sound, to their ears, a bit old-fashioned. Need I say that I didn't have enough of a handle on my mother tongue to tell them that all the Japanese I know had been distilled in me by the time I was six or seven. Keep in mind that my mother's Japanese was shaped towards the end of the Meiji era and the beginnings of the Taisho era and that's the Japanese she taught me. What has been grafted on down thru the years is, like my mother's English, rudimentary. Right here and now I want to say that there's a part of me that is taken aback by the fact, the ironical fact, that I am telling you all this in English. Which proposes to me that, whatever my true colours, I am, to all intents and purposes, a white anglo saxon protestant, with a cleft tongue.

Everytime I find myself talking, talking about anything under or even above and beyond the sun, I feel the very pulse of my thots in a North American/West Coast dialect of the English language with all its tenacious Indo-European roots. Now, concomitant with this recognition is the feeling that, when I am most bereft, it's the nameless Jap in me who sings an unsolicited haiku in voluntary confinement. I don't want to go on moanin' the old 'yellow peril' blues the rest of my days. Gawd save us all from that fate. For what it's worth I want to say that it's the N.A. Blackman's (African slave) Blues together with the Gaikaku with its grave intonations of an inexorable fate which holds me close to the earth. Talk about our 'aural' confabulations. Talk about the soul inherent in the heart-beat (the errant pulse) of a language. One day I want to tell you how music forms a linguistic bridge across the endless chasm of speech. One of these days I'll come by to play my dulcimer.

Everytime I look up at all of you I am astonished by how the very words we go on uttering all the days of our lives, together with all the different modes of silences we gather, like a harbinger, around ourselves, leave their myriad tracings upon your divers faces. I would go so far as to suggest that they have to all intents and purposes become an indivisible part of your very postures. I've been talking of how my mother gave me my first language, a language I began to acquire even as I suckled on her breast and what a motley mode of speaking it's all become in time. Need I say that she couldn't save me from that fate. But I have seen a look on her face that told me she understood (wordlessly . . .) the ardour of all such displacement. Thus it is that I always speak Japanese when I go home to visit her. More than that I can, for the time being, become almost Japanese. I realize that it's one of the deepest 'ties' I have in my whole life.

Here I want to say a few words about my father. He took pride in the fact that he had been able to shape a mask for the Asian in himself to speak thru by learning to read, write, and speak a no-nonsense English. He who kept a keen eye on the prairie politics of William Aberhart and the evangelical Social Credit party and spent the spare time he had left over from working his arse off in a garment factory reading. He who tended the flowers in my childhood gardens and prided himself in the fact that he never wore eye glasses thru-out his long life. Lately I've come to realize that I don't really know much about him or how he felt about the shape of his life. It was mostly an unspoken sense of the familial that tied us together. We spoke, when we had the occasion to, in cadences of silence, augmented by simple English or Japanese. I would remind you that the city of Vancouver wasn't much more than a forest clearing when he landed here in '04. Like the typical Asian immigrant of his day he had heard tall tales of a N.A. which was not much more than a mythical wilderness surmounted by a tall gold mountain and a handful of Indians, etc. You all know that hoary story. It's a part of our legacy as erstwhile North Americanos. Anyhow, I must have learned the efficaciousness of silences from him as he was, for the most part, a quiet, unsurly sort of man.

Now it's taken me all these years to understand the gravity of his silences and to abide the depth of my own and where it might take me. Let me add here that, where I'm coming from, silences are the measure of all that remains unconditioned in our lives. My father died of old age in his eighties. For what it's worth I want to say that we took a trip thru Honshu's Backcountry together in 1969. That brief memorable trip was the first and last time we travelled together since my youth. And I've spent a decade trying to see its shape. Write his/our silences. Like everything I've shaped in my life, it isn't what I intended, it isn't quite good enough. Such as it is, it's a homage to him who planted the tree-of-silences inside of me. Such as it is, it's the hard-won language of familial testament.

It's become a 'best seller' these days to say that everybody under the sun has roots, a trunk, and branches. That, therefore, everybody is rooted in the particulars of their own etymology. Preferences, hence all of our so-called references, tend, in the English I've learned, to take these things for granted. For instance, racism, as everybody can and does know it, has something to do with cultural dispositions and, despite all the rhetoric, it has its roots in the language of our fears and is, to all intents and purposes, wholly irrational. Hence our own vulnerableness in the face of it. Nonetheless, I am on the side of those who hold to the minority view that we have to attend to our own pulse and extend our own tenacities. Like they say, 'God helps those who help themselves.' It's right here that 'art' (in any tongue) can and does get into the act: like how do we cause the leaves on the topmost branches of the old family tree to burst into flower, sez it. Sounding all the old homilies (again), I want to insist that everybody is a bona fide member and an activist (each in their own way) in the ongoing histrionics of a given culture. Everybody's 'bearing' is, in that sense, equal and we N.A. Asians ought to act forthrightly on our own behalf. We shall have to remain vigilant if we are to insert ourselves in to the W.A.S.P. scheme of things, albeit their histories.   Thank you.

Nov. 21st '75 AD

May 8th, '81
356 Powell Street

Joan Dear:

Got the book abt Jock & his students. Glad I snuck in there with Irene W. & thanks for calling attention to the fact of my illustrious career as an erstwhile teacher. Like the proverbial 'gifted' ones, I had the vocation from the very beginning. It was given to me as a gift and my teaching has always been a means of honouring that gift. Like any true gift, it is given almost gratuitously and to recognize that fact is a serious matter. Education, at least our form of so called 'education,' mostly disguises if not denies the heart's knowledgeability. The quarrel that Jock seemed to be involved in viz the painter & the teacher co-existing in him, with the latter usurping the energies that should have gone into the former, just doesn't make sense to me 'cause I don't (never really have) believe in the notion of an utter specialism. I mean that (for me) everything I do wants to hang together. This includes the writing and the music I'm into. Keep up the good work.

Has Oshawa banned Japanese cars from their streets yet?

May 8th, '81
356 Powell St., Van. B.C.

Dear Gerry:

Got yr letter. Got the message. Like I sd, brother, it's up to you: the start of the trip & the Hinomisaki section page 27 is ok with me. It's a slice of the whole anyhow. *West Coast Review* & *Island* of which Daphne is an editor will do other sections. The whole thing will have to wait till Coach House does a manuscript edition, then a book. Getting thru the last draft took me three months, and I literally haven't been able to face a typewriter till now. But then isn't the moment of writing about anything always & inevitably now? Been down to Seattle to participate in a J.C./ J.A. Symposium. Wow! whata eye-opener that was. I mean that Japanese Americans speak American English which ain't the same as ours. & furthermore, there's more of them all up & down the West Coast, so that they've got more of a sense of an actual community than we have. Otherwise, we all look similar and tend to honour our mutual backgrounds alike. Joy K. was with us. By now she'll be back in Toronto and you oughta phone her up as she has wind of an External Affairs (writing) project about C.A. writers which could be something for you. There's good money in it too. Me, I'm just coasting. Or rather I'm gettin' my summer wind up after eight months of school. There's the remote but exciting prospect of going to Japan in July for the opening of a big Canadian Painting show. Then there's a show coming up at Scarborough College in Toronto this fall which I'll have to work like hell towards. It will be a photo show with a poetry reading and my first exhibition outside of Vancouver for a number of years. And so it goes. Hang on to the 'sacred' even when the going gets tough and the beatific will take care of itself. Ok that's enough. Say Hi to Rosalind. Say Hullo to Toronto the gook.

yours truly

May 14th, '81

Dear Sharon/Fred:

>better late than never? better never than
>too soon? better silence than cheap
>talk? better walk a brisk mile than stare at
>another similitude? better get it on.

anyhow, you have several choices if, as i imagine, i'm not, as they say, 'long past the deadline.' it'll all depend on how may pages the magazine as a whole insists upon. it'll all depend on whether you do or do not like it. though i might insist that your decision hasn't much to do with my need to get the writing to say what my feelings tell me about the whole truth as the language itself remains a perpetual witness to. one) use 'We Asian North Americanos' all by itself. that is 'intact.' if you think it's too dense in the dance of the pages, you could: two) use any *one* of the sections from WHEELS (depending on how many pages you need). or use all the sections (they're from different parts of the book) if that's what the issue needs. three) you could use W.A.N.A. and one or more sections from WHEELS. they don't even have to be side by side beside my name. like they could be sandwicht between other modes of writing/s. whatever you choose, please leave each piece intact. don't try to reshape it to fit yr paginations. a brief explanatory note concerning the sections i've sent you of WHEELS: whereas the W.A.N.A. could be sd to be 'self contained,' akin to, say, the classical notion of a well-rounded essay, WHEELS is a continuous trip in many discreet & various sections. like, you've just got a couple of slices of a rotund thing. i think this needs to be sd in, say, a discreet footnote and that a manuscript edition of WHEELS will be forthcoming from Coach House Press in Toronto sometime this summer.

>good luck to you
>it must be some kind of adventure

June '81
Edmonton/ Powell st.

sonja and her daughter samantha

presiding over an informal tea ceremony:
informal in that she who knew the ritual to a 't' shared the
tea making with the other three, including
samantha her daughter who had just come home from school.
each took the bamboo whisk up and frothed up
their own tea and then drank it as they pleased, while sonja
talkt abt comparative mythologies . then,
their cat walkt in and sam pickt it up to give it a hug and
click—another snapshot. if you look intently
you might be able to see me whisking my own tea
in their eyes' surmise. the official school portrait of sam
commemorates the end of another school year. sonja sd,
sam liked her school picture. what do you see in *it* that isn't
in the rest of the picture?

sam: you might like this
i thought of you thinking of your mother.
we all know who POOH is—
ask your mother about the TAO in
each one of us.

                              the next time we see each other
                              you could read it to me
                              but if it's an awful bore tell me so and
                              i'll try again . these words
                              want to line up into little groups and become
                              their own story so I had better stop

                                                          Luv,

Edmonton, June, '81

especially for *moe* sam's father & basho's irascible heir

sam & her pussy cat

caught in a fraction of a second, forever.
but 'forever' is no place they could abide. forever is
that fictive place nobody has ever been to.
even the pussy cat with its nine legendary lives knows that.
moments later the cat walks out the back door
while sam whisks up her bowl of tea. she's just walkt home
from school thru a downpour, her blonde hair is
still wet. can you smell the lovely dampness of it by staring
intently at the photograph? can you feel the pussy cat
's soft thick fur on your arms? weeks later—
i'm non-plussed by the enigma of their frozen presences—'who'
are they? what are they, in their unbecoming presence,
telling me? sam will never stand and look at me this way again.
the pussy cat sees thru its own cat eyes. i am also
my eyes: i, too, see what i can, and do. the camera is,
of course, deaf dumb blind & mute

dear Richard

      i finally got around to printing up your wedding portrait. it's going to be a piece in my Scarborough College show which opens in late September. i'll ask Lora Carney who organized the occasion to send it on to you afterwards. if you happen to be in Toronto during October and have the time, do look in on the show. whatever else it is, it's a slice of life in images since the late seventies. now that everything costs more than it's worth, or 'worth' itself is nothing more than an abstract kind of value, i find it impossible to make anything for the market place. i mean, given the ongoing monetary dogmas that support a nonsensical affluence, i go on making 'art' because i have a need to—how it is with me. B.C. behaves as usual: part English colony, the veritable last frontier of that kinda sensibility, part a northern hemisphere kinda lotus land with a single tree of knowledgeability, part orient, part Indian, and a branch of cedar (not laurel) waved in front of the nose of capitalism. so what else is news?

dear Lora

       first i thought i heard it as 'laura'; then it became, for whatever partially heard reason, 'lorna'; now i know better than to trust my overhearing and know from your letters it's 'lora.' anyhow, here's where we're at. first, an aside. it's been several long years since i put a show together and now that i've almost got this one together . . . i know one of the reasons i gave up exhibiting: it has something to do with the hype of producing & everything that entails. i estimate that i have put in about 750 hours for this show. not to mention an easily comparable figure for materials.

i didn't have the time to think thru their relationships viz their 'hanging' from your gallery walls, together. don't be taken aback by the diversity of images—they easily fall into several distinct groupings. for instance, 1, 3, 5, 9, & 10 are all variations on a kind of 'serial' portraiture. no. 4, 7, 13, & 15 are, among other things, abt the face as a mask/ & the mask as a face. no. 8 & 12 likewise. 11 & 14 could go together. they celebrate different summers in different places, tho i think i would like to see no. 11 with a small wall all to itself. it's the second most complex grouping of images i've made. it's also the most recent. anyhow, i leave up to you to find your own 'ratios.' the above is just a kind of clue.

. . . you mentioned over the phone that you'd like to get the exact sizes of the plexi-glass i'll need to cover the photographs so you could go ahead and order them for the show: i've been making a note of each set of photos i've mounted with 'size' in mind and do intend to get 'em to you on time but i've also had this thot that i could order the plexi here and put 'em together with each set of photos and send the works out to you.

get into low gear for writing. hear the motor hum. wait for the words to make their discrete appearances. let them tell you what i happen to be abt. all my life i've been a sedentary man. all my life i've moved discrete substances into shapeliness. i ofttimes think i am as much their peculiar shapes as i am anything. every thing in so far as we can call it 'this' or 'that' has its shapeliness. the movement of the mind likewise. like stones, a blanched thigh bone of a small bird, a gust of wind or the torrents of spring . here in vancouver it's a bright clear beginning, it's 'labour day.' ah well, there's no rest for the wicked, no honour to be defiled, in being an artist—nothing but the penetrant blaze of a late summer sun to addle the tongue   nothing but incubated heat.

Dear Lora

   speaking of Okinawa & particularly a tiny island called Obama : the last pictures i took and the most recent piece in the show originated there. as i have arranged them, the 35 frames ought to tell a whole story about one small place. there's the portraits of some of the people i met and there's the snapshots of the island they inhabit, not to mention their trade. & to set these off, there's the frames i took in Kyoto of classical images of Japanese women seen thru the reflections in the bank window. the images of the old man that reoccur stress his importance. he is the fishing community's elder and an outstanding folk musician. i've insisted on his importance (in the double exposures) in particular because he sang us the tales of his tribe during a 5-day typhoon. i would sooner trust his wind & weather acumen than any short-term politicians. he had only retired in recent years and had gone fishing well into his late seventies. you might wonder about the frames, the ones that are horizontally scored with aberrant white lines. i've included them for their image first (despite the scoring) and finally came to the conclusion that these essentially ruined frames had their own thing to contribute to the whole. the arrangement of all the photographs (glyphs) in these varied works is very important and i've spent hours getting their alignments (the way they inflect each other) true. the notion is to let the eye find correspondences. i wouldn't be able to do it in some other, less than optimal, arrangement. & so it goes on & on.

Frid., Sept. 18

Dear Lora

      i've just finisht mounting (made a fucken mess of it) a summer piece called 'our daughters swim like swáns, hornby is. summer '79.' it comprises 15 mostly double exposures taken of the Ngans, their two lovely daughters & several of their friends. it's the set i mentioned yesterday. as for the show, some of them will have names or titles while others won't. it all depends on whether or not something 'apt' will whisper to me. the same with the 'prose' accompaniment. i don't see the need for an utter completion anyhow. things have a perverse way of hanging on. i mean these days everything i make seems to have been in the making for a long-long time. nothing wants to get to where it's finisht. how a thing began & how it will end of times seems both fortuitous & fated. over the weekend i shall have to make a selection and, holding the gallery space in my mind's eye, i'll work out their actual arrangements on the walls. then i'll pack 'em up. there's an apt word or phrase somewhere that could serve as a title for the show but i haven't found it. if it happens to fall into your hands, will u pass it on?

                      we're havin' a lovely fall
                      the utter clarity of light & air just goes
                      on & on; even as i've spent
                      most of it inside my black box. thank
                      whomever i got to Okinawa for
                      awhile for the tropical sun

356 Powell St. Vancouver
midnight, Monday 21st, '81

Dear Lora

Pacific Art Services are comin' by at 9 am tomorrow (Sept. 22nd) to pick up the big packet I've spent 2 whole days packing up. they're going to slip the packet into a light crate and get it onto air express. hopefully you'll have it by the middle of the week. I'm sending it on to you 'collect.' this evening after a short nap followed by a hot shower then the dishes I'm down at my Powell Street studio determined to get some kind of (ongoing) letter off to you. as I sit here I find that the pressures of gettin' the show on the road are beginning to slip from my shoulders. ah, now I've had a good toke I'm beginning to tip toe. as light as I am I feel even lighter. having, as it were, gorged myself with divers images, I now wanta wipe my visors clean. in short I want to attend to a host of other things. like putting a 90 minute cassette tape of divers sounds together. one which could be played during the show by setting up a portable deck (complete with instructions). the idea being that anyone who wants a complementary sound while viewing the works could simply turn it on and, after viewing, turn it off. (pedagogically) I'd like to use the occasion fully. I mean to be able to demonstrate how working at the interfaces between all the arts is the most serious game I know these days. I live these days to find callit the ratios between the auditory the visuals, & the tactile. it's all about 'proportions,' hence 'harmonies,' 'pulsations,' & the vibrancies of 'touch,' something like touching the grounds of the familiar in the Paleolithic man I also am. my inclinations tend towards the beatitudes of the mundane, the mutabilities.

hope you will be able to get Vicki to Toronto for a performance. & if you do I hope we'll be advertised. apart from the students & faculty at Scarborough, I'd like to be able to show 'those' on the Toronto Art Scene Who Might Remember Me what I've been up to since the middle '70s. but it doesn't matter, we would give it all we've got for a handful of people anyhow. as for the reading, I'm hoping that the manuscript edition of WHEELS (my Japan book) will be ready. & even if it ain't, I'll read a portion of it anyhow. as I type I'm listening to the cassette tape of this morning's music session with my friend the flautist Don Druick. I'm of course playing a dulcimer. we've been playing Mondays since late spring and, dozens of cassette tapes later, I can hear 'our' music. I am pleasured by our concord as much as by our different tempos, different pulsations, all of which reminds me again that the act of making anything with another is among the deepest pleasures I know these days. I loathe the ongoing (false) 'Romanticism viz the Artist as The Solitary Hero' which even photographers (who should know better) pander to. photography for me is nothing if not a kind of tacit consent, a visualized mutuality. I for one wouldn't go after it if I didn't get a glimpsing of an inexorable kind of mutability.

furthermore

. . . if you need another photograph, you could phone Mike &/or bp and ask either/both for the ones they have. I'm sure they wouldn't say no. I haven't had the time to get in touch with Vicki (or you) to see if we're going to be able to perform together. assuming we will, I'm going to have to start thinking of the kinds of configurations we might together shape. I'll begin by playing back a lot of my music to hear her agile presence in among the sounds. then I'll gather a lot of the sounds together and make her a cassette tape. she will listen to them and respond. we'll work together on choreographing the performance by mail. if we need any props (they'll certainly be minimal), I'll let you know before the occasion. Vicki & I know one another well and we're going to go for the most intense performance we can put together. Lora, dear Lora, the secret, if it can be named, of being an artist (which is to say being utterly permeable) is to remain constantly vigilant, particularly when it comes to repeating one's past successes. these days I'm as deeply interested (involved) in the subtle intelligence of my finger tips and the exact nuances of pitch they can evoke. &, photographically speaking, I'm totally into the abstract harmonies of the 'grey scale.' not in any one photo as such, but in their myriad combinations. today was our first intimation of a grey wet winter day. the cold suckt. the wind whirled the falling leaves along Powell Street. why, we even had to turn up the thermostat for the first time since early summer. I hope we'll still have a few more Indian summer days. if I've got more to say I'll write later. these words also address themselves to that long ago interview we never had. above all, they're meant to harken you to get the ol' show on the road.

                        regards

list of (mounted) photographs tor Scarborough College

1/ Francois & Kristina, Montreal, March '81
    63 x 13 3/4

2/ Powell Street Promenade, July '78
    40 1/4 x 32 18

3/ David Bolduc & Eric Gamble in their studio, Toronto, '80
    37 1/4 x 32 1/8

4/ David, Gladys, Max & Daphne, double-exposed, '80
    34 7/8 X 32 1/8

5/ Raf & Kit at the P.N.E., Vancouver '77
    33 1/4 x 17 1/2 (cibachrome)

6/ Gold Windows of the Sun, '79
    24 1/2 x 17   (cibachrome)

7/ A kid I know tries on my masks, Wreck Beach, '79
    40 1/8 x 11 (cibachrome)

8/ Her belly : their hands
    32 X 22 1/2

9/ Joy Kogawa & her mother, Vancouver, '81
    35 3/4 X 10 3/4

10/ double wedding portrait, Ottawa, '80
    40 1/8 X 16 1/2

11/ 35 *frames from Obama:* Homage to a small place in the sun, July '81
    60 3/8 X 30 1/4

12/ Torso, Vancouver '80
    40 1/4 x 23

13/ Summer & Smoke, '78
    32 1/2 x 30

14/ Hornby Island Bathers
    53 3/4 x 26 3/4 (cibachrome)

15/ self-portrait among shadowed rocks, '76
    (i packt it up without getting the dimensions)

Friday, Sept. 18th, midnight

Dear Victoria & Richard

    since gettin' back from Nippon seven weeks ago I've been (shall I say it) a technician of the sacred in my dark room. I've been workin' like a manic devil in his black retort gettin' my Scarborough (Photo) Show together for Lora Carney. Vicki—have you, by chance, heard from her about our dulcimer/dance performance on the evening of the 19th of Oct.? anyhow, as soon as i untie myself from my darkroom, I'll put a cassette together for you. it'll (of course) be of & abt my recent music. both what i make and what i listen to. that abt to be made cassette tape could be a way into whatever we do. meanwhile, drop me a line & tell me you're still willing. I mean, let's begin to choreograph an occasion by correspondence & mail. let's knock our heads together, etc. as you know, I am not adverse to improvisation/s. I mean, we could make the whole thing up that very evening, couldn't we? this wee note is to break the (inevitable) silences that cushion the callit cacophony of our busy days. now it's time to re-enter the domain of darkness. P R E S T O I become a squint-eye'd mole with a gimlet of light to entrance an image with. write or phone soon.

                                                luv

                                                Friday, Sept. 25th, '81
                                                365 Powell St., Vancouver BC

Dear Vicki/Richard & Lora at Scarborough

    I am both listening to the cassette tape of a marvelous nite in Kohama while making a dup. of it & writing to the three of you. I'm doing this because it's time for me to begin thinking about a 'dance & dulcimer' performance. I'm doing it to re-enjoy a lovely (never to be repeated) night of drunken friendship. I'm (curiously) listening, listening to my own laughter. Like they say in the press, there ain't much to laugh about these days given our fossil-fuel distress: this era of Kadulfys & Reaganmaniacs. All of which proposes something like this for our performance. Are you ready? For starters: use of the gallery space. Ideally, with cushions for whatever audience, on the floor. Otherwise, simple non-squeaking kind of chairs. & for us, minimal props, for instance, a round table about three feet across with sturdy legs so I can hammer the ol' dulcimer, & two office-type secretarial chairs with wheels on all four legs to enable us to move quickly from a sitting position to a standing one. Plus a shaded table light, an ashtray for me and two glasses filled with ice water. Plus someone who knows the gallery lighting system and could monitor it at our behest. the table ought to be about 34 high ideally—to be able to sit down to, & stand up at, my dulcimer. O yes, & a few discrete flowers in an unobtrusive pot. Then, just in case we might want to do some rehearsing, it would be nice to have the gallery to ourselves for a few hours before the performance. The rest will be up to Vicki & me. I'm still listening to that cassette of Kohama and one way or another it'll surely become a part of whatever I/We do. I mean that my part in all this proposes I bring everything that's deeply pleasured (or even pained) me to the very next occasion, the very next thing I make. Which thought leads to another one that goes like this. That anything Vicki & I do has to celebrate, first and foremost, our friendship. I want to say our love affair to propose what's surely involved. There's a wealth of experience we share which must, given the occasion, find itself a shapeliness I can't, don't want to, foretell. Which does remind me that the deepest, most abiding, relationships I have with another have nothing of the mercenary about them. Not even a tiny bit. I see our collaboration as such. We shall enact something. We shall do it together. We will always be ourselves. We will, if we're lucky, touch a well-spring in each other. Now let the dulcimer/dance unfold. Let it become entirely 'us.' p/s the next thing I'll send is a cassette tape filled with (mostly) my music. If the so-called 'future' can continue to hold such occasions in front of my nose, I'm going to goad myself on. Let's simply do it. Truth, ah truth, you must be the sound that finds its echo. You must be the gesture that arouses. Take care of yourselves and give the occasion some thoughtfulness.

Saturday, October 3rd, '81, noon

Dear Vicki

last night Don Druick & i went to the Japanese community centre to listen to Tota playing his jamisen. this a.m. i am listening to him again, via the cassette i made the night before. right now he's singin' his heart out and all the old women in the audience are clappin' their hands. he's a contemporary Japanese troubadour and, like 'those' before him, he has spent a decade traveling the length & breadth of Japan, learning its inimitable music. he's a young man (33) who's music goes deep. he's my link with the old man of Kohama i mentioned earlier. despite, despite the handicaps, the inseparableness of a song from its mother tongue, i like to think i am part of that lineage. o warpt tongue. o my nonetheless waspish proclivities. these days it's only music that enables me to be in touch with the sacral. i've meant to phone you about our upcoming performance. i've meant to but, given my dislike of using the telephone, given my funny little apprehensions, i haven't. besides which i do want the whole occasion to simmer within each of us. i do want that space that silence/distance/ & letters afford to think about what we shall do. think of it this way: all the moments, all of the times i will have played music, all of the times i will have listened to it and all of the times i have sat down to write you a letter are nothing if not an ongoing rehearsal of that night. i mean it could, simply enough, begin by the two of us sitting at the aforementioned table and go on from there. well, the tape i began for you the other day is just about finisht. it's just another anthology of sounds i've been making & listening to. . . . am i ever going to hear from you?

Saturday, October 10th, '81

dear Lora

got yr note abt receiving & viewing the photos. got yr message (response). thank you. tho i did have the thot of sending you a wall plan showing how they ought to be related, i'm glad i didn't have time to get around to it 'cause it's always more interesting to come upon someone else's arrangements for sequences and juxtapositions. i literally mean, how anything is out there in the world (photos in particular) is beyond an artist's control. anyhow, i am looking forward to your hanging. & i am at work on Vicki's & my performance. i am tuning myself up:

clusters of feelings via clusters of sounds via clusters of movements, yet, to keep the whole occasion, utterly, up-front, utterly, spontaneous. Vicki & i are limbering up in our distinctive ways three thousand miles apart. now, just as soon as we have a bare schema, i shall write again to ask you to get us some basic props. props like the aforementioned table, two chairs, an ashtray, a pot of flowers, a large projection screen, a projector with remote controls & a wide-angle lens, & perhaps a video deck complete with tripod & camera. otherwise, i'll be in Toronto next weekend for sure. i'll be probably staying with David Young & Sarah Sheard. more later .

                                                                     356 Powell Street/ Sat., Oct., 10th noon

dear Vicki

            i've been hobbling abt with a fuckt-up left knee for over a week. i've been, as you might well guess, taken up by my lack of mobility, nothin' quite as draggy as a bum knee. nothing quite as wet as this October. nonetheless, i've been working towards our erstwhile performance at Scarborough College by playin' my dulcimer several hours each day and listenin' to the tapes i keep making along the way. D.D. & i put on a live improvisation thirty minutes long on co-op radio last night. i've been listening to it as i write : i've been attending to its modalities. have you had a chance to listen to the tape i sent? does your body respond to it? what does it think and what will it do?

            i have a tray full of frozen lava slides from Hawaii. i will be sorting & arranging them next week. & i intend to sit down & make music to them. something like a *frozen lava raga*. i want the music to elucidate the aural experience and i'm wondering if you could improvise something to both slides & music in front of a large viewing screen. the *f.l.r.* could be abt 20 minutes long & could be the middle movement or piece. *tripartite*. a classical *three-part performance*. something *before* and something *after* like a finale. dear Vicki, i'm just thinking out loud, as it were, for us. i'm doing this in lieu of our getting together without time for rehearsals. i'm doing this, even as i keep in mind the *astonishments* you will bring to the occasion. p.s. do you think we ought to have the occasion videotaped? i mean i could ask lora if they've got the facilities in the audio/visual dept at Scarborough. dear Vicki, despite my immobility, i am in a good space and i hope you (4) are too. luv

dear Vicki

            i've been nursing my knee & cursing ay derelictions. like they say, if it ain't one thing, it's another. thank gawd i don't have (touch wood) arthritis of the finger tips yet. Daphne sez i'm an awful sight to see, bent over & hobbling about. the more so given the usually nimble man i am. for good or bad there's been one decided advantage in not being able to get around: it's enabled me to get into the music, it's enabled me to think about us. i hope i won't be gimpy when we meet in Toronto. i don't really want to have you see me impaired.

            i've spent the morning getting set-up to make a tape to go along with the frozen lava slides. i've been reviewing all the slides again & again to tighten up the movement. & i've been watching them flick by while strumming my dulcimer. i have it in mind to synchronize the two of them. then, i want to sit down to both slides & tape, not to mention your movements, and improvise on my jamisen. hopefully, we'll be able to evoke a kind of frozen music/ dance. i can see that it will be this evening after supper before i make that tape. it's gonna take a whole afternoon of fussing about to get in tune with the lava goddess's awesome coruscations. otherwise, i feel bereft of ideas for us. for instance, i haven't got any other 'visuals' we can use. or, rather, i won't get around to sorting thru them to see what we could use. thus our performance could be said to be open-ended. like i've already suggested, we could simply begin by taking our places at the small table and open up the evening by quietly talking to each other while i add a 3rd party to the conversation with the sounds of my dulcimer warming up. it'll enable me to tune up and sound out the room's acoustics. then, depending on what happens to flow out from us, you could get up and walk off into the darkness and slowly begin to unlimber. at which point i'll be watching you and, after getting a drift of your predilections, i could play a tune for your agilities. the first movement could have the emotional quickness of a (shall i say it) pair of lovers who meet again in a strange city after a number of years. both dance & music ought to image their instant recognitions, as well as the usual strangenesses that their apartness, hence their changes, propose. dear Vicki, you can take all this with a grain of salt. you can attend to it or not, it won't matter. i am, needless to say, making it up. at any rate, i do want some feedback viz the shape of our performance. the third movement ought to be, if it seems possible, an extended solo by you, with or without my own music. a counterpoint, if you will, between movement/s, stillnesses/ silences, song, &/or rhythm. then, if we want to round off the whole thing, we could reassume our positions at the table and let the whole occasion end in, callit, whispers.

   now i know that the time is coming. i know because i have begun to worry a bit about what instruments to take and whether or not i'll still be hobbling. at any rate, i am determined to travel as light as possible. do you think you could make it to Scarborough for a day-long rehearsal on Sunday?

luv

Wednesday, October 14th, '81
356 Powell St. Vancouver B.C.

  dear Vicki

   it's already Wednesday. all the things i wanted to do before leaving for Toronto will have to wait. including the further cassette tape i've been making for you to listen to. it doesn't feel like my knee is going to heal in time. it doesn't feel like i'm going to be able to do cartwheels, let alone walk on air. all of which turns out to be a blessing in disguise as it will keep me at a standstill to tune myself for our performance: something i've been doing for the past few weeks. nothin' quite like a fuckt-up knee to give the lie to my own adroitnesses. nothing, given the old bod's frailties, but wit & stillness, even the mind's agitations, recognize the portent. (stop) Dale came by to say hullo. she's been sharing my darkroom for a coupla years and now she & Jim are building a place for themselves on a high bluff on Main Island. they're going to move there and settle down. i'm gonna miss her. anyhow, Vicki, i've decided not to worry about us. i've decided, given our years of mutual experience as performers, that we will be able to make up the show on the spot. 'improvisations' are what i'm about anyhow. sometimes i feel that my whole life is nothing but an unruly kind of improvisation, one which has its moments of alacrity as well as awesome doubts. i'll be phoning you from Toronto, say, on Friday night. do you think we can get together on Sunday to enliven each other? luv

Friday, Sept. 25th, 1981, 10.30 pm

Dear Francois & Kristina

    since i last saw the two of you the most memorable thing that's happened to me happened in Kohama, Japan. the days pass . . . the years seem to be more fleet these days. if i had my way i'd try to live untrammeled by the drift of time. odd to think that there'll come a day when we won't wake up. anyhow, this is just to say that your double-portrait will be seen in my photo-show at Scarborough College during October: after which i'll have Lora Carney send it on to you. so what's new with you two? what's older than love? come to think about it, i have the feeling i've been here before. hang on for dear life. hug the terra-firma. don't of course know when we'll meet again but rest assured you're as close as my thoughts of you. ain't affluence cum inflation grand? ain't it, to say the least, a consternation devoutly to be forgotten? marmalade & tea. mammalian affections. salut .

here's my statement for your piece on the varied members of the Order of Canada in the Vancouver area.

(please use it exactly *as is.*)

if the O.C. means anything to me
it must have something to do with my parents' silent pride
and how they have always stood behind me.
if the O.C. means more than this
it must have something to do with my own children and how
they have abided their father's prolonged absences
with an equanimity which is another name
for love. otherwise, i am pleasured for being honoured
for doing what i've done most of my life.
art & the intricate terrain of the familial is easily worth
a long lifetime of endeavour.

        written at 356 Powell Street
        Vancouver B.C. Sat. Sept. 26, '81

Monday, Sept. 29th, '81

Dear Victor

    ah i remember Kingston—i gave a poetry reading there: i had bought Mike Snow's two discs in Toronto and, wanting to spread the news, i played several cuts from them. an ancient Andre Beiler was in the audience. he distinguished himself by sitting very upright with a long slender horn held to his ear. like New Westminster, i thought, Kingston's most notable chunk of architecture was the ol' penitentiary. nothin' like the monumental architecture of our grand punitive systems to make nonsense out of the romance of the ol' sod roof'd log cabin of our erstwhile forebearers. anyhow, glad you have a decent paying gig for a change. this is mostly to tell u that i am in a good space these days. this is to tell you that i'm having a photo-show at Scarborough College during October and that i'll be at Scarborough on the 19th & 20th for a performance & an old-fashioned poetry reading. i won't be able to get down to Kingston, but if you need a break and can get away, maybe you'd like to join me at Scarborough, or David Young's where i'll be staying. i'm not into any music these days i can't make for myself—i'm thrumming a dulcimer & other string instruments to find my own sound. it's something like finding your own colours, your very own language. it's something like that kinda appetite. & inevitably, how hungry we are. i won't say a thing about my Japan trip but, to say it again, it pleasured something that goes deep in me. Daphne, Kit & i continue to be an equilateral triangle. the so called geometry of our now eight-year old relationship is ofttimes crystalline. keep in touch.

Sept. 29th, '81,
648 Keefer St.
Vancouver, BC, V6A 1Y4

my dear Syuzo & family

     my four day stop-over in Hawaii which included a small poetry reading in the 'volcano city art centre' and getting real high on Hawaiian gold was an unexpected pleasure. nothing quite like the tropics, whether it's Kohama or Honolulu, to make a body feel good. nothing quite like a body that feels good to want to go on even as i know i am dying. since July 1st i have spent almost all of my time inside a dark-room busy printing & mounting a photo exhibition for a college in Toronto this fall. it's only been the last few days i have been clear of photographies & already the leaves are falling from the tall maple trees around Oppenheimer Park. remember the tiny micro-cassette recorder i got there? well, it's been playing back all the sounds i caught tripping about. though i keep on losing bits and pieces of my trip (already) and i'll soon find myself having to make it all up, i am pleasured by all the different company i kept. p.s. i have been strumming my jamisen every day and though i'm not happy with the sounds i make i am learning day by day. the enclosed cassette tape is especially for you. i shall follow it up with a packet of photographs. let's keep in touch one way or another.

     with gratitude,

Saturday, October 2nd, '81, 5 pm

dear Mike/ & Linda when she gets here

    got the colourful ah Hawaii prints of yours truly. gotta a lovely whiff of the tropics, not to mention my brief tan. i'll tell you about my stay in volcano city and show both of you my 'lava' slides—why i don't know, it must be something like show-&-tell. it's got somethin' to do with sharing a view. meanwhile, i've been assiduously listening to callit scraps of another brief summer via my micro-cassette recorder: ah the cheap thrills of Proustian remembrances & all the Faustian wit. even as i am listening (again) to the old man playing his jamisen, i am listening to nothing but echoes, sonic re-verbs that continuously relapse into oceanic silences. i'm looking forward to my gig in Toronto and i'm looking backward to Hawaii & Japan. these wee words want to teeter-totter. primate: primemate: cremate: dissolve. Daphne will be there before me and we'll meet on Saturday night at David & Sarah's (17th). she leaves next day while i do my thing on the 19th & 20th. shall we all get together, then?

Thursday, October 15th, noon

Dear Jim

I'm off to Toronto Friday noon for 1/ a dulcimer/dance performance, 2/ a poetry reading from my latest book of pomes, WHEELS. Both occasions, together with my *photo show*, will be at Scarborough College, University of Toronto. I'll be there to check proof sheets, rehearse & do my thing thru to the 21st.

Otherwise, I'm still keen about getting a 'paid' sabbatical for the '82/'83 season. There's so much I need to have time for to gather together. There's also new projects I have in mind that require a concentrated period of unhurried time. Will you do what you can for me?

648 Keefer Street
Vancouver, BC, V6A 1Y4
Oct. 23rd, '81

Dear Sarah

    Was I in Toronto a few days ago? Did you catch sight of me? Now that I'm back, I keep wondering if I was really there. Someone who knows the real 'me' said via long-distance that they thot they saw somebody with a gimpy leg who lookt just like me. I don't know why but I want to say that I'm a little pisst off at the thot of having an impersonator. Particularly one who talks too much for anybody's good. My informant in Toronto told me that the gimpy one kept putting his big feet in everyone's face. Anyhow, here I am in Vancouver and, for some reason beyond the frail litanies of passion, I find myself wrapping my heating pad round an imaginary bruise on an imaginary knee and I am wondering who I am and what that guy that is impersonating me has to do with it. I'm not even sure which one of us is typing this letter. All I'm sure of is that it's meant for you and you alone (unless you want to show David). It's terrible to think that all I have to fight the Ubu Roi armaments race with is my own alacrity. It's terrible to read the latest issue of TIME and discover that the latest injection in that dullard's game called ECONOMICS (Free Enterprise Style) is the old munitions game. & it's equally terrifying to feel my own impotence at doing anything to stave it off. Hold onto your britches 'cause marriage, music, friendships, & poetry are about to dissolve in ideology cum propaganda. The next war won't be debased by anything as irrational as racism or ethnocentricity. No, it'll be the hairy hand of naked power. It'll probably leave us totally mindless. As over against this menacing scenario, your wearing something unorthodox at a wedding is a grace-note I would hearten to. Say HI to David & She for me. Tell 'em both I love them. luv

saturday. october 24th, '81

Dear Vicki

at this very moment i'm listening to the tape we made and it's being recorded (for you) simultaneously. listening to it, i thot we got off to a slow start. we probably talkt too much, etc. now, your singing, your invoking, and we've finally taken off. sing sing your heart out for, among other things, your unborn child, your irish ancestors and your own & my beguilements. now i'm talking to you and despite myself (as i sit here writing) i wonder what i'm all about. i'm wondering about our performance, out loud. ah, now we're into the performance wholeheartedly. i can see you dancing in my mind's eye. but where is the music coming from if not from the huge sky dome just outside that giant waffle skylight we found ourselves looking up thru? where o where are your movements coming from if not thru that same panoply? now our audience is clapping and the first movement has completed itself after i stopt playing and you gathered your movements up into yourself in silence. heartlessly the world goes on and now we're about to begin our second movement. frozen lava (raga) movement. remember all those faint abysmal slides? remember how they in all their faintness created a shimmer of light for your agilities? remember my variegated laughter? even as i hear myself laughing i am saying to myself that laughter, unprovoked laughter bordering on mirth and madness, is itself part of the script. anyhow, even without the tape to replay it all, i am pleasured by what we did. let's find a way to do it again. let's keep in touch in whatever way we can. now the last of the faint lava slides are flicking past. now the music and the dance are about to return to silence. golden waffle silences. pat your tummy when it begins to bulge for me. love

648 Keefer Street
Vancouver, BC, V6A 1Y4
October 24th, '81

Dear Victor

your last letter arrived the day after i left for Toronto and, tho i've been back in Vancouver a coupla days, i just got around to reading it. i don't know what i can say in reply that our brief but intense visit together at David & Sarah's didn't say for both of us. reading about the legendary lives of all the famous & infamous poets & others all my life i've often wondered if they were in the habit of speaking their minds with their close friends. or did they save it all up to put into a pome or a letter and go on talking nonsense because they didn't trust what passed thru their mouths, given the fact that they knew their mouths could be foul? anyhow, it was good to see you well. good to see you with (yet) another fine woman. ah i can imagine you when you're almost an old man: you'll be sitting down with all the women in your life and as each of them reinvents their life with you you will write a chapter to commemorate their varied enchantments, their prodigious skills. like i've already said elsewhere, we are all the women we have known as much as we are ourselves, etc. autumn here is a riot of colours. i am, despite my limp (remember R.B.'s limp dick, etc.), a small but vivid conflagration. reading the latest issue of TIME magazine while flying high over the prairies i suddenly had the thot that the Yanks could have us blowin' to smithereens without batting 300. i suddenly saw the magnitude of free enterprise aggressiveness and i wanted to puke them out. heart o murmuring ol' heart. why o why do you find yourself a flutter? if i read another word about how good 'we' are for the 3rd world with all its deprivations i'm gonna get really angry. it's a pack of lies. or a can of lye poured down into a clogged up toilet. it's nothin' but waspish propaganda.

648 Keefer Street
Vancouver, BC, V6A 1Y4
Oct. 25th, 3 am, '81

Dear Richard

    'we' had a lovely time. we put on a performance i'll not forget 'til we do it again some day. i mean that only a comparable occasion can erase its (illustrious) predecessor. why, from the very moment of our arrival at Guildwood station (quite unbeknown to each other) thru till the mad-cap cab ride out to Scarborough the following day, the whole occasion was memorable in its claritas. i mean, Richard, that we were meant to do this thing together. like they say, it was in the cards: if not written in the stars. & like medieval lovers we've been impossibly, but memorably, chaste.

        heart. the horst of the heart. its travails. its rallying call/s. hearth. the plenitudes of earth. its furrowed & rutted sorrows. frozen dreams. withered testicles. tractless wonderments. a faint whistling in the dark. aching silences. etc. Richard o Richard, it's the earth, the huge earth itself that enlivens our mutabilities. we're nothing without the surcease of its plenitudes. keep up the good work. keep all the senses open. p/s, guilt ain't anything but the black Maria racing thru the empty street of our nightmares.

        love,

Dear Lora

      one has to eat their words for the pome's sake, i thot as i found myself facing all those shining young faces. one has to speak their mind (at my age) or forever hold their tongue. i don't know if i got across to them, but i meant everything i sd. including some things that weren't even in the script. *discourse,* as i find myself engaged in it, is a continuous act of improvisation. the quest seems to be 'insight' into the thots & acts of one's life. furthermore, my notion of discourse includes photography & such music as i can make. it's a whole complex of inter-related acts. acts including wit, laughter & silences. & tho i am a member of the academic community (having taught for 25 years), i haven't much sympathy for pedagogy as our educational institutions deal it out. it tends to leave the 'spirit' as well as the 'feelings' out for the sake of methodology & a narrow-minded specialism. at UBC i often have the feeling that (speaking of faculty) so-called 'professionalism' is nothing more than knowledge tacitly accepted as 'private property.' like i've often thot to myself, nobody owns knowledge. i've even wondered if it can be possessed at all. furthermore, i tend to mistrust 'knowledge' that does not consult all of our senses—'intellect,' in my sense, simply being one of them. i mean there's nothing more monstrous than a swollen head without a consciousness of its friability. having said all this, i must add that i've known so-called artists who were equally monstrous. salut.

Nov. 4th, '81, noon.

Dear Lora

      Mike telephoned 'long distance' to say that he & Linda got out to Scarborough to see the show. Which pleases me: as i made it for folks like them. One doesn't need an audience as much as, say, a witness or two to verify their 'take' on so-called realities. I've often felt that sheer numbers had nothing much to do with what I'm about. I mean that whatever I do will tell itself to somebody. Anyhow, I seem to have my work cut out for me. I seem to almost but not quite 'know' what I am about tho I can't prove it except by doing what I did at S.C. This lovely November morning I drove out to the airport to pick up my photos. Air Canada had delivered them twice but we weren't home, etc. I'm going to package up the photos I want sent on to (you know whom) and Daphne will be delivering them to Mike or you. The packet contains the piece that is meant for you. Say Hi to Terry for me. Say Hi to Scarborough.

December 7th, on campus at UBC, '81

Dear Phil:

Here's a few takes on 'The Space Between' which as a title I do like. I say it's o.k. in so far as it would seem to derive from your thoughts about the act-of-painting, of & for itself alone. I mean that your paper seems to me to be consistent with how you do make paintings. However, the way your paper comes across bespeaks an awful kind of subjectivity, one which the academic mind could find fault with, given the notions attendant upon a university-trained artist with all that that implies. I simply refer to the fact that there are no *referents* outside the terms of your dialogue with painting. No sense of 'who' & 'what' you are beholden to. No sense of what you have 'looked' at & been taken with. No sense of the domain of literature surrounding art. In short, no quotations, no footnotes & no bibliography. Nonetheless, I for one am more than willing to assume that you have incorporated this callit 'scholarship' into both the painting & the writing and thus rendered it invisible. Given the sheer energy you brought to painting and being present, wholly present to that act, I regard the paper as itself a footnote. The icing, if you will, & not the cake. p.s. Hope you find a way in these troublesome times to keep at it. Given an ongoing openness and a bit of luck, you ought to come into your own as a painter. I'll look forward to seeing your work up against a wall one of these days. Take care .

Yours sincerely,

December '81

Dear Isamu & Kazuko

    'time' lapses. or, rather, we seem to stand still while moving on. i was going to say, a treadmill—like one of horizontal escalators you find in international airports. my kohama is a 'freeze frame' of a mid-summer typhoon. the weather remains as vivid as your faces, a portrait in time that declines all exactitudes. broad as the pacific. small as a sand island. or a tea drop. water. moving water. elapsed time collapsed that. every distinct thing i remember about kohama displaces a thousand vagaries. where am i? and what am i doing there? if i could say these things in japanese, i might say them differently but mean the same things in english. the power of politics resides in nomenclature. its abuses can lead to, among other things, felony. the weather here drenches. it washes the portrait of your faces. broad as the pacific. small as kohama. don't waste time crying over spilt milk. throw away your watches. time elapsed parents unborn time. every thing i remember about kohama replaces a drop of salt sea. southern climes. northern predilections. the residual powers of a noun turn into stone which in turn holds the heat of summer. if i could say all this in japanese i would say it. a tongue-tied nissei often forgets to cross his 't's' and dot his 'i's'. hang on for dear life. give the children their due. dope debilitates the pater nostrum. remembering the old man remembering his youth i remember my own ocean. a sea of waving wheat. a delirium of sky. i came down to kohama to take a good look at the two of you and the magnanimous ocean. what i hold in mind i hold to be true. time collapses the view. nothing like a hot ofuro in the middle of a typhoon. you might not believe it but i haven't laughed or got as drunk since i was with you in kohama. laughter is dirt cheap. the sands of time decline all measurements. fuck the computer if you want to birth peregrine statistics. use 'radar' or 'sonic' scanners if you want to wipe out all the salmon. use a spear if you want to laser an eel. maya koizumi listened to all the tapes i made in kohama. she sd it was like being right there with both of you. if you toss a green bottle with a message in it into the ocean, it will float into someone's future. i came to kohama to see both of you. the pictures are an exact replica of the ghost of you. flesh & blood. brine intelligence. a sea of waving wheat. the myriad creatures of the sea writhing under our bare feet at low tide. islands sand islands singing in the southern sun. the language of sentiments is a lapse into amniotic time. memory gloss. cadences of a summer. fuck the consumer society. debits and liabilities die daily. if you toss a salad in the air it will tumble before it hits the ground. doors of enchantment. windows of suppression. hang onto dear life. if you could see me as i am now you would say that he's changed colours. chameleon. comic disguises. remembering the old man playing his jamisen, i have been playing my own. no two musicians can make exactly the same sound—'once,' let alone twice. three blind mice. three blind mice (us?). see how they run. see how they run. they all run after a mytho-utopia with a laugh in their bellies and a tune to hum. three blind humans with a thumb to suck. a sun to suck. i remember your sunburnt faces as a portrait that declines all exactitudes. if i could say all this to you in japanese i would have been born in kyoto or umagi. language sucks. every breast begets another tongue. i wonder what language i would speak if i had been born green. i hear the sea awash in my ear. i see myself, inexorably, veering towards it.

saturday, october 31st, 1981 (already)
(almost, but not quite gone

three months have gone bye the bye since i was in kohama. time flies. an ocean of particulars dies into each word i write. what's left unsaid? what's left, mired in silence, haunts these words. if i did write to you in japanese i would put parentheses around our laughter. even as i sit here on powell street writing to you i can hear all the children say sake! sake! SAKE! everytime i find myself telling somebody about my week in kohama i invent myself, everytime this occurs i find i have to invent both of you, not to mention all the others. what's left of my brief passage along the beaches of kohama informs all these words. i've printed countless pictures of it. i've listened to all the tapes i made during the memorable typhoon. everytime i hear the rain falling on our roof here in vancouver i feel my whole body laved in your ah warm tropical rains. 'no man is an island unto himself,' sd a famous english poet. i wonder how many languages in the world hold that thought in mind. ah, but here's the rub: i had to go all the way to kohama to renew its veracity. no one except a handful of now-aged Indians remember the huge sky over an immense prairie overrun by buffalo. billy the kid was nothing but a gun-totting medieval troubadour. history is nothing but a choice of alignments in time. points on a grid. itself an illusion of order. these simple words would decline all hierarchies for the sake of tropic plenitudes. if i could write to you in japanese i would try to say the same things. mired-in-silence these words want to rise above my small fears. fuck the computer if you want to birth the monster of calculus. i felt the whole beach move under my feet and i felt the myriad organisms moving through me as indivisibly as my blood cells. what gets left unsaid also moves through these words. there are colours embedded in these consonants and vowels i have never seen. they lure me on.

i'm listening to the tapes, again. i've been re-attending the drunken evening we shared during that mid-summer typhoon. strange to be here in vancouver at the beginning of the winter rains and hear all of us as we get drunker and drunker. strange to hear myself speaking japanese while laughing with you in english. strange, yet utterly familiar, all the dialects of our laughter. how many tongues do each of us speak? and aren't we all a basket of water? if i ever return to kohama i will have to re-invent my sense of self if only to be the perfect stranger. keep an eye on the yanks stationed in naha now that reagan presides in the (sic) white house. fuck ideologies. close your shutters against the typhoon unless you want to lose your roof. if i could write in japanese i certainly would. what is the ideogram for a tear? how do we escape from the coercions of a language? is taped-laughter real? hang on for dear life. let it go if you have to for your children's sake. *sake! sake! sake!* when the venerable rice god distilled the first brew and tasted it he must have had in mind our memorable night during an equally memorable typhoon. rain nothing like a tropical rain storm to wash the big-city blues away. inundated. inundated by a plethora of memories i am, among other things, their faithful savant. now we are laughing our fool heads off and our children are laughing with us. i tell myself that i would like to die amongst such ebullience. strange to be listening to the old man singing and be moved to song. i'm having the time-of-my-life without going anywhere. kohama a speck. canada a larger one. if i could speak an impeccable english i wouldn't necessarily use it to address the two of you. heart's small song hides parentheses. the wrathful gods have been awakened by a lethal injection of malignant chromosomes. i'm almost afraid of their satanic fury. i'm almost fearful of being a man. ironic mankind. nothing like laughter in the belly of fear. nothing like untapeable silences. hullo kohama .

Dec. 16th, '81

Through Familiar Eyes
Proposes, amongst a Host of Recognitions, that
What the Photographer happens to be looking intently at and Whatever it is that
Happens to be looking back are co-equals. I'm not (these days)
Interested in the anti-Capitalist's notion that a camera is just another tool
(or weapon) in man's conquest of Nature. Even as I am stupefied
By the continuing rhetoric of its obscene insistences, viz the razz-ma-tazz over
The latest computer & all of its programmatic agilities.
Through Familiar Eyes speaks—in so far as pictures can be said to speak—
Of How Tacitly Both Parties Consent to be Recognized within
A make-belief world of images. I take this to be true with a barndoor, a pebble,
Or a face. Through Familiar Eyes proposes that an eye is nothing
But a Prism-of-Light (I was going to say, 'prisoner of light'). These are then
Pictures of all the different sorts of members of family. Plus
Those of immediate friends. Strangers, necessarily, are among them. You may have
Seen one or another among them, whilst walking down Granville St.
Jungian 'synchronicity' and Photography meet at every intersection. My neg. files
Are filled with a Host of Familiar Ghosts. My mind is filled with their
Undefiled presences. Through Familiar Eyes, hopefully,
Embodies both.

kit & his buddy rafael

they are no longer these images of them. they have moved on,
even as they tore thru playland on a hot august afternoon because it was
something to do. they had already been friends for a few years
& even now, several years after these pictures were taken, they continue
to be so tho both of them know it won't last much longer—you
see it reflected in their eyes if not their very postures. they are,
despite these pictures, despite themselves, no longer children.
(perhaps they never were.) see, see how their expressions change from
frame to frame. see how the tall one looks away from the camera
while the short one hams it up. they are not brothers: it's not as simple
as that. given all the endless hours they've played together, each
will carry an image of the other inside themselves for the rest of their life.
these pictures of the two of them are nothing but a brief respite.
moments later, they caught a bus home. it was already night. move on.
move on. nothing stands still. even my own eyes see them (now) in
a different light. playland. playland bathed in its own fictive light.

February '82

dear unheralded issei
    nissei, sansei, even yonsei:

they used to call this block the heart of *Jap Town* even though there's only a handful of Japanese-owned shops left today. hell, everybody knows that it's the goodly Saint James (bless his religio-pragmatism/ his monetary proclivities) who owns most of both sides of the 300 block, Powell Street. now that the finishing touches to the brand new pre-trial retention building across the street from Saint James' concrete bastion have been completed, all the discretionary powers of God, Law, and Order dominate the west-end of my neighbourhood. all, all the *social fiction* based on incontrovertible hierarchies, all the gross inequities begin and burgeon within the domain of these 3 and their imposing brick and concrete edifices: their ofttimes arcane statutes (now monitored by computers), their law enforcement officers, their surveillance corps and tax collectors, together with the ledger-domain of a tribunal of law-makers and their advocates; all abetted by the Biblical Tales authorized by another religio deity named James. all these histrionics prime the pump of the labyrinthine plot at the vestal heart of any modern age megapolis. *REDRESS*, the rallying cry of an awakened Japanese/Canadian conscience, will to all intents and purposes be arbitrated by their God and his anointed jurisprudence. the issue for us J/Cs is HOW WE CAN HELP TO SUNDER THE INEQUITABLE WAR MEASURES ACT and How we can (collectively speaking) as part and parcel of the Canadian Mosaic lift ourselves above the thraldoms of a bestial 20th century of appalling ideologies. i have had a nightmare in which our mechanistic-minded, commodity-riddled age of insidious nuclear wastage got shat out of the arse of that giant of giants, that satanic god whom the ancients fearfully named Mammon. neither redemption, pride, or filthy lucre means much when everybody has sanitized hands and television eyes. . . .

on *NO NUKES DAY*
the neighbourhood children's
variegated voices
enliven the Ides of March

•

how is it
that the word *pollution*
never toucht
the lips of my Dirty '30s
childhood . . . ?

i can't recall
hearing *it* sounded till the
ecological '60s
unearthed it to point
out a plundered
imago mundi . . .

how come a
ravening Stock Market
precipitated
the Great Depression . . . ?
what does it
teach us about wanton
usury . . . ?

born of
the ravening technologies
mid-wifed
by 20th century dialectical
materialism

the combustible
ascendancy of the petrol / chemical
multi-nationals
has injected *pollution* into our
body / politic:
our very nouns

nothing unscathed
even the last child tilting
a No Nukes banner

inside earth and in outer space
a nameless toxicity
corrodes our very metabolism

don't talk too loud about
acid-rain fouling the skies above our
children's fouled hearth
hang onto your logistical epiphanies
your carboniferous mind

will Doktor Faustus take a bow

this foul language bears the imprimatur
of its ideological debasement. watch its solemnity
slowly dissolve on late-night television
then listen to *it* re-surrect in the mouths of these
hapless children enacting their parental
misgivings on No Nukes Day: their ebulliences ride
the warm currents of an undismayed Spring
•

these bright, insouciant pundits
these daffodils
and pink cherry blossoms ignite an
agog green world

the pear tree's white blossoms tessellate the sky

                                                                           march 82'

March 19th/'82, U.B.C. Fine Arts

Dear Fred / & Ricardo:

First a tally of my expenses for the week in Nelson:

Air fare to Nelson & return (enclosed receipt)		$181.45
Taxi to & from 648 Keefer St. to Airport		$30.00
Expenses (@$20.00 per day, as agreed)		$140.00
	Total	$351.45

Then:

I asked the big lady who did the video-work at both my seminars & performance to send me a copy of the video-tapes. & I asked the tall kid with long hair for a copy of the cassette tape he made of my performance. Both agreed I would get same but there seemed to be a problem of duplicating either well, so I suggested they send them on to me (particularly the video/cassette of my performance) & I would get them duplicated here, then send the originals back, pronto. Now, the sole condition of their further usage by DTUC consists in my getting these. Otherwise we'll have to make other arrangements for their actual usage. Could either of you look into this? (I mean, it's not likely I shall wail the way I did that night again, and I want to have a record of the feat. Ok?)

Last but not least:

Need I say that it was a great week: one I got a lota energy from. It told me (again) that such occasions as a mode of pedagogy are right up my alley. To be (demonstratively) an 'artist' is far better than being just another academic one. Fuck the encumbrances. Fuck the 'recession.' Hang in there & make a big bang. Hopefully, I'll see you towards the end of April.

yours truly,

March 31st/ '82
648 Keefer Street, Vancouver, BC

Dear Gerry

Stan B. & I were in Nelson B.C. recently to talk abt divers things. He (bless him) brought along several copies (hot off the press) of *Paper Doors*. Need I say I luv it luv the fact of being sandwiched in between my Canadian/Japanese peers. Need I say you've done a great job, one you've been at since that (equally luvly) CBC job. (Any chance of getting a copy of the tape (in the CBC archives?) of the occasion for my callit history as a C/J?) If making books means anything a glut-world, it must mean such books (wee books) as P.D. How about getting everyone together for a reading at the Japanese Cultural Centre (or whatever it's named) in Toronto this fall just as a kind of kinship celebration? (Wild thots, the more so given the work involved.) Scarred by the 2nd W.W., we C/Js are a small tribe, one I'm proud to be (my kind of) spokesperson for. Whatever else I'm abt, I'm clear at that. Meanwhile, another year at UBC is coming to an end & I feel a bit like a bent bewhiskered ol' man with buckets of rage smouldering under this late March rain. Hi to Roz for me. & D. Aylward.

March 31st, '82
356 Powell St.

Dear Sarah:

Got the small box full of 'paper doors.' Got a real lift from it: The more so since I've been down-in-the-dumps 'cause I've been given notice to leave my Powel St. studio. It ain't the leaving so much as the mountain of stuff I'll have to pack up and take somewhere else. No one told me when I was a kid that adulthood would be, amongst other things, a huge encumbrance. Ah but 'paper doors' is something else. Everyone who had a hand in shaping it up at the ol' Coach House deserves to be congratulated. It's a fine piece of the art of publishing. It's the ah so fine edge of a samurai's sword cutting thru a morass of thick unreadable books. Say 'Hi' to Stan, the true book man for me. Tell him I got off on the breakfast we had together that last morning in Nelson. It's almost midnight (April Fool's Day) and Daphne & Kit will be leaving to join Mike & Linda in sunny Hawaii. Back & forth we come & go & where we'll all end up is anyone's guess. Suffice it to say, this does seem to be our year for moving with (1) my having to move from my Powell Street studio, (2) Kit's moving down to Seattle to be with his father for the upcoming school year. It'll be a real big occasion for both of them now that he's turned thirteen. (3) Daphne's extensive travelling together with her going to the U. of M. this fall to be their resident poet. God knows, the world's a huge place with extraordinary sights but I seem to be almost rooted here (like a unpulpt tree). & my thot is that some young guy/girl just might come along & carve their signature on my gnarled skin. Did you know that the Globe & Mail has invaded Vancouver? Did you know that it's available daily at every crossroad in the entire city? I never thot I would find myself reading it with my morning coffee, but it's nice to be able to keep in touch with the Eastern Establishment's take on our/their proclivities. Tell his lordship I'm keeping an eye out for all of our hearsays, ad nauseam. p/s Coach House could simply run a manuscript edition of WHEELS as it stands & I'll take it up from there when Mike gets back to Kanada.

your reigning Japophile,

Dear Phyllis/

        Hurrah   another school year drawing to an end (again). Given the fact that I started teaching way back in the '50s, it's going on 30 years. I'm not quite at the end of it tho: I don't have much that could be called 'insightful' to speak about. I have no intention of being treated like an old academic hack, let alone a senior citizen. & as of now I don't intend to stay till I'm pensioned off, tho gawd knows what's around the next bend in the ol' O.P.E.C. fossil fuel Ekonomicks. That old pea-under game the oldest con game ever. Anyhow, spring's here. & if it ain't a blessing bestowed on everybody's head, i don't know what these words are worth. I hardly think of the world today without that thought passing through, somebody I love. No real world news without ol' 'referent.' Otherwise, I am almost but not entirely alone. It's as if some God went PRESTO! & Lo & Behold, most everything pertaining to the 'domestic life' has fallen away from me. Daphne, Kit, my own daughters, others, all caught up in the ol' 'march of time.' Remember the Saturday matinee 'newsreels' of everything that was, or seem to be, exciting? Anyhow, here I am with nobody to throw my arms around. Nobody to touch. & Yes, I feel like an old/new place. I seem to have fallen away from the years ago and have, simply, been brought back to. Nose to the grindstone, my own smell around the house, the endless prevarication of mind, & yes, those fitful moments of an acute sense that my end is rushing towards me faster than a cruise missile. Came across this, in R.C.'s deeply felt memoir of V.S. in the *N.Y. Review of Books*. The memoir concludes (movingly) with these lines from Conrad: 'Life . . . will close upon sorrow like the sea upon a dead body, no matter how much love goes down to the bottom.'

for sonya, long beach, august '82

riddled by demon time/the diamond of space: love
is a piece of the cloth-of-life two solitudes coming together
weave for a little while even as each will arise in the
early morning from their own side of the bed 'perfect strangers'
beholden to their own loomings and prefigurations . who
said love was nothing but a current in the mind's own rivers a
turbulence or eddy in its estuaries . like our friend
salmon i am nothing but wind star salt/air oceanic hunger .
with my poised fingers 'demon time' looms a galactic net
of blinding prismatic colours . behold! the leaping salmon the
unloomed threat i am . behold! your own luminescent thread .
love, you ought to know i don't test your warp without
fingering both harp and loom .

IN THE STUDIO DOORWAY ON POWELL STREET

huge steaming brown mound of
shit in the doorway i nearly stepped into
offal smell even at the top of
the steep stairs   couldn't get homo sapiens'
excremental smell out of my nose
hair clothes   couldn't compose anything
let alone myself. went home   had
a hot bath then composed the following notice
which i'm gonna post in the doorway.

<u>THE NEXT GUY CAUGHT SHITTIN' IN THIS DOORWAY IS GONNA GET HIS FUCKEN NOSE RUBBED IN IT</u> !!!

Indian guy in blue jeans avidly picking up
bits & pieces of garbage & stuffing 'em into a green plastic bag
at the annual japanese festival sez i do this
every year for them. they (the japanese) like things neat & clean.
i smile   crumple up my obento box & hand it
to him   he walks off   grinning

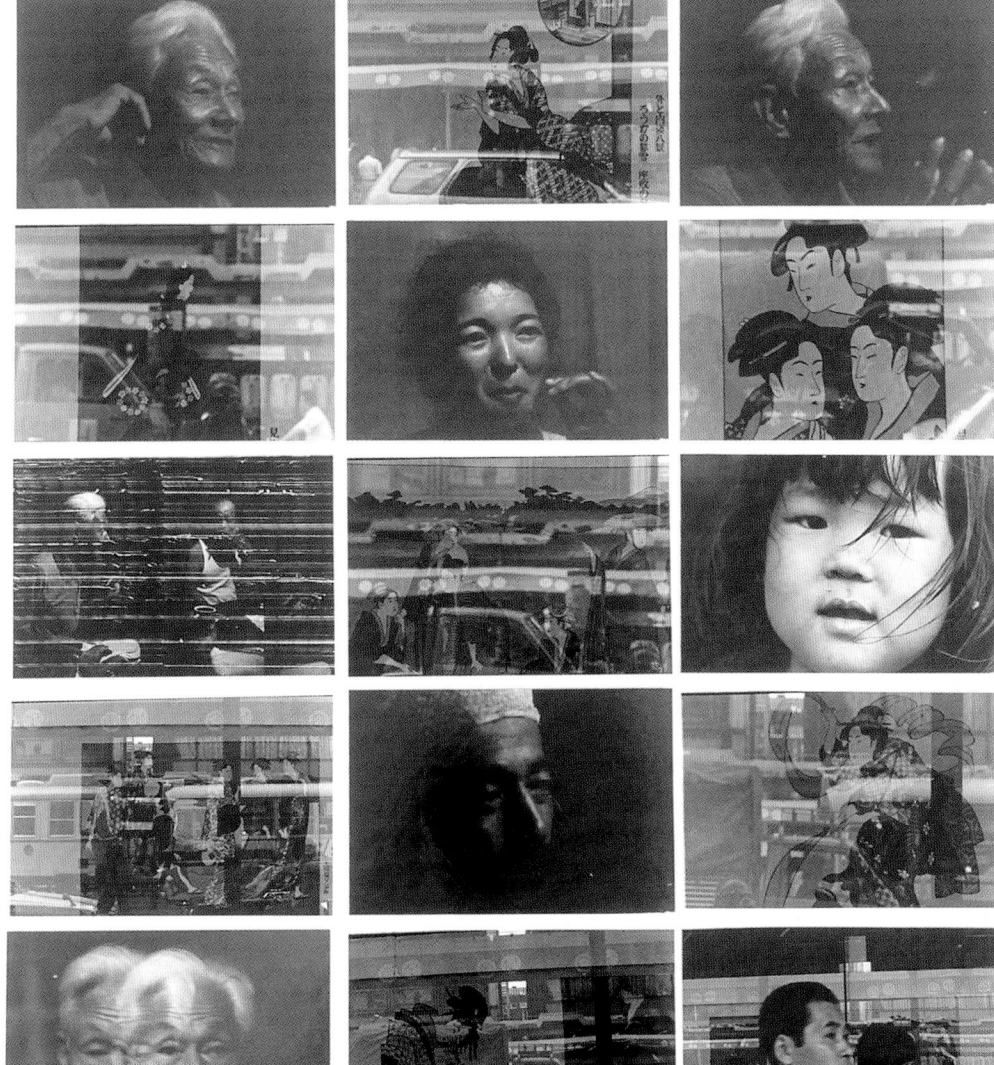

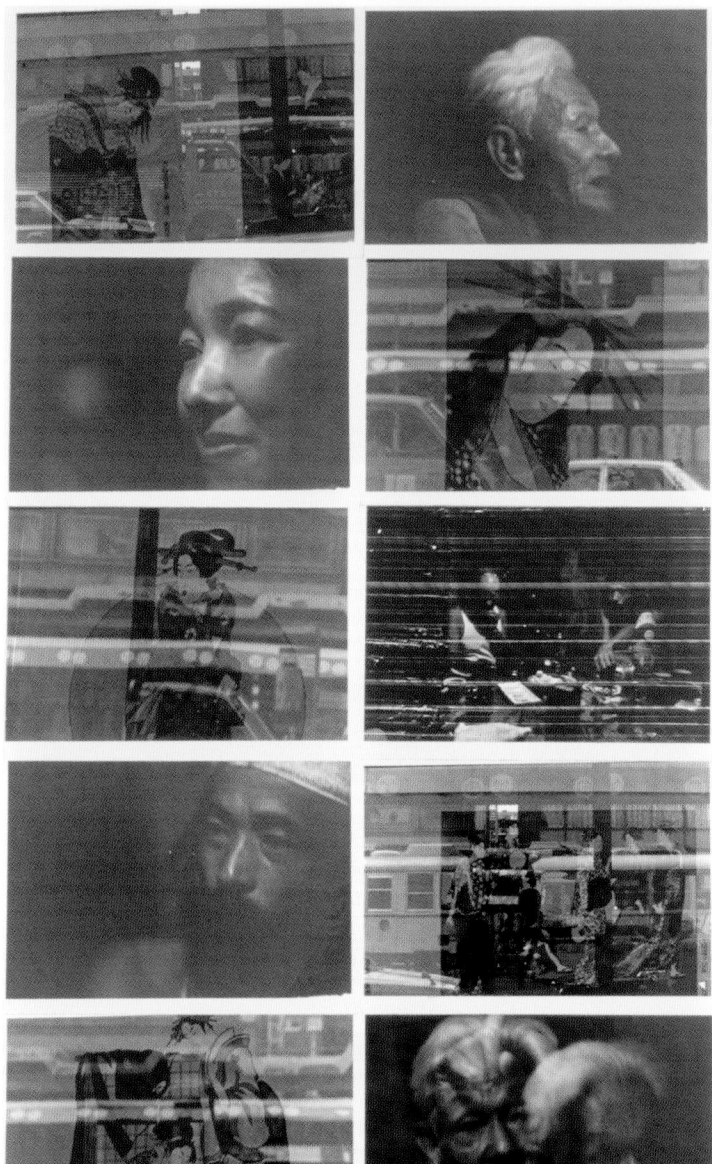

3.9.82

Dear Joy:
    . . . to resume my correspondence after a long hot
    callit 'kinky' summer, to simply say that i've come
    thru (heart's derelictions?) more or less intact,
    is to say nothing, nothing new.   i mean 'who' hasn't
    put themselves thru it & lived to tell abt it.
    anyhow, do use 'me'/ my name for your father's honour
    sake. i mean tell the O.C. folks i more than consent
    to back him up, etc. otherwise, it's back to school
    & in & back of all the unsaid words i seem to become
    more the gnomic fool daily   hang on to language:
    it's at least as credible as our debased ekonomicks.

    regards

9. 20. '82 11 pm

no frost here
yet. no sudden diminishment
of summer tidings

no untied feelings to burden
september's airs
there's a small bird singing in the pear tree

Daphne
i like to think it sings
for you

•

surrounded as i am by your boxed & pact belongings
i'm no longer troubled by their mute presences.
i mean in my mind i've simply added them to all of
the other things that clutter the casements of
callit mind's eye.   i just think of all of it undertaking a seasonal hibernation till you come back
and make it all come alive. p.s. found your other box
marked 'winnipeg.' will get it & your mail off to
Winnipeg soon. say 'Hi' to Bob K. for me. tell 'em i'm
dumbfounded by the thought of existence.

•

the hottest romance in the neighbourhood is the one
between Linda H. and John G. that tiny lady with
the mean growl in her lusty voice not to mention her
snub nose and brown freckles goes on living up to
her legend. come to think of it so does our young Adonis.
like we both know it's been a season of falling into
and out of love with no diminishment of either pain or
consternations. i wonder what's in store this winter?

~

how tell *anyone* when
each occasion is, to say the least, particular, how tell

the truth about 'feeling' when each feeling
turns into a scheme of words . like, how many ways do I think I
want you when some part of me doesn't want
any part of you . how tell anyone anything   this
mid-summer equinoctial tide doesn't compel .
how to get clear thru to the other side of language seems
to be the acid test of this unquiet summer   .
remember the blood-stained sacrificial stone in the temple
of the sun ?   how come we were at our best when
we were wordless travellers in the Yucatan ?   this body
remembers all the moments of silences when both
of our bodies simply toucht to meet the oncoming night   .

lattices of summer : Billy Holliday singing
'i cover the waterfront' .   there's no bluntness no scar that
this permeable light this golden exultation of
bodies down on Kits beach doesn't annul . one way or another
i say to myself, there's an unaccountable 'ace'
maybe even a hidden 'joker' in that deck of cards we stackt :
and the next one to cut the pack will break thru .

27.9/ '82. midnight

midnight conjectures washed ashore by the lapidarian tide

riddled by Demon-Time:
two solitudes can choose to weave a piece of
callit   The Cloth-of-Life
together even   as each knows the other will rise
in the morning, 'perfect
strangers' beholden to their own breath their
own intricate loomings

who sd, 'Love was nothing but the mind's
own feverish currents   a froth   or turbulence
in the estuaries of Time . . . '?   riddled,
i am nothing but   wind   star   insatiable hunger

p.s.
'who' are you and how did we come to meet at this cross+road?

Dear Syuzo & Family:

Since we were together—was it two years ago already!—I've lost my 2nd family and for the 1st time in my life I am unencumbered by all those familial obligations. I am almost, but not quite, 'free' as I never imagined I could be and that's, shall I say, terrifying. Anyhow, it goes on being impossible to tell anyone more than a fraction of what happens from moment to moment in our lives without forfeiting that very life in a total obsession to write it down. O I have had hours of pleasurable thoughts about the three of you via the cassette tapes I made of all the divers sounds that only the tape heard and the tape itself portrayed. Just yesterday I found myself listening to *the bunch of us sitting out a summer typhoon in Obama* with 'oji' playing his jamisen and singing the Okinawan songs, songs of an ancient bard. I'll never forget the choruses of Kazuko & Isamu's children chiming in between our drunken laughter and buoyant conversation, etc. Even tho I've been living a mole-like existence, I can keep in touch with some of those things that have touched me in the world via the tapes I go on making. Believe me, it's more real and certainly more vivid than almost any television / movie / newspaper / magazine reality. I mean that I can authenticate my presence in the world by actually monitoring this moment, this movement, these acts by simply pressing a button and letting the built-in microphone become my very ear anywhere I sit or stand in the whole continuum of sounds that surround us as surely as the air. One way or another, Syuzo, you are my callit *Japanese Connection* and I am therefore writing out of my sense of familiarity. In other words I say what comes to mind and simply assume you will fill in the silences that stem from the same ground as these thoughts. O it's such a lovely April 30th with all the nuances of spring and mid-summer trembling in the warm air tousled with the vocables of the nearby school children.

Sept. '82

dear Syuzo & Family

    there's so much to do daily, one barely has enough time to do nothing. 'nothing' is equal to the time it takes to write a letter. nothing is what i'm doing now. it's been a whole year plus since i was there with you and, since then, my small world has come apart again. i've lost a family, lost my studio, and yes i've misplaced my young manhood for good. it's taken most of the time since i was there to find myself, living, alone. find myself another studio and, yes, tip my hat to my gawky manhood and without grimness salute an ebullient old age which in my fancy consists mainly of piss, vinegar & yes lovely women.

time passes . water moving water: haunting these words this bag of skin holding lotsa water . autumn here   the starlings scream in the bare pear tree branches   the last ripe pears have fallen off   i am 56 this summer . how shall i tell you my own small world   my own family   has floated on   downstream   without me. that Daphne & Kit have left   by their own consent : heart's consensus .   that all of this had begun to unravel last spring . time passes . everything becomes water, again . & it's taken most of the summer to untie myself & in that very act tie the end of my frayed line onto another line   & so it goes . bobbin' spinnin' heavin' sinkin' thinkin' a small whiff of podded-breath along (it must be) an ancient celestial trail. slime trail . glistening mind . dazzlement of days more than anything you can buy on the installment plan. 'breath' a baleful retort.

anyhow . . . the music you'll hear on the tape is without exception music i've helped to shape . &/or music i've attended & taped. me playin' dulcimer, harp/s, zithers, bells, even voice, together with others, or by myself plus records & tapes. different combos for different occasions : taping/ mapping/ tracing all the levels of   callit   heart's sonorities its pleasure/pain .

19. 10. '82

Dear Syuzo & Family:

We have had a brilliant October. 'Indian Summer' it's called here in Kanada, tho I can't for the life in me understand *why*, unless it has something to do with the first white men who lived thru a comparably brilliant fall and had had the thought that the Indians who had been here for ages had seen 'it' all ways a long-long time ago. Had in fact their very faces weathered by their passage thru all the seasons. I love fall. I had had the thought years ago in Halifax that of all the seasons it was my favorite. But now I'm not that sure 'cause I can clearly see that each season has its own miraculous sights & smells & a host of unforeseeable consequences. Besides which autumn doesn't quite fit me yet: I mean I haven't got to that time of my life. I still feel at times like a spring chicken or maybe a summer fowl. Even as winter is my birth season . . . Would you believe me if I said that this is the umpteenth time I've started a letter to you? Would you believe me if I said I have started a letter to you each season since we last got together? Anyhow, it's quite impossible to leave anything out of a letter if one goes on writing it long enough. How many Languages/Seasons can each of us actually think in? How many of our feelings ride the same currents of air? Have I mentioned that I am planning to go to Japan next spring and if I'm lucky (which is to say I've saved up enough money) I'll be able to stay thru-out the whole summer into fall? For the present I seem to be thinking about taking up a small house or apartment in around Kochi beside the Pacific and just go right on doing what I do with lots of going to & fro. Like down to Kohama & right on up via water to Hokkaido. O I'm getting carried away. . . . But there's really nothing to hold me here at the moment, nothing but a need to be rooted somewhere.

19. 10. '82

mother was with me for a month in august/september. she turned 86 in mid-august & tho she has slowed down a lot she is in every other way intact. it was the longest period of time we spent together since i was a boy and both of us were quite amazed to be together. mother got around to asking me to take her to japan next year if i had thought of going which i of course had. i said i would have to think it over seriously 'cause i hadn't planned to take her, hadn't planned anything out of the ordinary except to do a lot of travelling and clearly travelling a lot with mother would be, given her age, very trying indeed. but as i sit here telling you this i have already made up my mind to take her or at least have her come when i get settled in kochi. it keeps occurring to me that each of us has an obligation to attend to our parents one way or another before death takes them. i'm sure you know what i mean. anyhow that's where matters are at the moment viz nippon & me. i don't know if you ever met maya koizumi or not but she's recently returned to yokohama after 16 years. she intends to become some sorta cultural liaison person and travel back & forth. one way or another you'll be hearing from/about her. time to head off to U.B.C. time to have a bite to eat before i do.

22. 10. '82

it's been an extraordinary sorta day. one of those late October days that begin with an overcast grey sky and lots of rain then abruptly shifts over into gales, gales of uncommonly warm winds (last breath of summer?) winds that toss all the trees' branches every/which/way divesting them of most of their leaves leaving the whole ground the sidewalks & streets plastered with colour. in short a stripping down to bare (naked?) essentials 'cause winter's coming. it's been a peculiar fall for me. i mean i don't remember waiting for 'this' day to happen in quite this way before. i've never quite felt the same poignancy. i don't want to equate the time of year and weather with the weather in my own time of life, but 56 isn't exactly summer any more . . . anyhow to make a long story as brief as possible 'i' am on my own once more & i think i can say that the heart-break has to all intents & purposes mended and the three of us (Daphne) (Kit) & i are on the best of terms tho we will probably never live together again as each is already forming, shall i say, new relationships. so all in all it's been a most intense year and living alone has been a quite singular experience. the thought curious thought that crosses my mind these days has to do with the seemingly unlikely, but none the less real, possibility that i'm going to be on my own till the end of my days. . . . or rather i'll have to live with all the wayward characters that live inside of me, i'll have to make peace with each of them and that's a big job all by itself. but i do miss a family and if i go on doing so i might one day do something about it   going into November the days have been dark darkly overcast and raining raining ever day . needless to say the nights get longer every day . it's going into that time of year here where we begin to dream about the tropics, all that sunshine & blue surf all the ways the heat of the sun caresses our cold bodies . this is a *lament* a typical lament of one born a northerner . it carries within the conventions of such lamentations an image of self dressed from head to foot in layers of cloth . it harbours an image of an undisclosed naked-self astonished by the sight of its own epidermis   . anyhow the weather feels like it's inside us . that kinda chill . what's it like in Hirakata City? seasons, seasons of the self in time . i am much preoccupied by such notions . such daily commotions . have i told you that i have been into music in a big way these days? have i mentioned that i haven't been able to play my jamisen since i broke the bridge the delicate bamboo bridge which lifts the strings up above the snakeskin box? not to mention the fact that i've busted one of the strings and the other two have become frayed . so that i have been playing my dulcimer and my harps and the pleasure of it is in excess of my own abilities . i have been playing with different musicians both western and oriental but most of all i have been playing with, for, & to myself . like hearing, wanting to hear, what my sound is . what is both particular & peculiar about its range & timbre .   anyhow the old man in Kohama is always there on cassette tape to remind me of what i am about when it comes to music . nothing 'talks' like song.

27. 10. '82

dear Syuzo & Family

      this letter long-long letter proceeds by fits and starts by writing itself when it feels like it. i mean there's really nothing to say that isn't a part of even the daily tedium. as for personal news, that is news about myself and my own world, the very act of writing to you fulfills that need if need be. it isn't as if i had anything to say. it's more like saying whatever comes to mind in whatever order prevails. all thru the day i've been working away on a suite of pomes called the *pear tree pomes*. all thru the live long day i've been weighing my pauses, weighing the words and what they intend. weighing the periods. my Japan trip is not very far away in my mind. some part of me is planning for it tho i haven't lifted a finger to get it all happening yet i intend to. ah yes, south to Isamu & Kazuko's island Kohama and north to Hokkaido with Kochi City as base. what i will do when i go this time i don't yet know, but i do intend to work at something relevant to being there. sometime soon you will be receiving a package in the mail with all the things i've intended to send. this packet will include another packet with things for Isamu & Kazuko, together with photos of almost all of you. let's just say it'll be a Xmas packet. i haven't any woman in my life these days to argue with or praise and i don't see anybody to even keep me company if i feel lonely. but i am not sorry for myself. i seem to be for whatever reason my own best friend. one way or another this is a threshold year for me and i'm thrilled to think i still have a future opening out before me. at this moment i seem to be preoccupied in having *one last look out of the back door* before i close it for good. i don't want to live off my past. i don't want to eat the contents of my memories. if i have any voraciousness left in me it's a hunger for the unrevealed.

30. 10. '82

dear Isamu & Kazuko

      Takeo Yamashiro came by yesterday with a copy of your N.A. Indian book for children . i remember your showing me the long scroll filled with those illustrations . i remember the other scrolls you showed me in Kohama . i've both talkt & dreamt about Kohama & even as i sit here writing to you i am planning to go to Nippon next year and if you're still there in Kohama i will come down from Kochi City to spend some time with you . it's curious to think of how huge really huge the world is and how little we're given to see of it . Kohama but a speck of fly shit on a map of the world the size of a football field . Vancouver but a few grains of sand . we have had a most brilliant fall which lasted well into October . we N.A.'s are in the grip of an *economic recession* which simply means that our ideology (capitalism) is unable to cope with the high cost of our way-of-life . and the joker is this, that we're in some respects unbelievably poverty-stricken . i mean despite our abundance we keep on grasping straws. & i for one find no comfort in the fact that the whole of the so-called 3rd world wants what we've got . or is that another piece of pernicious propaganda? i sometimes think that 'polis' therefore 'politics' is the price we have to pay for being homo sapiens. god knows i've payed my share of it and no doubt will continue to do so as long as i'm around. but here's the rub: is it possible to be in the world and therefore 'political' without causing suffering or other forms of human deprivation/degradation? i of course do mean to be vividly present in the world and act/be acted upon. blessed are the so-called 'meek' for they shall inherit the earth, etc. i'm just ramblin' on for want of something to say. i know i'm not sayin' anything you 2 haven't felt or dwelt upon. i mean all things considered none of us is that different. those lovely typhoon nights we spent together with 'oji' old man with his jamisen and songs continue to delight my ears via cassette tapes i made. one of the things i think i learned from him is how all the days of our lives can be packed into one small song.

18. 11. '82

Kazuko & Isamu & daughters

    got the copies of your little book about North American Indians . it arrived (miraculously) at my front door scored with your address in Okinawa . it carried in the empty spaces between each page a particular odor of it must be the tropics . i found myself remembering that ecstatic late-night ofuro i had outdoors in the middle of the warmest downpour imaginable . having my belly full of hot sake helped . and you can't imagine the number of times i have played those cassette tapes of that long night of a summer typhoon with oji playing his jamisen and singing his heart out . whatever else tape recorders are about they are to me *magical boxes* with sharp little ears and a mechanical tongue sufficient to bring any kind of sound back home alive . gee whiz they've just got to be one of the technological wonders of any age . apropos the little Indian mythology book i remember Isamu unrolling all the illustrations in front of my eyes . ah the many many lives we all lead . like Isamu and i have both come to know the 'Indian' we also are . not to mention the 'Eskimo' i know in me . we are into a west coast winter with lots of grey sky & rain more rain than sun or wind more rain than anybody wants . in other words it's that time of the year when we dream about Hawaii, the Caribbean, Okinawa, anywhere on earth that's hot . i have wondered if those who are native to the tropical regions of the earth ever dream about living in the cold . & isn't it a small miracle that hot or cold, black or white, our body temperatures remain a constant? isn't that part of our survival equipment? anyhow, i am committed to going to Nippon next summer and i am saving every cent i can towards a 4-month long stay, mostly in & around Kochi City & Kyoto . when i say i am committed i simply mean that i'll be taking my 86-year-old mother home for the last time . that, and what i want to do while i'm there, for myself .

which includes lots of travelling south to Okinawa and north to Hokkaido with lots of stops in between . need i say that if you remain in Okinawa i will certainly come down to spend some time with you? meanwhile my stomach sez i'm empty, come fill me up .

Pre-Xmas, '82

my dear Isamu & Kazuko in Kohama:

     well here it is, almost the day before Christmas and all thru the house not a critter is stirring not even a lousy poet. it's so cold here this Dec., even w-o-r-d-s congeal as soon as they hit the frozen air. whereas i imagine words melt like butter on hot toast in Kohama, Okinawa. i can see the two of you brown as the top of my mahogany table and almost naked. i know, for instance, that 'we' northerners seem to have a subliminal dream of basking in a tropic sun and, given the unusual cold at this time of the year, those who can afford it flee like migrant birds to Mexico, California, Hawaii and south-east Asia. you can't imagine how much 'we'll' pay for a good tan. not to mention sun and surf romances. all of which has me wondering if 'those' who are born in a summer climate or, like yourselves, migrate there ever dream of icicles hanging from eaves, miles of crystalline white snow, and a cold so intense it can burn a white-hot hole in the mind. do you think a native in, say, the jungles of New Guinea even has words to tell of it? i've heard it sd that the Inuit (Eskimos) have a large vocabulary pertaining to the snowy domain. how abt the Okinawa people? the ancients i mean. did they, for instance, ride the vast Pacific currents both northward and southward? they were/are a sea-going island people, but is there in their mythology a now forgotten language of ice? i know that the Japanese are familiar with callit the snow kingdom, tho i can barely speak it. it does seem to me that northerners have an altogether too long a winter season for contemplating both tan and utter death. dying, as it were, into the mouth of the new year, i am nothing but a derelict—one that hasn't tasted the salt of a woman's body for so long that *it* too turns into crystalline flakes of snow. . . . . i don't know about you tropic-types, but we're really good at withholding ourselves, we're really at home under layers of clothing to keep us, separately, warm. 'puritanism' as i know it in my own bones is inseparable from ice, cold, sleet, snow & abundant clothing. it fuels our dreams of a naked Eden wherein the body stands utterly revealed, utterly at home within itself. that fantasy and a comparable dismay of the pallid whiteness of our swathed bodies. it is the geography, the abode we are born into, that defines us as much as the language born out of the same circumstances. ethnocentricity is a vast collective fable when 4000 vast miles are scoured by a persistent arctic wind.

January 18, 1983

my dear Syuzo and Satchiko:

     i am 57 today! i don't want to believe it, tho the face looking at me from the bathroom mirror wants to confirm its quotidian countenance. with all these years behind me you'd think i ought to know something about the carryings-on of this our world but the truth of the matter is i often feel more ignorant than i ever did when i was young, tho i might add that it's an ignorance that has finally come to trust self. hopefully not that 'self' regarded as a hindrance, but a more palpable self that has been shaped by the scourings of time. anyhow, i do have some good news for you. mother and i will be coming to Nippon in May and will certainly look you up. we intend to spend a month together in Kochi City, and, if it's possible, it would be nice if you could come and holiday with us. mother will be returning to Canada in June and i shall stay on thru the whole summer with a special trip down to Kohama to spend some time with Izamu and Kazuko and their children. otherwise, spending a part of my birthday writing a letter is just about my proper speed these lachrymose days. ah! now that the cleft darkness of Capricorn's bleak season has begun to break open, can the darling buds of spring be far behind. . .? regards,

Thursday, March 3rd, '83, 1.50 am

My dear Syuzo and Satchiko

How to say 'time' passes without saying it & a lot else? It's been 1 year and a half since I was in Hirakata City, and many a time I have had pleasant thoughts about you & your family. I've turned 57 this January and ever since I got back from Japan I've been busy putting the pieces of my life together. I've been busy looking for a number of missing pieces plus laying tracks down into an indeterminate future. One in which *you* willy-nilly figure. Figure, because I am bound to turn up in Japan sooner or later. Anyhow, I am alone (again) these days and it's been, to say the least, a dipsy-doodle kind experience relating only to oneself. I'm often on the very edge of laughter as I watch myself pick my nose. Not to mention watching the tape-loops of my mind like television. One way or another I am becoming rather accustomed to myself. Is this a prelude to my old age? Time passes . . . but *mind* is, it seems to me, timeless. It's always both young and old. Spring has come to Vancouver. The cherry blossoms all over town tell me so. The slight balm in the air sez so. Already I've taken off my long-winter underwear. Any day now I'll stand at the front door and watch the snow recede from the North Shore Mountains. Or rather one day I'll look up and notice that the snow disappeared into a yawn. Early in the New Year I had thought that this is going to be a hard winter but as it turns out it's been one of the best in recent years. I mean among other things I got through it without 1/ taking a daily nap, 2/ getting ill or having some kind of trouble with my back. In short, I've had a nice run of creative energy. Even this letter I'm writing to you is evidence of it. And, of course, evidence of passing time. I often ask myself, how come we're so clock-bound? Is it because the earth itself turns in its relationship to the pivotal sun? Is it because we can hum? One thing seems to be sure and that's the fact that our life will pass away when the time for its transport comes, and whether we're rich or poor, busy, incessantly busy, or just plain idle, our own time will run out of numbers . . . Meanwhile, let an exchange of letters pave the way till we meet again. Which, if everything goes well, could be this summer!

with kindest regards,

my small 'i' seems to say i can be anything i want

to be i can't for instance be 'bruised' and/or 'half-eaten' but
the 'me' in me says 'be careful you're just the poet and not
the burden of where these words point towards.' thinking about
all the 'eavesdroppers' e.g. the poets the birds in the
pear tree's branches that monitor the daily round of silences for
a small pome's sake. thinking about all the bruised half-
eaten pears hugging the ground nobody wants to stake out. thinking about a 'me' bearing my own fruit every summer: the old
midden at the foot of the pear tree said in unsurpassing rhetoric
'I compost the Language-Tree. Take your cue from me.'

running the old words thru again
& again, as in the notion of 'a draft.' the ofttimes
impossible impulse to make it better.
running the old experiences thru time & again
as in, these very words, these words, these thots.
impossible the impulse to penetrate them deeper
deeper than 'will' can possibly go.
now that i've got that off my chest if not back i'll
simply wait to see what's next. perplexed,
nothing comes. nothing comes of itself into the matrix
of language without a nudge, it seems. like
this one. o will the next one come,
unattended?

                      now that i've come to the end of
                      the line with WHEELS the Pear Tree Pomes
                      are next. apart from letters then
                      i'll not be writing till the summer
                      in Japan.

                                      vext, these words look ahead to
                                      spring's renewal

there's a kind of madness at the very heart of language:
i mean it wants to be 'simple' in the face of an utter
bewilderment. it simply wants to posit the movement of breath
syllable by syllable & leave 'meaning' to fend for
itself. Mike: i ofttimes feel an incalculable ignorance in
myself, faced with the breadth of the unspeakable.
        a finely etcht circle as in 'iris' would make
          a fine logos if you come across one.
i've spent the most solitary winter of my life: it's been
an eye-opener.
                                      i wonder when i'm going to
                                      blunder next.

                                late october sunday morning on keefer street, '82

with the first bright patch of sunlight in many a day laving
the dew on the last handful of bruised pears we sit quietly over
our second cup of coffee attuned to the chattering starlings
as the newest family in the neighborhood across the back alley step
out onto their back porch to renew an ancient covenant and our
washing machine spins the grit out of our soiled clothing underfoot
just as jim the ace mechanic tows another derelict automobile
away to the giant automobile crusher then because it's friday the day
the giant orange garbage-gobbler comes to chomp up our leavings
the bent old lady with a shawl on her head comes out from between
the two garages cum repair shops and peering up and down the alley
walks across and deposits her own green plastic garbage bags in
our dented but not overloaded garbage tins and turning disappears
between the garages till next week. later we shall gather up all
the unpecked pears to preserve for the long winter ahead when we
will sit down to a bowlful of preserved pears and yes! spoon an
infinite particle of the sun into our craven mouths .

o   the englobed fruit!
the mixed choir next door singing
Hosannas to the lord!

17. 11. '82
Vancouver, B.C.

Dear Michael:

    here's the pear tree pomes for what they're worth. have a good look at them and make your own selection. the pomes come under different headings, and a group of pomes can be lifted from the whole under any heading. as arbitrary as headings can be given the whole thing. as you can imagine, 'headings' as such have no place in the actual conception of them. i mean that the structure of the whole owes something to pome no. one of the key (visionary) pomes, that is each pome is a branch or spoke of a big wheel. in which sense the composition of the whole is radial/axial rather than linear. to my own amazement the pear tree pomes turn out to be the most traditional pomes i've yet written, and this in spite of my once incorrigible modernity. all of which tells me that if i keep my ears open i'll also hear the archaic buried inside of language. & in this way touch it in myself. the book will be dedicated to Daphne & Kit with whom i traversed the '70s. i'll send a curriculum vitae later.

my coming to Monreale over Xmas seems impossible at the moment as i'm going to be in Toronto from the 29th thru dec. 8th with no time to hop over to see you. and i can't extend the time because i have my obligations to my students etc. traversing Kanada is all by itself a big project. perhaps we can get something together that will enable me to come in the spring. meanwhile, let's keep up a wanton correspondence .
                yours sincerely,

17.11.'82, 3.45 pm

Jim:

just a note to tell you that

1/ I'm going to be giving an extended rap provisionally titled 'a thin slice right off the top of my head,' or 'the notion of the history of self as a series of callit "intimate" distortions,' to the M.F.A. student body & others on the 24th of Nov. It'll be a long afternoon, & if you're free or even vaguely interested, come on by.

2/ I do want to have a year off, that is reapply for a 'sabbatical' with pay. & it's got to be 83/84.

3/ My annual trip 'east' is coming up soon. I'll be flying to Toronto on the 29th of Nov. & coming back on the 8th of Dec. It'll be a Canada Council sponsored trip to give a series (3 to date) of poetry readings with music.

4/ I'm applying for a Japan Foundation 'short-term grant' to enable me to work in Japan next summer & I'll be needing your good name to represent me.

5/ p.s. my truncated 181 class comprising 8 students is working out fine. They know they won't be getting a how-to-do-it kinda class but their intellectual acuity ought to be improved beyond their youthful knowing. Ask Elspeth.

         that's it for now.

dear Elliot

    Sam Tata the well-known Montreal photographer took the photo.
give him 'credits' if you use it . otherwise, keep it
clean and neat 'cause i do want it back . it's a gift from Sam,
you understand . i'm lookin' forward to my
stay in Toronto . p.s. i first hit Toronto 'the good' back in
'49 after leaving art school . i lived at 272 Parliament
Street for awhile and used to glimpse Horse Varley at Angelo's .
those were the days when the Canada Council didn't exist
as even a glint in a Cancuck's eye . my o my, whata an unwieldy
dominion we twinkle in . anyhow, i'm 56 and don't have much
time for playin' pick-up-sticks . see you on the 29th.

    yours sincerely,

Winnipeg - Nov 22/ '82

Dear Roy,

          i really subscribed to *MusicWorks* for *you*, you know. so i'm sending this copy back to you with the renewal notice in case you want to keep on getting it.

i hear from Elliot Lefko that you're going to be reading in To. on the 6th, so i guess your eastern trip has been moved ahead. actually you'll be out east the weekend i return to Vancouver. do you know, too, that Michael is reading in Van this coming weekend? Friday i think at the Literary Storefront. he's probably been in touch with you by now in any case.

we had our first blizzard here on Saturday & the snow looks wonderful in the sunlight. folds of ice on the inside of my bedroom window every morning now. it took John & me 1 1/2 hours to unfreeze the locks on my car so we could use it—matches, cigarette lighter, boiling water, hair dryers, ethyl alcohol. i'm *so* glad i'm coming home soon. also glad not to be driving as i've been hearing hair-raising stories about coming through the Rockies in December. think i might take the train. bus would be cheaper but my legs start twitching just thinking about sitting on one seat for 37 hours.

when Michael was here he told me that you & he & Josee are thinking about sharing a house together in Japan this summer. sounds wonderful. what will you do with 648 when you go? Bob & Smaro want to spend the summer in Vancouver & they would be interested in renting from you if you're gone then. they need a place for 2 months. would that work out for you?

just interrupted by a series of phone calls. it's crazy, now that i'm going everyone at the last minute wants me to come to classes, do readings, etc. 2 full weeks ahead till i go.

let me know what your plans are & when you'll be around in December.

                                      love,
                                          Daphne

dear Daphne:

        i have had to go off to Julie's studio in Gastown to have a look at her work. (11am) just a reminder to 1/ get Kit's bed and bookcase from the upstairs room. 2/ don't forget the bed & things downstairs. 3/ the cinder blocks on the front stairs. 4/ we'll deal with both pictures and books of all sorts later. be back in the late afternoon. have a good move and let's hope your new home will turn out to be fecund. p/s take whatever plants you want. luv

                              thank you, Roy—
                                with love,
                                    Daphne .

24.11. '82

mike & linda:

        daphne & kit came by: we had a lovely evening. there's no doubt in our minds that we'll go on being the very best of friends. no doubt about that 'cause there's no lying or even a grievance between the three of us. odd to think of us as apart rather than simply emptied of all talk and all sex. ambidextrously, we're all moving into a fraught future. i mean, even i have my fears facing a fervent old age. d. & i both agreed that we had dear friends in toronto in common and that in fact they were at least as dear as our common friends in vancouver. perhaps more so, we thought, given the estrangements, the inexorable changes, in our assorted friendships here. otherwise, i have a new/old lady (a norwegian-canadian / japanese scholar) in my bent life and tho we seem, even to ourselves, an odd coupling, we're keen, not to mention wary of each other & our propensities. shit, you two should know what i mean. these days i'm thinkin' that 'l o v e' is like 'fool's gold' unless leavened with salt and laughter. thus the 'spiral,' the 'spindle,' & a 'lute.' all this is just a preface to the pleasure of your company during my stay in toronto. being with you reminded me of being at home with monica & my three daughters years ago. or, again, being with my mother & my three sisters. not to mention daphne's mother & her three daughters. linda: thanks for the pear tree jam. i'll not read the pear tree pomes better than i read them that night at your place. love,

25.11. '82

Dear Nancy Townshend:

enclosed 1/ the rewrite of my Norman Mackenzie art gallery homage to Max Bates. like i said over the phone the printers made a hash of it then. the new version is substantially the same: hopefully better. 2/ a xerox copy of an extended sorta letter (taken from my *transcanadaletters* of '75) to Max & Charlotte Bates from New York, '61. use either or both, intact. neither, otherwise. i haven't sent any of this on up to Edmonton; i wanted it to go through you first. make a copy for yourself and send it on to Dave Ponech if you think it'll be useful. i found that i didn't really have anything further to say about Max and that these 2 occasions you have before you said it all, all at the time of our deepest, tho often silent, friendship. make sure i get a copy of both your catalogue and the 'newsletter' when they come out.

yours sincerely,

~

Max Bates was the first painter I met as a student who impressed me as being a real painter. I met others that continued to do so but he was the first. This was important, for I discovered then that 'every artist's strictly illimitable country is himself.'*

He has painted and I have seen

Droll males with clay feet and dumb red hands
Songless green faced children buoyed to light as lead balloons
Pregnant females with ochre passions pushing perambulators
Stern daguerreotype families packed into chromeless living rooms
Red pubescent girls among mute crowds on sunless fairways
Clapboard houses banked with weeds in mindless grey suburbia
Grey protesting cathedrals with ungothic spires
Black truncated butterflies poised on treeless umber horizons
Sunday parks with mindless lovers embracing speechless statues
London Paris & New York street scenes leavened with wit
Austere still-lives with equally austere women in Sally Ann clothes
The escarpments of the foothills wreathed in snow banks
Edge of the sea cleaved through a rear window of a parked car
Paltry puppets and tatterdemalion scarecrows

The proletarian 'I' divining the human comedy with a jaundiced eye.
The 'faraway flags' fluttering above a German salt mine.

He continues to paint and to reveal that
'every artist's strictly illimitable country is himself.'

These paintings I suggest are for 'someone.' No anonymous political 'anybody' is worth painting for.
*e.e. cummings, *Six Non Lectures*

                                        Roy K. Kiyooka
                                        Vancouver, B.C. 1960/ '82

~

                        late Autumn on 57th Street, N.Y. /
                        Montreal, '67

for Max and Charlotte Bates at
the other edge of the continent—

the layers of tin hovels   hidden away from
the blue surge surf / sea-side promenades tell me

how cheaply i purchast a silver medallion at
the San Paolo Bienniale .

there's not much difference between Art News   or
Le Devoir when it comes to silly art reviews . you pay

yr dues and git yr name list'd among
A/rtists A/nonymous, John Diefenbaker or a Dow-Jones .

and a man named Manfred i've never met writes
again for my autograph . i scrawl it on the back of a postcard

of the empire state building with my ball point pen
and send it off to him . 'anonymity is death'

'destroy those who make us invisible'
'black (cunt) s beautiful' and 'fuck you, too'

selections from the definitive collection of Graffiti—
on the last train to Brooklyn .

a timely New Yorker sez medical-science hasn't found
the definitive pill to kill off P/ ublic R/ elations yet .

'have you tried our crest'd toilet papers . . .'

.

i danced at the Dome :
Claude sd he had a gun pull'd on him there .
Emil the manager of the George Washington Hotel sent
congratulations . his Japanese wife

Barnett Newman, Pat Martin Bates, Edwin Dickinson
and Tim Deverell all showed up .

too bad we couldn't get drunk together
at Max's Kansas City .

all   my Ellipses   i hope yr having swell dreams under
Oldenburg's vinyl and kapok machinations .

Grippi-Waddell Gallery
West 57th Street .
.

frm the avenue of the nations :

he saw himself thru the blackout with
the candles from his birthday cake

spent ten yrs in a cold water flat five stories up
on Madison Avenue: his cupboards filled

with a decade's work .—How cld i complain abt
the cold/ early/ morning/ racket/ s?

.

yr name O Liberty! writ in blank ledgers fill
a million warehouses

even in Aklavik/Alaska . she sd
'Central Park's a terrifying place after dark'

rubble rumble everywhere——
rust corrodes yr stainless towers

yr Cries   Echo——
thru concrete underground

corridors   into the putrid sea
where Dawn waits

patiently——
for the 'A' Train .

.

i want my own children
their friends and other children to

be the measure of my acts .
as for Those who wld have us use

their yard-sticks——
go measure the light suffusing this room

and leave us to devise our own
measurements.

.

he tells me he's astonisht—!
seeing   her light yellow pubic fluff

'cause further down   her
long black-hairy legs, bristled .

the Biggest Show in Town :

M. Ernst's
Remains
Archetypically
Surreal
His titles
Cryptic

Recent work/s
Show a Gloved Hand
Fastidiously
Lifting scraps frm
Libidinous
Id's

The
Veritable
Bottom
Of the Un-
Conscious
Garbage
Can
Long Live
Surrealism's Brute
Fantasias
Andre Breton
Hans Arp &
Sigmund Freud.

+

i want the restoration of Magick
magical incantations any number can hum

i want my baselines
the rituals i plumb from

if only a black/ white/ yellow/ red or/ green Goddess wld
abide in me and show me the secret colour of Mud

colours
don't lie . . .

+

Rene Levesque—
i love you a bushel and a peck and
a hug around the neck   But i
won't stand behind you when you raise
Separatism's flag—remembering
how the rising sun nearly bled to death
when the great bald eagle swoopt
down on it. if, however, you want me to
stand at the curbside waving as She
rides on by i'll come running
running to your side .

+

some days Monreale's snow looks as if
some God had wiped his arse on armfulls of it

+

sun/light   over
my left shoulder spills

a precise triangle
on the polisht wood floor
to live in
the presence of

these words
this breath enables . . .

+

fuck Marcel Duchamp's Descartean Ploys   I'll take
W.C. Field's crooked billiard cue any day

+

Libidinous Dreams shall destroy
All yr IBM D-A-T-A

Theres gonna be a Reign-of-Shit over
Everything till Kingdom Cometh

I remember Virgin Country
No surrealist nude ever steppt onto

Visions of hell-flowers   clutcht
In the hands of a Beatrice Claudia or Monique

High embankments of primary colours
The Red Yellow and Blue 'stains' of Paradise

+

to eat/ sleep/ love/ work/ and sing
what else is there

Orpheus? i believe in my feelings when
i feel like 'a song'

+

                    Vermicelli
                    Max
                    - - - - - - - - - - - - -
                    How's yr
                    Daffodils
                    Charlotte?

14.12.'82

Dear Jim:

Got into Solkin's *Richard Wilson*. Don't know what all the flap is about. I mean it seems to me fairly obvious that R.W. meant to paint an English Arcadia based upon the best sort of continental models and that he painted them with an unerring eye for the tastes of his wealthy patrons. Furthermore, that such enlightened forms of patronage were sought after seems to me to be self-evident with or without Solkin's text. The fact that the ubiquitous system of patronage has for some time now fallen from favour simply adds a poignancy to it all. The 'history' of painting in & for its own sake is clearly open to critical scrutiny these forlorn Capitalist days. Wealth, hence power, images of an unsullied landscape complete with guileless peasants, the lucky painter kept like an expensive household pet, all this and more form an indissoluble link in a complex history we of the late 20th century are called upon to witness. As an aside i would simply add that our current economic malaise seems to make clear how money mediates even the most esoteric of professions, e.g., painter, spy, politician, or historian. p.s. Richard Wilson's portrait of David Solkin standing beside a tumbled ruin would also make good sense. Anyhow, the acid test is have I learned anything and the answer is yes. Though I would add that I wasn't given any real astonishment.

15th. 1 '83

Hi Sam

just got around to getting the candy i promised to send you and because i promised to send it on right away and didn't i've bought you 3 rolls, one yellow, one green & one pink. if you suck one a day they'll last you 54 days but if you happen to forget some days they'll last even longer than that.

when i was a mere kid your age i had a sweet tooth my gawd did i have a sweet tooth! it now seems to me to have been so sweet i've repeated the word sweet 4 times! anyhow my favourite candy was Macintosh Toffee and i used to do errands for a Mr. Furusako the barber and he'd give me a dime which was enough in those far-off days to buy 2 boxes at a nickel each. suck, suck, suck a square at a time till the whole box was empty then i would start again. and though i hardly ever buy a chocolate bar these days i still have an unappeasable sweet tooth which i swear goes all the ways back to my Macintosh Toffee Days. if everything works out i'm going to be coming up to spend the February 4th weekend with the two of you and i'll bring my dulcimer with me so we can play together. maybe i'll even learn that song you were trying to teach me the last time i was there. have you got into reading any of Durrell's animal books yet? they're a good bed-time read but even if i may say so a better long-afternoon-with-nothing-to-do-read. give your mother a big hug just for me and i'll give you a bigger one when i get there.

love,

Feb. 6, 83'

Dear Mike:

Well, here it is, thwarts, farts, belly-aches, tree and all. I've had it, for sure. Like I sd over the phone, whatever you finger viz line, sequences, or whatever, that's for the good of the pomes is good enough for me. If old friend David the Bold Duke wants to illustrate them, that's O.K. with me and I'm sure the tree won't mind a bit. I haven't got a picture of a book in my mind, tho I'm sure the pomes have their own picture of themselves embedded within them. Like some distant but utterly particular echo of, say, a Persian /Indian miniature. One way or another, I've had the longest spate of dwelling inside the belly of language (such as I know it) I've ever had and I'm both glad for it and rid of it. I don't know what the summer has in store for me but I'm not thinking 'language' as much as super 8 movies complete with sound tracks. Otherwise, I have this thot: that all the arts I practise are but separate strands of both the 'particular' and the 'mythological' ground of self. And that it is to all intents and purposes a pure Gift. More than I ever thot possible that gift alone divines the future and gives it the shape of my becoming. Which I take to be just as important as, say, Bill Bennett's or Margaret Atwood's. Or else it's just another shadow-game, another video production. To wit, the P.T.P.'s

A few last words. I've been working towards a language/voice, an articulation (formal of course) that might enable me or somebody else to sing them. I mean that simple yet complex. It, in this sense, ties in with my music making. I mean the formality of them, their simple language wants to be sung. All the 'echoes' of older songs and sentiments in the tradition are manifestly a-part of their presentation. All the 'echoes' of an older perhaps more heraldic language are part of the instrumentation. Even the disenchantments of love have their echoes, etc. Therefore, the sequences, the layering of 'em are integral tho not necessarily completely articulated. Otherwise, let 'em find a place in the world like anything has to.

Will you let Sarah & Stan in on these letters if you feel like it 'cause I haven't had the time to write them separately. Anyhow, give 'em my love. 6th. 10am. '83

Feb. 8th, 12.30 pm, '83

Dear Maya

got the quite vivid impression from your letter that you had a lot of sex on your mind . got that uncanny sense it ain't easy to simply get fucked . 'impotent.' . . . does the work ethic of a micro-chip, robot, and cherry blossoms society make Nippon men impotent? or have they all learned to get off on a noon-hour masturbation trip? anyhow, my dear Maya, given your wide-eyed North American love-boat experiences, i'm sure the *codifications* back in Yokohama feel as tight as a 2-tatami room without Billy Holliday to soothe your blues. besides, i hava feelin' that a high percentage of workaholic men in all the so-called technologically advanced nations feel impotent despite themselves 'cause they burn up their sexual calories pushing buttons, making long distance deals, and watching the old stock market retort without ever gettin' off their fat bums. to think that 'those' who sat around on their fat asses and got rich by keeping their hands clean by only handling laundered abstractions became the princes of the land, the archetypical *capitalist*, and those who handled the picks and shovels, not to mention the garbage collecting, the butcher, and bruised old wino deserve what they can barely scrape together, and they, too, because of the fetters of their lot, literally turned impotent. like nobody wants to go through the commotions of copulating with another, whatever the vexations, whatever the sex. dear Maya: my callit small balls kind of sex ain't gettin' much exercise these winter days. almost as if lost in an ancient maze, 'love,' disembodied love. the sheerest glance of it casts a stone shadow on an amazing floral cul-de-sac. Maya: mother & i are definitely going to Japan in mid-May and do want to see if not stay with you. my Chinese oracle tells me these days that 'moon-faced' women (like you and Sonja for instance) are the best for me: he says i'm through with long-faced women and they're through with me. why don't you keep writing me regularly?

love,

Feb. 8th, '83, 11 pm.

Dear Linney:

      got your change-of-address card. got your postcard askin' for a letter of recommendation which will follow shortly. just the other evening when i was packin' up a bunch of books i'll never read again, 'this' decade old out-of-focus *snapshot* fell out of one of them. staring affectionately at it, i thought to myself, 'GOLLY DIDN'T WE MAKE A HANDSOME SORTA COUPLE?' and 'who would ever suspect they lusted after each other and laughed an awful lot?' i've still got that custom-tailored Monreale suit which i've lately taken out of the closet and wear about whenever i want to feel like a dude. i can't remember what was on my mind when the photographer clickt the ol' shutter but from the look on my face i surmise it had a lot to do with the pleasure of your young company. and that ah so white piece of paper (was it your graduation diploma?) you are holding in one hand certifies the fact that you are on your own in the ol' Atlantis of the heart. dear Linney: i can't for the life of me imagine another writer with as much experience as you when it comes to CanLit/Eroticism. do keep writing and painting up the proverbial storm. remember i saw the flaming hair'd hag behind the round wistful childlike face. now that Daphne and i have split up, all the women i love seem to live in distant parts of Kanada. have you met up with Francoise & Kristina and Richard & Vicki Sommers yet? dream of me to keep my old soul company and i'll reach out in the dead of night as if to caress your breast. p.s. my 56th winter hasn't been un-kind .

                                                love,

February 14, 1983

The Director of the M.F.A. Program
Nova Scotia College of Art and Design
Halifax, Nova Scotia

Dear Sir:

> Re: Recommendation for Grace MURAO—
> Graduate Studies

A few words in favor of Grace Murao and her ambition to go on to graduate studies. One will not go deeper than one does in their youth when to touch the bottom of the well (of self) was never an intention, never a programmatic thing. Sometimes it happened quick as a wink and as often as not went unrecognized. But the memory of that momentary transport suffuses the well springs of a life. I believe that 'those' who are young among us and know this experience have the best chance of making 'art' their lifetime vocation. I believe (however obscurely) that Grace has had an intimation of this sort and, given her ongoing diligence, not to mention her open attitude towards life, she ought to become one of the precursors of the yet-to-be-born art of the 21st century. Needless to say, I am wholeheartedly in favor of Grace Murao and recommend her to you without reservation.

Yours sincerely,

Roy Kiyooka
Professor
Department of Fine Arts

19. 2. '83, 2pm

To Phyllis Webb

Dear Paper Doll, the CanLit Establishment's most intelligent moll:
      How's that for starters after all the silences? Love the callit texture of our anti-ghazals, the ofttimes wry wholly inimitable speaking-out voice. Love the small precise gestures. Sometimes these February rain days I feel there's
      really nothing else to attend to but the *myriad precise gestures/* the *syllibant hiss of sylla-*
bles. (An excess of winter
      rain pisses on callit the dolour of these stoned words.)
Anyhow, one way or another I've been a middle-age Mole this wet
      winter. Like an oriental Proust I've been mining the callit
image-bank of my life and putting it together with the daily
      weather the sodden ground of my intrepid soul. If gazelles
are emblematic of the soul's swift purity, are anti-ghazals
      therefore the intrepid round? How does a fine lyric voice
ripen with the passing years into the long wail of any man or
      woman's true psychic life in its rotund fears? How to voice
the depth of innocence while digging roots deeper and deeper into
      the earth till root trunk and far-flung branches utterly
merge in the cosmic mirth of a world without beginning or end we
      can know anything about? Phyllis: is 57 some sort of
threshold for callit the next psychic leap? (Hopefully the long
      hop before the last one of all.) Having been, one way or
another, a family man most of my life, I can't begin to tell you
      how appalled I've been being all by myself for weeks on end
with nobody to touch let alone talk to. Like I seem to be saying
      57 is decisively Proustian, though I would add that in some
unaccountable way these days I also look forward to callit the
      future. p/s I'll be going to Japan for the summer with my
mother. O irony of ironies. I just recognized what I've said and
      it doesn't make sense to look forward to the future by
returning to my ancestral past holding my mother's frail hand and
      so it goes. Anyhow, if you would like a weekend guest almost
any weekend let me know: Old Mole gotta start diggin' his way
      outa his long fecund tunnel . Write if you feel you're up to
it. I'll do the same .

sonja/ the small hazards of tic-toc-time. i mean february has had that peculiar distinction of, indubitably, being the shortest month of the year. and yet it sometimes (quite unmindfully) feels attenuated. as if each of the subtly lengthening days imperceptibly stretched the duration of a second minute or hour. on the whole i am having a very good february as i have been able to sustain a high level of energy. energy enough to make a number of small things work together (like word/s or frame/s of pome or film) in other words sustain a very particular, very peculiar, up close kind of concentration happening, and hold my health firmly together. like the ol' op song sez, 'who could ask for anything more.' march is waiting— almost like a green thumb sticking up even in front of my typewriter. i, too, am waiting, waiting in my fashion, for you. august's fair child .

~

Dear Sonja:

it's Sunday, February 20th, 1.05 pm

mired in my own thoughts: the mud-impacted lot of them. including the sometimes crystalline thought about you, hence 'us.' i am learning to be patient with myself without becoming just another statistical mental patient. i'm learning (again) that nothing reveals itself without the most subtle forms of patience practised upon oneself. oneself and the large world. thinking about you. thinking about the distances between us. not to mention, callit, the obdurate silences that fall between us. . . . i am nonetheless caught up in my daily round of work and the obsessiveness of making it cohere. that very coherence includes my ofttimes vagrant thoughts of you, hence us. if i let the weight of our February silences utterly obscure what we are all about, i am, needless to say, lacking in the aforementioned patience. i wonder what you are doing at this very moment. hang on to dear life. i'll do the same. Sonja: if i am to be your '2nd husband,' does it mean that i'll have to spend most of the rest of my days without actually living with you? does it mean that i'll have to continue dwelling in my ofttimes mired thoughts as if you were outside of their boundaries? 'patience' i'm told would enable me to forgo such questions. don't forget to practise your calligraphy.

2. 21st, '83

Dear Mike or bpNichol:

                                   i'm abt halfways thru callit the final version of WHEELS : one way or another i've needed the time since presenting the manuscript to attend to those moments of awkwardness in the body of the text and one way or another it all takes a lot of time to divine if you don't know the grammatical rules. anyhow, father has been dead for a decade and, given the little trip we made together, i have had to account for my feelings about him since his demise. nobody ever told me i would find myself writing a chapter of the oldest book on our fair earth. what's copyrights and authorship all about? anyhow, i want to see this book go to press first. i'm including a number of photos, each with their designated place in the body of the text. perhaps as chapter (or section) beginning/s. father's photo thru the windshield is one that has to go in. the rest is up to you and the formal discretions we all know books are bound by. otherwise, i don't want to see even proofs if i can count on your vigilant attention thru-out. any day now i'll start on the definitive alignments of the *Pear Tree Pomes*, but first things first and to everything else an operatic kiss-of-death. Dear Mike/bp i am thinking thinking about how i had thot i was walking along one branch of a forked road until i came to a cul-de-sac and turning back walkt straight into a sunset converging in the crook of an uphill road. where do you think our separate but common roads will take us?

                                              bless it with your breath thru
                                              the machinations of the Coach House Press

February 24, 1983

Chairperson, The College Board
College of New Caledonia
3320 22nd Ave
Prince George, B.C.
V2N 1P8

Dear Sir or Madam:

It has been brought to my attention that Barry McKinnon is going to lose his position at New Caledonia because of the ongoing 'recession' and all the SoCred cutbacks, particularly in the field of liberal arts education. I for one don't always know how seriously to take the ofttimes infuriating pronouncements of a Bill Vander Zam or a Pat McGeer, but I would nonetheless ask you to take the actual presence of an authentic poet and teacher among you in Prince George seriously. I've known both Barry and Joy since their undergraduate days at Sir George Williams U (now Concordia U). They were among the small group of Western Canadians who converged on Montreal in those years. Remember the Great Computer Bust & Separatism?

It's important, in all those subtle ways that count for a community (any real community that's not just a ghost town), to have a poet such as Barry among its varied citizens just to keep, call it the warp, exuberant. I mean that Everyman has to (whether he wants to or not) do something for the common good and it just happens to be the poet whose goodness consists in listening, ardently. The true notion of a Democratic Education, the one we often give lip-service to but in truth seldom take the time to think through, would make of each human being such a subtle ear for nuances that all acts of deception would be instantly recognized and ceremoniously dealt with without fear or humiliation. I am wondering if the 'nuclear age' with all its unbidden portents doesn't therefore ask us to re-examine the very tenets of our educational system and what its collective aim ought to be for the sake of our collective survival. Like I say, poets like Barry do have, call it, an unseen hand in shaping a community of beings. And it goes without saying that his work as a teacher and small-time publisher also contributes.

The question is, how is it that we have such a heartless economics and what can 'you' and i, together with Barry, do about it?

Yours sincerely,

Roy Kiyooka
Profesor
Department of Fine Arts

Feb. 25th, '83

my dear Michel:

      got the tri-part postcard from Germany. ain't
geography the cat's meow. anyhow, spring is on its way here.
the cherry blossoms in front of the house tell me so.
among other things, i've been working on the final draft (is
there such a thing?) of WHEELS, a travel pome
set in Japan which i began in the winter of '69. it's, among
other things, a sidelong look at my father with whom
i travelled thru Honshu's backcountry. if i can keep up callit
the zest, i should get it done by the end of Feb. then,
it'll be the pear tree pomes, their final draft.
let's say that i'll get the manuscript to you by the end of March
at the latest. i've now read them on several occasions
and have a sense of how they ought to, particle by particle,
sound. what's left to do is a matter of visualizing them
as they fall on the page with all the exactitude of a bird's flight.
meanwhile, Nippon begins to beckon. needless to say,
i have no clear plans except the fact that i'll be going over
with my mother and we'll be keeping each other company
for the month (mid May/mid June?) she will be there. after that
i'll be largely on my own which means (unless i get into
some work!) i'll be ready to travel most anywhere, including
south/east Asia. say hi to Daphne when she hits Monreale
for me. remember 'us' together even tho we're now just pals.
Michel, let's you and i strengthen the bond between us which as
you well know is 3000 miles of wind-scoured tundra.

otherwise, my love and i live (not by choice) far apart, and i am,
as always, left to my own obsessions.

sunday, february 27 '83, 2.30 am

dear sonja: mike de courcy & a couple of friends, old '60s drug fiend friends cum poets from mendicino county in northern California, came by tonight, like they say, out of the blue. one round of their california pot & i'm swept ass-backwards into the vintage '60s. nice middle-age guys who'd hustled all their lives, takin' a long car ride all the way across o kanada and droppin' off here & there to give a poetry reading out of the trunk of their 63 cadillac—all because one of them is that untypical kanuck of the '60s who went south and didn't come back till the day before yesterday when he heard about the kanada kouncil and being a good kanuck applied for a grant and willy-nilly got one. the other guy lookt a bit like an english country squire who had once sung in the choir of handel's messiah but turns out in fact to be a polack/americun who spun classic discs & ground coffee professionally in mendicino county. talk abt 'cycles' like 'On The Road' goaded by none other than Captain Poetry 30 odd years later in an amazing 60s cadillac & all that kinda stuff. i don't see michael d. very often, let alone his ofttimes amazing friends, but, given the fact that our friendship (also) goes back to the '60s, we got our way of obscurely diggin' each other. anyhow, at one point in the laugh-a-minute-talk-it-up evening (just a few scant hours ago) i thot to myself, well, this is gettin' to be just a shade too boring, i'll have to make the signs that will tell them it's time to leave. which i did, and they read, and presently left. among other things, i got to laugh a lot which i don't get to do very much these days. i had almost forgotten that laughter is in fact if not deed cathartic.

sonja: will these long silences therefore be an integral part of what you and i are about? and will 'it' be a pebble or heavy stone?

love

~

28. 2. '83

midnight right after your phone call and our conversation:

rain yes we've had our share of it during february and yes i suppose it got into my february letters tho i hope my speaking isn't as bleak as a typical feb day. the rash of letters i've written to you since late fall all have weather in them: i mean i don't know how to keep it outside. several of the women i have known have told me that i could certainly be uncomfortably bleak and that that bleakness took the form of a sometimes harsh silence. 'big earth' frozen over. no matter: these days i keep all such bleakness to myself. in fact live with it as part of each day's occurrences. geez i keep wonderin' what happened to my '60s laughter. that quickness of wit that could turn stone into feather and feather into a quill. anyhow, sonja, what can a 2nd husband do but wring his hands at the very thot of holding you? any day now spring will renew both the surge and the trepidations. i wonder what Ikkyu would do in my shoes.

goodnight

Dear Dean Will / Jim Caswell:

A few words concerning my un-updated CV. I suppose that it is to my own detriment not to have kept up a resume of my activities since '75, but I do have my own peculiar reasons for letting it slide. Simply put, I have for a number of years felt the burden of being my own historian. That is, by the very act of recording my own activities, I was, unwittingly, demarcating myself. And all along the artist in me kept saying, but it's too limiting, self-limiting. Even the pedagogue in me wants an open-ended discourse. In other words, the artist in me wants to go on fingering the very premises of art without the hindrances of my own achievements. Furthermore, I've quite recently discovered that there is, callit, a gift-of-time-in-anonymity, and to go on doing things discreetly seems to be what I need at this time in my life.

Anyhow, here's a casual Listing of some of my activities, together with commentaries as they occur, since the late '70s.

midnight, March 3rd '83

To Daphne Marlatt

Reading Rich's 'Diving Into The Wreck' I am
given to divine the very self that lies at the bottom of it.
Out of the fierce carnage we have shaped out of
the atom there is a self to be shaped. If we could come fully
into our senses and praise the fragrance haunting
this spring night, simply praise it as if there will never be
another spring, we might begin to heal ourselves.
'Talking. Talking thru my hat again,' I thot, putting
the book down. Reaching up thru the wreckage of my own life I
found my long-lost fingertip: the very bluntness of
its severance consecrated, an unspoken pain .
What I have to tell about the Wreckage has already been told.
Visiting you in your new place in Kitsilano
is another *telling*. Take care of yourself .

& may the Ides of March mark you well

2.50 pm. mon. march 7, '83

sonja/

my thot is that you haven't time in your busy life for us, whereas i've got all the time in the world. my thot is that if you haven't time for just the two of us, how can i give you a piece of my time? and if i can't do just that, what can i do but go on making us up in my mind? my thot is of no account unless it can make you tangible. it is, itself, nothing but air & a little bit of water. my thot is, itself, sheer momentum. call it a surge of breath, whatever. anyhow, what all this seems to come down to is how heartless i can feel feeling that you don't really need me in your life & (true or false?) you will probably never ask me up for a weekend given the fullness of your days in Edmonton. no matter. sometimes i feel like the proverbial mad hatter cum middle-age lover who'll never know what's good for him. sonja, sometimes i say to myself, my days are numbered. shall i count them out monitoring the endless distance between us? shall i go on counting on my small resource of words to parachute you across the mountains into my arms? no matter,
the plot thickens & my heart has been quickened by our heart-to-heart talk. p.s. my thot proposes that we don't need to be in one another's life unless we know that we are, thereby, enlivened.

what happened to that roll of film? i mean how come i don't even have a snapshot of you, & then, again, does it really matter?   ah, 'love' the unspeakable 4-letter word. quite unlike your 5-letter name or my 3-letter one. think of us.

~

3. 13. '83

Sonja: it's midnight (again) & tho i didn't intend to mention it, i was half-waiting for your midnight call. now it's 1 am *there*—it's more than likely you've gone to bed. have a good sleep & if by chance you happen to dream of 'me,' don't let me know, i say petulantly to myself, 'cause i feel that i am absent to you when i am not there. out of sight/out of mind, sez it. anyhow, i want you to know that you nonetheless flip thru my dailiness: sometimes like a big smile, other times a frown & above all else a handful of air. blessings on thee o gnomic oriental scholar. one dim-wit middle-age ho-hum escapade artist nonetheless draws upon your absentee affections. he is, to say the least, learnin' the hard way about the truth of long departures in the hinterlands. anyhow, here's a few fragile blossoms to perfume the envelope of this letter to you. p.s. the whole town's a bloomin' pink .

luv

noon. 13. 3. '83

Dear Mike:

We're into spring here. The callit 'balm' is in the air. All the cherry blossoms in town tincture the grey ah lengthening days & dwindling nights. Methinks I'm becoming more & more a wind & weather man: not that I think I can read 'their' signatures any better than I can read my own. No, nothing like that. It's more the way I ride the currents of my feelings than it is like 'knowing.' Anyhow, spring's here and already my own ah stiff bod is beginning to limber up. I don't need any more 'grease' in my life (fuck O.P.E.C.): what my bod wants is more S-U-N-N-E! Ah Hawaii!

. . . emerging like a seedling from a long winter compost, the dream of a summer in Japan begins to shape itself. One thing I know about the forthcoming trip is that I'll be taking my old mother. W-H-E-E-L-S

Otherwise, I just want to say that WHEELS is in your hands to see thru the ol' Coach House Press. For what it's worth I've spent the whole of the past month going thru it with the proverbial fine tooth comb. Re-addressing the Text again, I sd to myself, this time it's really had it. In other words, dear Mike, what remains awkward will have to stay that way. I mean I can't belabor it any longer. There's too much of a thronging in the wings: callit the unvoiced cry of the hirsute future, whatever. After 14 springs, it's time to go on with the show, etc. Whatever else I'm about as an erstwhile 'writer,' I know within myself that the whole quest has been to claim some small portion of, callit, the verities of English which is, among a host of other things, not my mother tongue. One thing seems certain & that's how 'language' will go right on shaping us, some actual part of our very substance, for the rest of our days. One day I would like to wake up with the feeling that I could walk away from it without a tinge of fear, let alone remorse. Ah the horseless carriage, a forlorn love & a mouth fill'd with the rarities of simple breath .

15.3.'83 NOON

Mike/

Movies, i thot to myself, are most like (my) dreams: i mean in their material friability. Most of the time these days 'neither' lasts any longer than the moment of their immediate recall after the experience. i have that sense that both used to be more of a clutter, but then hindsense is itself a warp, ain't it? i read somewhere years ago that none other than Krishnamurti sd that he thot dreams were of no importance, that they just cluttered up the ol' psyche which is moving towards the light. Movies likewise? It's the threadbare gaff of narrative that's mostly been wrung dry at least since the Forsythe Saga. Like sticking another 5¢ in the nickelodeon to hear the latest, therefore oldest, heart wringer ever. i guess there's no way of getting the sexual act onto the screen without it turning 'blue.' O the fucken boob tube is at root so fundamentally obscene in its heartless stereotyping, its avaricious use of, is it our, callit, need for images of self. 'Ghandi' was a waste of the tax-payer's lucre: nothing like epic tapestries to fuel a belated capitalism. 'All the dreams money can buy' almost always turn out to be Fool's Gold. Mike/ at least since Sir John A drove the last spike into the last tie, tying this continent together by iron wood, steel & mail, we've been disenfranchised by a false History & one way or another i mean to lean on it. Fuck movies. Fuck dreams. Luv the smallest gesture a thing can make. To break each new day open like a soft boiled egg & see the yellow yolk run before you spoon it up is square one where i'm coming from these March days.

> hope the Ides of March runs
> its brisk fingers thru your beard
> your hair/Linda

My lovely Lady cum dealer friend is spending March on Big Island. She is intently drawing its flora & fauna. Thinking of me her long-time dope fiend friend, she sent a small box full of hand-made Hawaiian (CHOCOLATE!) Fudge for Valentine's. Ah, nothing quite like a toke of Hawaiian Gold first thing in the morning with a cupa coffee plus a piece of toast with genuine Iowa Pear Marmalade to sweeten the tooth of our endlessly divisive economic caveats. p.s. the Queen & her Consort have been in town stirring up the natives.

A good friend suggested that we ought to try & get the Pope & the Queen together on a worldwide tour for the sake of an impossible PEACE. I suggested we throw in either Peggy A. or Wayne G. as Kanadian escorts.

More on layout (re: picture/captions) later. Just have to get this mss off before it turns into another misnomer.

Mike/ don't let WHEELS become another laid-back summer book with lota erratta.

> luv to all from 648 Keefer

15. 3. '83. 5 pm

Sonja/

      got your letter Tues. 15th morning: what a lift as i had also got the final draft of WHEELS finisht late that night. after over a month of intense scrutiny word by word / space by space, i got it xerox'd today to send it off to the Coach House Press. a mere 60 pages & 14 yrs later i'm washing my hands of it for good. i don't at this moment know its worth except that i've needed all along to get it down & out. i'm afraid what it sez about father could be put in a thimble but then, being a quiet sorta man as i remember him, it's impossible to see how he could have taken up more space in the body of the text, without my talking too much. i've had to be diligent to keep both the homilies & wit in there—without either foreshadowing the underlying seriousness of my intent. i mean it mustn't sound like another damned translation of the sort we've both read too much of that leaves the fun of the colloquial out. anyhow, so much for WHEELS. at least 'that' turn of it. where it'll spin me (us) next is anybody's guess.

      like your I-Ching toss it feels like it fits me too.

next it'll be the *Pear Tree Pomes*/ Japan/ & Mother, which should keep me busy thru to the end of April. p.s. Michiko tells me that Maya intends to come back to Kanada, probably to reside here. she sd it'll be this coming May or, if not then, later, in Sept. So you better write to her to let her know your intent, again.

                                                                                        keep in touch

24. 3. '83. 8.30 am

Dear Mike/ Linda

. . . pausing to toke up this Thursday 7 am . pausing to genuflect on my impossible writing habits which include pausing to say this and yes to look out of the study window while wondering about using 'i' or 'me' instead of 'he,' or is it 'it'? anyhow, this is an interim report on the *Pear Tree Pomes*. i've been into them since WHEELS, and just this morning i'm as it were filled with unconfidences 'cause the Text if you will has already, shall i say, solidified. or, do i mean that it's untamperable? codified. complete with its built-in seemingly obtuse kinds of awkwardness, slurs & peculiarities. anyhow, it's going on to 8 am and it's time to get myself a bit of breakfast before i go out to UBC. i've been re-playing the reading i gave at your place, going back and forth. i've been listening to every little nuance to get it right on the page. etc. p.s. the actual heat of the pomes as they were written has already been put on a slow back burner. that much is clear. i love 'em and hate 'em and i want to let 'em go to wherever pomes get to but before that can happen i'll have to pry them open to let in a little bit of the new year air. my deadline is Easter. time to resurrect a brand new batch of words to tickle my fickle self with. all winter long i've sat with my back to the ocean but now i am slowly turning towards it and putting my back to these ah snow-capt mountains. Japan beckons. where will my forked tongue lead me? shall i pack my toque and begin to think in ideograms?

April 1983

Dear Richard & Vicki:

I have often had the thought that I ought to tape a piece of my dulcimer music for the two of you but I haven't got anything like the measure of the music it's capable of. O I've been strumming it twice a day almost every day since I got home & needless to say it does pleasure me in ways I can't tongue but I am not ready to record it yet. You would be pleased to know that D.D. & I have been playing together once a week and we intend to go right on doing so till either or both of us reach our limits. Anyhow, I promised you a tape and will get it together soon. It's been an unaccountably wet April, almost a belated winter complete with daily downpours. Great to hibernate and strum inside.

Jeezus, ain't the news appalling these days? Ain't it familiar as 'paranoia'? Ain't it inflated? I am pisst off with the mendacity of our local real estate, its gross opportunisms: that the notion of supply & demand has got out of hand when a mere shack down the st. is worth a hundred thousand dollars. I mean we will deserve whatever is comin' at us. Despite the illusion of well-being, we seem to be feeding the war machinery: Thanatos is about to walk on to center stage and flash his rapier of doom. What is so monstrous is the awesome fact that we are all a part of the complicity despite ourselves. Shit, the morning Reagan got shot, Don & I were playing together in Kitsilano. One thing at least is certain and that is 'we' have to do what we 'do' to help keep a balance.

11 am. 5th. 4. '83

Dear Michel:
_____

        well, here it is, for what it's worth. meaning, i'm thru with them, for now. i've spent the better part of 2 months going thru them, re-writing and re-wiring them, changing their interconnectedness, their geometry. my mandate was (is) an utter lucidity, meaning, 'it' ought to be capable of song and, like song, carry everything along on the wings of a (syllabic) melody. like a 'plain' chant or 'blues' a la Billy Holliday. like a new-told 'renga.' if you remember my reading some of them to Josie & you when you translate them into French, i'm sure you will find their 'key-note.' the order in which they come to you is simply the last chance i took with their interfacings. another look (yours, for instance) at them could affect their semblances. for your sake, i'd say use any of them in whatever sequence you want them to fulfill. for the sake of my pages in the anthology, let me say that i can't imagine a more auspicious way of getting translated into French than thru the bonds of our convivial friendship. it heartens me to know that in and thru our friendship my ongoing love affair with Montreale will surely (breathlessly) continue. while i'm with you in this way let me tell you about an old/ ah yes, still young, (30 year old) girl friend from the early '70s who has recently (3/4 of a year ago) moved back to Monreale. her name is Linda Vanesse and i think you two ought to get to meet each other. here's her phone number & address for what it's worth. (Japan on the horizon. leaving mid-May. let me know your plans or whereabouts. let's hope our paths cross.)
p.s. i know 'our' words, one way or another, will. love,

6. 4. '83. noon

Dear Jim Caswell:

    Well, it's almost the end of another university year. I say 'another' because it's (yes) 30 years since I got into the old pedagogic game back in Calgary, Alberta, in the '50s. Jim, I didn't intend to be a teacher of any sort given my lack of credentials, etc. but I soon discovered I had a knack for it and, about this time, I discovered that my knack for it was, shall we say, 'entwined' with my propensities as an artist. I am one of those who have really never been anything else but an artist/teacher. Do you know what that means? Does Dean Will know what that means? Does he, for instance, really care about art? Not that it matters, but I do wish he had the perspicacity to trust my intelligence when it comes to art 'cause it's a riven path I know something about. Which brings me to the real reason I sat down to write an unbecoming letter to you. I mean why doesn't Dean Will serve me notice one way or the other? I mean, here it is going on into April and given the seriousness of my request with all its implications for the coming summer, not to mention the rest of the year, you would think that in all fairness to one of his faculty members he would have acted upon his decision by now. I mean, given the callit intricacy of the whole system of which I'm just a small cog, I should have thought he wouldn't have had the time to ponder on my is it 'justifiable' sabbatical so long. Anyhow, I want to say that if and when he does let us know and the answer is 'no,' I would like you to make an appointment with him for me so I can find out 'first-hand' why I've been told 'no' twice in a row. Otherwise, I've had a good year despite the ongoing animosities. I mean I have had a number of keen students which is what I most get off on. Please keep me informed.

                                                                                Yours sincerely,

Easter Sunday / '83

Dear Mike:

It's Easter sunday with Bach boppin' in and out of one Easter ear and out of the yolk of the other one all day long and me mostly stoned dancing an old time sexual fantasy on the penumbra of a hopelessly perpendicular ego while awaiting, haplessly awaiting, wanting Sonja. meanwhile, i go on waltzing with whatever Matilda comes along. . . . if i were a true christian, i would no doubt use E.S. to meditate upon Christ's passion and pray that i might be imbued with it. it's all a question of choosing and/or believing in a religio/mythology and sticking with its callit abiding principles. or else find an embodiment via the etymology of the very roots of what we call consonants and their twin vowels: it would seem to lie in the very praxis of language and its intricate modalities of callit life's brine psalm. anyhow, i feel that it's fitting to be able to tell you that the pear tree pomes (such as they be) have completed themselves. i mean anything in them that doesn't mean exactly what it says has to be a lie and to get every last bit of the old lies out of the text has been a remorseless quest. as for the sequence, they are numbered but it's still an open-ended sequence of events. mike, if you feel the script could be tighter, let me know and i'll consider it. otherwise, it's an old Text i found in the language tree which believe it or not grew out of my open mouth via the tip of my tongue, etc. otherwise . . . it's waitin' for Sonja . . . waitin' to say, 'hullo, how you been, well, it's nice to have seen you, good bye . . . again.' 'ya can't live without them and you can't live with them' is one of those old myth-maker's tales that abound in all the translations into the English language. & being a prairie-born boy with more grit than wit when it comes to girls, i go on believin' it. leavin' for Japan with my mother come early May. be a goner for at least the better part of 3 whole months. give me news of whereabouts till then. one of them high gloss super colour kodachromes in a slicko magazine ad of a 'pear' close-up with its curved stem straight up and its green rump square to the table would make a great cover. i sd to myself just as i began to run out of 2nd hand words. Mike: will you act on behalf of T.P.T.P.? and it goes without sayin' that none of this has anything to do with how we use our friendship. that's got to be its own thing or nothing else.

and windin' up i wanta say that the notion of namin' one's feelings is mostly a bag of metaphors. nonetheless 'i' does feel like this pale green reticent April wind, etc.

April 11th thru 19th, '83

Dear Dean Will:

    Jim Caswell informed me that my request for a leave of absence has been turned down, again. It makes me wonder after more than 30 years of an ardent pedagogy whether I'm playing in the right ball park. Add to this a considerable amount of doubt concerning what team I'm playing for and 'who' if anybody the coach the pitcher and the bat boy are—and presto! You've got all the bases loaded down with, callit, my bag of perturbations. Anyhow, I had been waiting for a word from you longer than I care to recall and as the end of another school year veered into sight along with the freshly minted green leaves I began to get the message and bit by bit I let all the pleasurable thoughts of an intense year of work all onto myself be tattered by the brisk March winds. 'So be it. It ain't the end of the world. It ain't nuclear missiles,' I thought, even as something in me that wanted to be released from these migraine thoughts whispered, 'Tell it the way you feel, you have nothing to lose speaking on behalf of your sense of art.' In early March I had heard that 3 of the junior members of the A.H. wing of the F.A. dept. had been granted their leaves of absence. I thought of my membership on the tenure & promotions committees and how I had been an advocate of their competencies (their socio/political, multi-lingual scholarship) against the conservative art historians and their dominant views. I had read what I could of their recent publications and, though I didn't feel I had been given any exceptional insights (which in any case are rare), I wanted to uphold the principle of a diverse intellectuality for the sake of the F. A. dept's well being and effectiveness. . . . These matters come to mind simply to underline the 'irony' implicit in my situation. I mean that I seem to have fallen head over heels into a large credibility gap which is to all intents and purposes not of my own making. Believe me, this is not the kind of letter I enjoy writing but write I will for the sake of my own self claritas.

For what it's worth, I want to say that the notion of an unspoken institutional containment, e.g., 'you were hired as a painter to teach painting and you had better stick to it, etc.,' doesn't make much sense to an 'inside' practitioner. Furthermore, it seems to me wholly unwarranted by the very nature of art with its myriad transformations. For what it's worth, I have from the very beginnings of my life in art/pedagogy held to an ideal which goes like this: any faculty member's own intellectual (albeit creative) growth ought to find a forum in the domain of pedagogy. All the more so in the Fine Arts where the unspoken mandate is : 'cast a keen eye on the riddled universe and paint or speak its coruscations.' Take my own writings for instance. I wrote a kind of poetry long before I began to make a study of it in my young manhood. Long before I ever thought to publish it. In fact, I've been a particular kind of writer (given my Asian/Canuck background/foreground) as long as I can remember. I simply mean that painting and writing have always been twinned in my life. They, along with all my other curiosities, stem from the same pan-Pacific sources, etc. *Curiosity* may have killed the proverbial cat with or without his nine lives, but let me assure you it's at the bottom of everything I practise in the name of art/pedagogy. In so far as it's an ongoing possibility, I'm speaking here of an *unbound curiosity*, that is one unconfined by any a priori notions (rationalizations?) of relevance or simple-minded usefulness. The artist/pedagogue in me begins here. All the things I have shaped and taught over 30 years bear the marks of Curiosity's Signature, if they bear any signature at all. Speaking for myself, I seem to have come to an age where every act is informed by the least act or gesture I've made in my life, and the consequences of it acting upon the world reverberate even in the spirit of this letter. I have no intention of trying to prove to you that my 8 books of prose and poetry, plus a couple of hundred poetry readings throughout N.A., have a special relevance to my effectiveness as a teacher or even painting if you haven't got the mind to deal with it. The true pedagogy, if such a beast is possible in these crazed '80s, consists in, callit, the acts of authentication of all we are called upon to witness in our lives.

For what it's worth, let me assure you that the painter you thought you hired was much more than that all along. I mean that the painter I used to be, and will 'be' again, is father to the middle-age man of the arts I seem to have willy-nilly become. For what it's worth, let me assure you that the poet in me is listening most attentively to all of these little words. Even as the pedagogue I am presides over another round of rhetoric. Furthermore, all these indissoluble parts of me become fingers and thumbs of the harpist I be who strums the tonic strings of an ofttimes ancient threnody. For what it's worth, let me say that I am not of the company of the Modern Age breed of highly-touted Specialists and have never aspired to be one. I, for instance, hold the view that the Industrial Revolution with its grand procession of magnificent machines spelled the beginning of the end of a hitherto 'ambidextrous' human being. I mean that bit by bit his varied skills got translated into a particular kind of quantification machine with a particular kind of keen machine-like 'will' and as each new machine came along 'our' man became less and less his fulsome (instinctually-grounded) self. etc. Another way of saying it goes like this: forfeit the archaic ground in yourself and you indenture the artistic impulse which is at least as old as the caves at Lascaux. All of this seems to be my way of saying that it is impossible for me to affirm the notion of art based upon the craze for specialization because it goes against the grain of my mandate as an artist. For, you see, I am one of the obdurate ones who have had to rediscover the truth of each art form within themselves before finding a language in which I could speak of it. I have no authority except in the minutiae of attention I bring to what we could romantically call my Heart's Work. My whole pedagogy is rooted in this. Given all the years I have been a savant of the arts and the particular ways (senses) of knowing, such attention proposes I am nothing if not my eyes, my ears, my mouth, my nose, my very prose. Believe me, I intend to go on using my eyes for the sake of painting as long as I have eyes to see with. Believe me, nothing completes itself in the domain of art till the maker and the thing to be made complete a circle of consciousness. I am, if you want, one of those who would become adept on the ladder of consciousness for the sake of the shapeliness of all the things I will go on making. Pedagogy is nothing if not relevant dialogue.

Believe me, Dean Will, I shall continue to hone my perceptions in the divers art forms I practise because it goes without saying that I have my mandate as an artist. Furthermore, I hope my reach exceeds the grasp of any institution and its nomenclature or containments because what's at stake is bigger than both of us. I for my part feel that I don't have any authority in these matters except for all the divers things I have shaped throughout my life (in the name of Art) and sent out into a fraught world to fend for themselves among a vast constellation of human artifacts. I mean that my own sense of credibility stems from a life-long dwelling in and among the ruins of a Language wherein I continue to struggle against my own ignorances. Art has no tongue but the tongues of those who have given their lives over to its speaking out. Meanwhile, I have to get my marks in even as the coruscations of another summer open out ahead of us. It comforts me to know that both of us will have an equal share of its beatitudes. May you also be led to feel idolatrous in its erotic embrace.

Yours truly,

mid April

Dear Isamu/Kazuko:

time passes . . . passes thru me. i am a one-way passenger, a *mote* riding (sometimes soaring) on its immense/invincible wings. the JAL 747 that'll be bringing me to Japan in mid-May is, amongst a host of other fables, the, callit, perfect embodiment of how all of us do 'soar' thru space/time. i imagine therefore that all the Russian & Americun cosmonauts who have walkt out in outer-space and watched the huge earth dwindle into something the size of a small glass marble have perhaps glimpsed another divinity of space/time and, except for a few errant remarks, kept the vision to themselves as if it were truly unspeakable. all these thots hover about as i write to you. furthermore, i have played & replayed the micro cassette tapes i made when i was there with you almost 2 years ago, and each time i play them i can vividly picture 'us' sitting out a summer typhoon with the downpour tapping out an incessant rhythm on your tin roof. i've listened to 'oji' playin' & singin' his jamisen while the rest of us laughed, talked, or joined in with pots & pans so often it almost feels like i had these little holidays with you, tho i am 5000 miles away. if there can be a magical place for an ol' skeptic like me, it almost has to be that tiny pin-point on the map of S/E Asia called 'Kohama.' anyhow, if you're still there come late June/early July, i'm coming down to spend a coupla weeks with all of you. how far away is Kohama? where will my breath take me? these questions come to mind as these words take their fated places in the entanglements of my own thots. believe me, all my miraculous moments are an unspoken Gift. i shall probably meet both Minoru & your Mother before we get together. p.s. Mother (who will be 87 in August) & i are going to spend a month beside the Pacific Ocean in Kochi (end of June).——the enclosed things are long overdue. i can't begin to tell you how much i am looking forward to the heat of an Asian summer to warm my Northerner's friable bones. you'll hear from me as soon as Mom & I are settled in Kochi City. say 'hullo' to Oji.

22nd, April, '83
10 pm

Dear David/Candice

David, it was lovely to hear from you. I don't usually go out of my way to keep in touch with my assorted friends, but those I love are never far from my mind. For you see I am one of those for whom the only meaningful basis of our necessary human relationships (politics?) is one that's rooted in empathy and love, albeit one that recognizes that all you can truly want of another lies in welcoming their being into your heart and be pleasured by their, shall we say, 'hearth.' Tho I am in my way 'adept' at playing the part of a man at large in the wide world and tho I wouldn't dismiss the myriad rituals of any Citizen's public office, I know for myself that the endless machinations of our public offices are fundamentally heartless. I would be part of that esoteric circle who act upon the world knowing the exactitude of callit 'accountability' for all my thoughts and actions, ad infinitum. . . . The huge orange garbage gobbler just went by and the thought crosses my mind that our gross-national-product-bent-consumer-society produces at the very least as much garbage as it produces the endless paraphernalia of our secret desires and silly pleasures. Not to mention the ongoing ideological language of *detente*, big bully monstrous fear of ultimate irreparable catastrophes, etc. I don't hear that proto-Freudian age word 'paranoia' booted about by the arcane society of psychologists but something very like it is fouling up the air. David: think of the P.T.P. as a collaboration: I scrawled the words, now you can scrawl the pictures including jacket/ & cover. All of them early 20th Century European Artists we so assiduously studied didn't do more. More than you perhaps know I have cleaved to the old-fashioned notion that all human works (however individualistic) were clearly acts of a myriad collaboration of which the thing, the book to hand, is but a luminous moment of perception's untold store of silences. I am to all intents and purposes 'alone' in the world for the 1st time in my life, or so it ofttimes feels. but even as I say this, a host of distant friends whisper an incantation of love in my soft ear. David: Gladys Hindmarch's Coach House Book with Brian Fisher's cover leaps to mind as a kind of typo/ design that could feel fine. I like the clarity of the large type. I'm one of those who don't like squintin' at language. Take care.

April 22nd '83

Dear Stan/Sarah:

    higher in the sky each day the ol' sun emblazons these little words on my small back. another school year almost but not quite over, i say to myself, stretching my arms onwards. in about three weeks i'll be flyin' across the sweep of the old Pacific on my way with my mother to reenact an ancient rite. i seem to have come full circle in that everything i feel feels like an old hat like the one G.G. gave me a decade ago an old panama with rumpled brim i wore all the way across o kanada. now it gathers dust on a basement hook having outlived its actual usefulness. not unlike a humble-pie sort of big game hunter's antlered trophy hanging on the wall of the ol' den. but wait a moment: 'what about the future?' a wee voice in me hoarsely whispers. to which another wee voice in me replies, 'ah yes, tomorrow is indeed another day and what it might bring is, to say the least, partially apprehended/partially incomprehensible.'

    anyhow, you've got WHEELS and you've now got the P.T.P. naturally I want them both (immediately!) to turn into inimitable Coach House Books. like PRESTO! you could ask G.S. to re-enter the *Paper Doors* (like be a guest C.H.P. editor) and both edit & design WHEELS but only if he has the mind to. i mean that all of our 'wheels' do keep on turning. at this point it's up to you. i mean that i've turned into a mere cog etc. as for the P.T.P. i've written to D.B. to tell him we're a 50/50 collaboration and as far as i'm concerned the pictures together with the cover etc. are mostly up to him. Mike has the final say on the exactitude of what is in some senses no longer my own text. i mean i've never been one of them poets who lean on their press to get the book out. i would be an arse-hole if i didn't trust in the two of you after all these years. etc. let me get this off to you. i'll send a postcard or two from S/E Asia as soon as i can splice two thoughts, one Japanese/ the other, English, together. etc. have a splendid summer wherever you be.

                                                            yours faithfully

26th, April, '83

Dear Minoru:

got your message from Fu who phoned to say he's packin' up to return to Japan and that he was studying acupuncture/ massage with you, etc. i have got a year's leave of absence from UBC and that certainly pleasures me. it makes it possible for me to stay on in Japan longer than the summer if i need or want to. to bring you up to date: mother and i are leaving here on the 14th of May for Tokyo/Osaka/Kochi City where we will take up all the strands of our past existences for a month before mother returns to Kanada and i move on, up to Hokkaido or down to Okinawa. that will be late June/early July. anyhow, i shall let you know where i am in Kochi City as soon as we're settled.

i've been playing & replaying the cassette tapes i made at my studio on Powell Street and at my home on Keefer. these tapes include your presences as a musician and singer along with all the sounds of other people we know in common. they're just about all i listen to these days, thus you're very much with me.

do you think we will be able to go down to Okinawa for awhile together?

yours truly,

2 pm, on Campus, April 28th, '83

Dear Dean Will:

need I say that I left your office feeling that we had had a fair exchange of views and that my letter (of grievances) had been effective. I didn't come away with the feeling that you had changed your mind about me and my work, but that didn't matter because I had already given in to your decision and now had to make last minute arrangements for my summer in Japan. next term was after all several months away. need i say that your phone call the following day almost but not quite blew me away. I mean it seemed to come out of the April sky as an omen, an unexpected omen, which I must act upon, steadfastly. An artist's life work intersects at all points with the body politic: I would be a fool indeed if I didn't write to you to express my gratitude. Like I've already sd, there's more at stake in this bequest than both of us know. I'm leaving for the Orient on the 12th of May. If there are any matters I should attend to (for the coming year of absence), please let me know.

Yours truly,

~

2.25 pm, on Campus, April 28th, '83

Dear Jim Caswell:

Need I say that I'm nonplussed at my good fortune. Need I dwell on what it means to me. Need I say that even a year of indolence is good for an artist if that's what he truly needs. Furthermore, the good Dean's confidence in me will prove to be beneficent when I come back, etc. For what it's worth, I spoke to Robert Young about my replacement. Because he was working on getting Peter Dagleish out here, I suggested he could replace me as I had complete confidence in Peter's assorted abilities. p.s. We knew each other from the early '70s when he was living in Canada. P.D.'s wit, and he has a natural gift for it in his art, could be to say the least salubrious. Otherwise, you could speak (personally) to Ranjan Sen who has taught part-time out here for many years. He has had a broad teaching experience in the practice of painting and graphics that could, given his thoroughly modern Indian background, be a distinctive contribution to the dept. I'd say, take Ranjan seriously as a replacement for me with my blessings. Needless to say, it's up to you guys and gals. I'll be leaving for the Orient on May 12th for 3months & 10 days. Be back in Vancouver come September with a mind full of pan-Pacific thoughts. Please keep me posted via my home address concerning important studio decisions, etc. (p.s. I'll be in next week to tidy up the ol' office and attend to last-minute matters that might come up.) Have yourself a bracing summer . . . despite the Voices-of-Doom impending holocaust.

Yours sincerely,

11 pm, May 1st, '83

Dear Syuzo:

For what it's worth here is a resume of my/our Intentions when we come to Japan. Mother and I will be leaving Vancouver on May 12th and arriving in Tokyo the following afternoon. We intend to go on to Kochi City after a night or two in Tokyo. Mother has written to relatives in Kochi asking them to find a small cottage for us to live in for a month to six weeks. We intend to stay there and visit our relatives in around Kochi and Umagi besides taking short sight-seeing trips around Shikoku. We will probably spend a few days in Kyoto before I see Mother back on the plane to Canada (mid/late June). I'm wondering if you and your family could come and stay with us while we're in Kochi City. We could even rent a car and do some travelling about if you thought it was at all possible. Otherwise, I shall certainly see you when Mother has gone back to Canada and I am on my own. Just to make the entire trip to Nippon this summer really interesting, I shall be getting together with Sonja and Sam (remember them?) after Mother has gone back home. We three also intend to get together and do a bit of travelling, like going down to Kohama to be with the Akinos. Maybe we could all get together, somehow, somewhere?

'WE' : mother, sonja, samantha & i arrive in tokyo on the 15th of may. will phone you when we get there and before we (mother & me) move to kochi city. sonja & sam are going on to yokohama to be with maya koizumi. remember her?

May 9th, '83, 4 pm

Dearest Vicki:
the days (daze?) before flying off to Nippon are catching up with me. I mean that the count-down has begun now that it's Monday, May 9th, about 4 pm. this letter will be my breather, between getting a pile of last-minute things accomplisht and finding myself at a curious intersection of my life with my mother, my daughters, Sonja & Samantha passing in and thru the old Keefer Street house. add to all them ladies the fact that Kit fell by on his way back to Seattle. lauded by all the ladies present he sd he knew why he was coming back to Vancouver after the school year. he meant that there was nobody outside of his school chums in the city of Seattle who would hail him on the street and say, "Hi, Kit." not quite like a 'son' and yet he's the closest thing to one I'm likely to have and, given his qualities, I would be an arse-hole if I didn't feel good about him. and, needless to say, I feel the same about Daphne: more than ever I feel, despite my previous summer's abnegations, that we somehow completed one whole turn of our karmic wheels and who's the *axle* and who's the *rim* has nothing to do with anything.

begin again. begin with all the 'hiatuses' since we last got together. begin with your recollections I have just re-read of our song & dance act at Scarborough and let memory have my derelictions. begin with the fact that my own mother (who is 87 come August) is sitting downstairs watching a soap opera while waiting for one or another of the aforementioned ladies to reappear. begin with her and the burden of memory she embodies and you have a forlorn poet cum musician who has wanted to forget everything and thus unburdened would live forever in the present tense. but . . . all, all of these women (memory's vivid mirrors) keep refracting the light back into my cerebral cortex. anyhow, this is simply to say that my callit 'mind' is active in a way it hasn't been for a long time. I mean, actively 'present' to them. anyhow, Nippon is beckoning with all its considerable elan and, like I say, I'm standing at another cross-street in my life and waiting for the lights to change. waiting for all the women who have gone out shopping to return so we may get on with what's left of the day. even as I write, a host of other 'graces' hover near and 'those' who are present and those who are, as it were, absent have their equitable share of all the silences to come.

the enclosed cassette tape (long overdue) will tell you where my kinda music is at these days. have a lovely summer all of you under Pinnacle Peak. p/s been in touch with Lora Carney at Scarborough, again. I've suggested we could get together this fall and do another number. . . .

luv

July 30th, noon

Sonja dear Sonja

Michiko and Koko were busy unpacking the latest shipment of goodies for the Japanese Festival this weekend: amidst phone calls, customers, and all the heapt up goods, Michiko says that she & Don are off for a month in Japan this Sunday. Don is apparently getting a customized t-shirt with the character/s for 'gaijin' silk-screened across his chest. i, laughing with her, suggested it ought to say, 'no. 1 gaijin.' anyhow, it's an occasion to have a letter delivered to you in, is it the 2nd or 3rd, person? this glad bag of words then to let you know i miss the 3 of you and, tho there are no regrets worth bothering abt, i go on wishing we could have laughed together more than we did. plangent. all the plangent intersections i found myself walking across with or without you, the three of you. i gave up thinking i had something special to 'do' long before i headed for home. i mean i could spend years sorting thru my heap of photo-glyphs, my cassette tapes and if i know anything abt myself i probably will. one way or another, what was/is special is the time (of my life) i spent there with mother, you & Sam. there were very few holds that were barred. a number of barbed wire barriers, and more than each their share of, callit, emotional congestion. none of us will be quite the same after this summer. Sonja: i couldn't go on waiting for you like an impatient young lover. i had to prove to myself that i could leave you (in peace and purposefulness) which, you sd more than once in different ways, is what you truly wanted of us. 'us?' 'we' were hardly ever that but when we were we implicitly trusted each other: didn't we also do that? it never really occurred to me to be in your life to deprive you of yourself. i mean if i had thot abt it at all i wouldn't have come knocking at your door. like i've already sd, every bit of it is worth it. it all makes sense. if you happen to find yourself talking to old friend Ikkyu, tell him i think i've got a leg up on the next rung of that parabolic ladder and any day now i'm going to break into song. o the ol' 'hesitation blues' will get me down unless i can keep my wit up. p/s Sat. July 30th, 3 pm: now it's time to hava hot shower and get myself over to the festival so that i can give this letter to Michiko who takes leave of us to join the three of you tomorrow morning. hope Sam has a great 12th birthday. hope Maya has been writing with the typewriter.

love,

July 30th, noon

Maya Dear Maya:

Right off: Many many thanks for your generosity whenever I found myself in Yokohama. Thank Suzy, too. The Gift of self is just about all we have and you gave wholeheartedly of yourself. You and I can never be lovers because we're like a brother & sister who feel the world impresses itself on our psyches in similar ways. It felt that way from the beginning. There's hardly been a sun in Vancouver this July and far more rain than a thirsty fir tree can gulp or swallow. I've had to put a sweater on since getting back and needless to say I've hardly taken it off. 'Drowned earth.' Don't know what an excess of 'water' means in this the 57th summer of my whiff of a life unless it means I need all the moisture I can get.

My own bod remains gladful for all the heat it stored up in Nippon this summer. Ah all those sticky nights in Yokohama, Tokyo, Osaka, Kyoto, Nomi and Gotenyama: how, how they bear the brunt of all these grey overcast days. Days that fill the page and drip down the pane like an exquisite opal tear. Sonja's heartfelt tears. My callit rusty tin drainpipe heart. Samantha's clenched little fists. Plangent downpourings. Enough salt/tears to scour an old wheel boat. Maya, my dear Mother left from Yokohama 65 years ago for good ol' Kanada and never lookt back except to remember her roots in Shikoku. Seekers of the Sun God have their way of getting to Tonga or Okinawa. Maya, let the crypt of language you have buried in you speak the truth. All acts of communication seem to embody the act of translation. The language of love can fall off the tip of any tongue. Yours, for instance. Even the weather, all the aforementioned 'blood, sweat & tears,' has to declaim itself.

Will you give Sonja & Samantha a big hug for me? With Michiko/Don & others arriving on your doorstep, you're going to have a lively send off. Please feel completely free to call on me and even stop-over on your way to Toronto. Daphne's latest book of pomes called *How Hug a Stone* has come out and what a lovely book of 'origins' & 'remembrances' it is. She sends her love and wishes to be remembered.

August 1st, 8 pm, '83

Lora dear Lora & Terry

got yr hand-writ letter days after i got back from the ol' orient, the orient of my mind if nothing else holds it. sounds like the kind of family gathering i ain't had for many a year with all of the trimmings, including sun, sex and lotsa beer. if i never spend a long summer weekend in Georgian Bay, will i qualify as a w.a.s.p.? will T.T. ever forgive me? i don't know what worth there is in it, but i'm just another Canuck who knows 2 places, 2 actual places in the world and neither of them has much to do with big Ontario or Northrop Frye. mind you, a lot of my very best friends have always hailed from there.

remember the yankee folk tale about what's his name and how he fell asleep for a long time only to awaken one day and find everything as it used to be or rather how he remembered it except his long beard which changed from black to white streaked with grey? coming out of the oriental time warp (lasting 60 daze), i've landed here on my feet and find myself with a surfeit of time to burn the riven summer away. tomorrow i'll have go to the bank and get a certified cheque with which to pay my taxes up. then i'll get my cable hooked up and watch the summer pass by. no fool like an old fool with suction cups on his soul instead of wings on his heels.

thanks for checking out the Harbourfront folks about a show of sorts. i like the idea of a tight but full showing of some of the blue mule photographers of now yesteryears. it could be a fillip for 13 cameras too. like the Vancouver' scene with beautiful B.C. tip-toeing in the background. that and a long evening of super 8 movies and performance del-arte. why don't you broach A.A. about it for early spring? you & Terry could co-sponsor it if they didn't mind. anyhow, i have lotsa pics to print & choose from and i want to show them some way.

otherwise, the writing about my 60-day sojourn lies ahead. it's better to be read than dead. better to be insolvent. say Hi to Mike & Linda.

Early Aug. '83

Dear Linney:

          I've been to Japan, the 'real' Japan and not the N.A. press's version of that place since I had your last change-of-address card. How are you? Have you found yourself a wealthy middle-age man with lotsa love left in him yet? Have you written another 'seal-of-approval' novel?

And how does it feel being among the Quebecois after a decade among WASPS out here in Lotus land? I mean, is it beginning to feel as if you've come home? Is it as real as, say, my Japan? Or our Cape Breton? Met Mona Fertig briefly at the Folk Festival. She said she had some fine times with you in Montreale. She also said that she was getting married soon. Sooner or later I'm going to be harried again but for the time being I'm on my own and making out. I'm trying to get at callit the heart of my 60-odd (to say the least) days in Japan and write it down. Sometimes it seems as if everything I've written, let alone painted, photographed & shaped into music, has the shape of the human heart. In other words, I'm piped into a circular dance and dance I will till the heart gives up. Linney: this is to tell you I'm in touch with you. Why, come September, I'm even thinking of flying out East to spend some time with you and others. What do you think? How do you feel? There's a Montreale I carry around inside me that isn't in the news out here. p/s I hear Bourassa is waiting in the wings to take over the Libs out there. Isn't politics the cat's meow? Write to me if you have the mind and inclination to do so. Oh that knoll called 'God's Hand'—a crazy couple I fondly recall blew the whistle on love on the installment plan. Cape Breton is as far away as Japan. Take care of yourself.

august 3rd, '83, noon

dear richard & vicki

    vicki & richard : i'm back in vancouver after 60 days in japan. i went there with a plan and actualized it before i knew i had: that is to say *the plan* took me by the scruff of my neck and put me thru. it all had to do with my own dear mother and a lady named sonja together with her daughter sam. needless to say, we travelled a lot and, tho we never fought, we unnerved each other. predilections, obsessions, & a thousand small awkwardnesses put all of us thru. it's a wonder we got to do the things we did. what we didn't accomplish will bear another kind of fruit. perhaps even another kindred thrill. anyhow, this is just to tell you i hope to come by soon (late august, early september). i have a whole year off and i do intend to get about as best i can. & will. odd to come to that time in my life when the gap in the familiar seems to have widened. i'm to all intents & purposes on my own and find myself peculiar to say the least. i mean there's a beast in me that refuses to lie down. even as it balks & barks, it paws the ol' ground. if i learned anything this summer it's, callit, the sacral ground i hail from: both mother & mother earth. i hear all the women's voices. hear the pulse of their beatitudes and pray for my own. my own forlorn beatitudes. let me know 'how' things are with the two of you & your large brood. and tell me if my coming by is convenient. there's a disturbance in these words i can't finger. there's an unrehearsed love bursting thru. hang on to dear life and it'll cling to you. i'm only a draft of august wind. . . . .

love

Mid-August, '83

Dear Mike & Linda:

     me has been back in Vancouver for a month after 60-odd daze in Nippon. me is working the trip outa his system divining words and pictures, pictures and words, ad nauseam. me hasn't become an 'i' since i flew over the ocean and almost drowned in a seance—or was it a trance of tears. i mean me is trying to get a handle on how i became the dutiful son cum avid but inappropriate lover. 'i' think i will have to reinvent myself, again. the language gap i've fallen into leaves me with, callit, the marginalia of self-hood. i haven't spoken a word of Japanese in good ol' kanada, tho i keep mumblin' nondescript words, lunatic phrases over and over—almost like my own built-in ethnic radio station.

how 'i' look and feel Japanese without being able to read and write a single ideogram has to find a Text in the writing to hand. otherwise, kith & kin are numerous and, there's no doubt about it, my roots are grounded in Shikoku: i mean when mother & i got there (we were there together for a whole month), we immediately heard 'where' our kind of Japanese comes from. and like all 'dialects,' ours is grounded in the particulars of her birthplace. why, i even found myself speaking out, particularly when i was drunk, in a way i rarely did in my travels elsewhere in Japan. even more important, i felt that i was clearly understood. in a nut shell the valences of my Japanese self. as for my Kanadian self, 'he' relished all the duplicities (of personae) wherever he went. and truth to tell, he often hid himself behind dark glasses and a camera, often found himself going for days at a time without speaking English: strange how a language can remain buried in one's larynx and all of a sudden burst out. anyhow, i'm going full tilt. there's a work-in-progress that i hope to bring east when i go thata way this coming September. it'll be my (hitherto unaccomplished) picture/word book.

what would we do without roots? not that we don't re-convene them in order to authenticate ourselves. i wish it were that easy. i mean if 'i' only had to hang from a thick ANCESTRAL LIMB in the vast Garden of Genealogy to become a troubadour! but 'we' both know nothing's that easy, unless you've got the grace of a singing porpoise!

went by the other night to have supper with Daphne & Kit. it was almost like old times the way we got off on each other. all that warmth felt good. driving home i thot, well, we fell apart as if the script we had written together had been surreptitiously edited and those edited pages got lost. but then again there's still a lot of cement to hold us together and i felt nothing but tenderness for both of them.

for what it's worth, Mike: i was forty years of age in Montreal and those were really halcyon years for sheer exuberances i abide by to this day.

                                                         Love

Late August, '83

Dear Char:

      you might have heard that we haven't had much summer here in Vancouver but now that we're into August it looks like we might have an Augustine light. one thing for sure, nobody in lotusland is gettin' much of a tan this year. or, at least, not so far. i didn't intend to begin by talking about the weather. rather it was my intention to tell you a bit about my sojourn this summer in Japan with you know 'who' besides my mother with whom i spent a month in Shikoku. as i sit here piecing this letter to you by picking my mind, i find that there isn't that much to tell that could be told in a letter without writing a hundred pages and that's clearly not what i intend assuming i have, as it were, an intention in mind. 'finders/ losers/ keepers/ weepers'—the ol' childhood spell went, and it comes to mind to divine something lost & something kept & somebody wept—is of course a simple abstract of whatever it turns out to mean, if meaning it has. Char: i think i did my very best for my dear mother but something in me says it wasn't enough. when it comes to playing the dutiful son i must admit it wasn't much fun, tho we slept side by side for a month. (like we used to when i was a child: 50 years down the ol' road doesn't break the ol' childhood bonds, sez it.) what was pitiless was all the (riddled) silences we couldn't cut thru. in short, all the things unsaid. otherwise, we dreamt both 'beginnings' and 'endings' in the bosom of our numerous if distant relatives and felt at home if home is a feeling of familiarities. i hadn't wholly graspt how venturesome my mother & father were till we were together in Shikoku. to this very day most of our relatives haven't even been to Honshu, let alone cross the Pacific at the turn of the century. mother, as it happens, was the bringer of 'the news from the new world' they'll never see except on television.

i was my own person, notwithstanding. even when i was with sonja and sam. to say that the 3 of us had both good, not so good, bad & very bad moments is only a way of saying we found it tough going at the best of times. nothing quite like a forlorn lover to make a muddle out of a small triad. nothing quite like the 3 of us to undo the banal sentiments. nothing quite right or quite wrong yet nothing much to hold us sez it succinctly. i don't know whatever made me think 'we' could divine a bit of ol' Nippon together unless it was based on false proclivities: my own, as it turns out, most of all. Nippon on the installment plan took us by storm. i mean we never knew where the next monsoon was comin' at us from but, i would venture to guess, it was inside of us all along. anyhow, i had to leave, left them at Maya's place in Yokohama after we'd spent a coupla (last) days in Tokyo. i had caught the shinkansen back (again) to Kyoto and, then, Gotenyama. tho we had provisionally agreed to meet in a few days in Kyoto for the Obon festival, i knew by the time i hit Gotenyama that i would surely go home and go home i did on the 11th, almost 60 days later. . . . and so it goes. Char: i wanted to say that i feel i've lost her but that can't be true because the truth (as she tells it) is that i never really had her at all. not, not that i ever wanted to possess her. lovers, middle-age lovers fall into the same hole they did when they were green-horns, if they love at all. Char: am i speaking nonsense again?

                                                              Love,

September 1983

My Dear Isamu & Kazuko

It's almost two months since we parted, parted in a break of the summer typhoon, on the shores of Kohama. Every time I find myself telling somebody about my summer, I tell them that the highlight of my trip happened to me in Kohama. Hardly a day goes by without Kohama tapping my head. I've printed countless pictures of it. I've listened to the tapes of that memorable evening we all got deliciously drunk together, and every time I hear that rain falling on your tin roof I feel my whole body laved in tropical rain. Something marvelous to 'look thru' into the future with. Will you give the old man & your one-eyed neighbour my warmest regards? I can clearly see that I had to go away this summer to prove to myself I'm a citizen of the world. &, furthermore, I had to rediscover the instinctual man in me 'cause he's the guy who keeps all my senses alive and tells me that I've acted on more than my own behalf. A famous English poet said that 'no man is an island unto himself.' Everybody has said or thought it. But here's the rub: I had to go down to Kohama to renew what it meant.

I didn't get out to the country to visit your mother but I do intend to send her some snapshots of Kohama. I didn't get back to Kyoto because by the time I arrived in Osaka I had decided that Kohama was what I had come for. Hawaii was a big HIT. I read poetry to a room full of 'unknowns' at the Volcano Art Centre and took a long bright afternoon's drive in my rented Corvair thru the lava ocean crater of the huge volcano and took lots of pictures. Nothing quite like a hit of 'Hawaiian gold' to embolden a faraway traveller. Nothing like dope to erase the Pacific jet-lag.

Regards,

sunday after pearl harbor, 1.30 pm

Dear Richard:

    got the big books. thank you for all the thots they bear. got another wallop, viz how tiny nippon must be among the most exploited 'exotic kulturs' left in the eyes of post-western european man with his inordinate sense of Otherness. as a long time purveyor of such books, i am nonetheless astonisht by their sheer outpouring and not a little harried by all the hirsute scholarship adorned by shiny kodachromes abt a wee domain i have very real ties with to this very moment. my 87 yr old mother & yours truly spent a whole month together there this summer. we re-animated all the old haunts & scents. the japan we know with all its preposterously/ pitilessly/ prefigured Ways never will get into the aforementioned books. and, if our trip this summer doesn't eventually get into a wee book of mine, i'll have failed as an erstwhile writer cum maverick artist. more & more i see how those of us who have always acted in/upon the world as artists/writers are given to accomplish those very things (. . . of the heart) that keep getting left out of Media's ugh collective texts. & as i sit here writing to you, the thot rises up before me that it will most certainly take all the psychic strength i have to go on giving it a compelling mundane shape, one embedded with all of life's vicissitudes & supine acts of (an often gory) Glory. i think we're both survivors in our fashion and are quite possibly vain abt that fact but the stretch of time/space that lies all around us into a hypothetical future . . . promises to be the catalytic test. it'll be at least as littered with humus debris & unaccountable corpses . . . but the thing i seem to be talking abt has to do with an, ofttimes, inordinate *subtlety*. we'll be thoroughly tested by our actual consciousness of all the thots and all the acts of our ongoing life and how even the least twinge of feeling will be, fragilely, hinged to the aforementioned dialectical twins. so-be-it. you were a newly wed man the last time i was in ottawa and the collaged portrait/s of the 2 of you were meant to celebrate that. i've lost a 2nd family since then and have fallen in & out of love. un-accountably, a-gain. still, it does go on feeling like a strain, if not a stain, keeping up the old familiar virtues. furthermore, i seem to have utterly displaced the luvly rhetoric of courtship & like a pimply faced adolescent with a lisp i talk abt the latest Hits i hear but don't really give a twig abt. one thing i feel urgent abt is i don't want to have anything to do with that highly touted form of in-fighting called Criticism in all its diaphanous sizes & shapes. i'm 'sick unto death' with the knowledge industry's glib repartees on every form of mass media. & yes, i'm tired of the chorus of fervid Feminism, its no less redoubtable two-bit criticisms of everything under the sun. . . . but then, again, my chinese oracular friend told me that this would be overwhelmingly a woman's year. their strength, he sd, would be peerless 'cause it's born of the re-birth of their intellect coupled with the primacy of an embodied Earth Goddess. but having sd all this, it occurs to me that all the recent women in my life have, in their turn, revealed to me some hidden aspect of the woman i also be. Dear Richard: i'll be headin' east come march. my intent is to do a number of performances of one sort or another in & around the toronto/monreale axis and i'd be pleased to give a reading in yr very bookstore. if you want it. otherwise, i'm going to make it an item with a star beside in my little notebook to spend a day in ottawa with the 2 of you. p/s the enclosed Xmas cards are 2 paragraphs in a wordless Visual Biography.

        taking the utmost care of W-O-R-D-S
        seems to be part of both of our Ventures
        write, if you're moved to do so.

                                                                   your

        West Coast Co-Correspondent

Mon./ Nov. 14th/ '83/ noon

Liz Amer/ Editor at *Canadian Forum*:

        here's a few prints of the original STONEDGLOVES. use them as you see fit. i send along the 'book' to show context. will you get both prints & book back to me, pronto— both are as scarce as the proverbial hen's teeth or is it comb. anyhow, i'm gladdened by the wee fact that my g(loves are still kickin' up the ol' dust in the backwaters of the CanLit (Laurentian) Shield. for what it's worth, i've got a coupla wee books comin' out when Coach House gets 'em out. the early one is titled WHEELS (abt a son & father making a trip to the homeland in '69). the other, more recent one, is titled THE PEAR TREE POMES. it's all abt a cycle of seasons in the life of a marriage/tree. it's also (not at all incidentally) abt coming to language: the groaning board of that act if you're born Asian. don't of course know whether you still have anything to do with Ward Island, but there's a warm green bower somewhere in the tangled forest of my memories reserved just for it. say 'hullo' to your big brother for me. we've been outa touch....

                                              sincerely,

14th/ Nov./ '83/ 1 pm

Dear Victor:

       when it comes to correspondence/s these tall-tale days i've been tight-mouthed. really nothing more than having little or nothing to say.—that cornea-size flare of light down at the far end of our nuclear tunnel ain't enough to even read by. as for the state of an un-updated feverish CAPITALISM, its 'rhetoric,' not to mention all its inherent contraDICTIONS, DOESN'T NEED A SEISMOLOGIST to tell us it's quaking underfoot. i sometimes wanta say, bugger the HI/SCI/TECHNOS/MULTI-NATIONAList/WAR MONGERING/ IDIOT MEDIA with its rush of 'future oriented addendums.' —but what the hell, i'm alive & kicking in this paltry world. anyhow, here's a cassette tape of miscell. soundings to tickle your ear. will you pass it on to Nobby when you've had enough? nothing makes me happier these days than fingerin' my old harp. no fool like an ol' fool barking his hoary head off while his fingers flick the strings. hang in there & keep yr head out off the ol' incinerator.

       any day now i'm going to burst into a BLUES, 58 comin' up. feels like the beginnings of the penultimate phase. 'love' just an ol' croak in a phlegmy throat. what's a cock for but pissing the time away. these days EASTERN KANADA feels further away than a Kiplinesque Orient.
                      HA!
see you come mid-March with no strings attached

16th/11/83/2 am

dear bob kroetsch:

                hey, i think i got yr naME right. anyhow, this is to remind you that i'd like to do something in winnipeg come march when i'll be headin' east to do a number of performances of all sorts. i've got toronto billed for the 12th thru the 17th. it could be, if it's gonna be at all, the previous weekend (beginning with thurs. the 15th thru to sat. the 17th or sun. the 18th). bob, it doesn't matter that much if it happens or not, so don't bust yr arse on my behalf. i mean, giving 'readings' no longer seems as relevant. besides, i do like to create my own occasions for reading or playing music & in such ways i am intently heard. the mac & stew canlit numbers game has never been my faintest wish. anyhow, the vast silences of this our country is in its incommensurable distances: there's light years of arctic solitude between us & all the words we would address to each other. in these callit fatuous days when the old-world chinese merchants & their immigrant children use both the abacus & the pocket computer with equal ease without drawing any distinction between them & their particular modes of calculation—knowing that it's the virtually effortless mode of pushing 'figures' around in wood or plastic really counts. in these steely lethal days when writers find themselves talking just as excitedly abt their latest IBM or APPLE as they might talk abt the NHL, or is it the NFL, i'm appalled to think of all the umpteen billions of words that will be pouring out of micro-chip minds programmed to dredge every known narrative, every plot & character in the whole domain of the english language to shape another 'best seller,' another minuscule 'variant.' ad nauseam. but then, again, i just got my first electric typewriter after 30 yrs—you could say i'm just lagging behind the TIME/s. laggard, braggard, haggard and worn, i'm puttin' these words to sleep with an aromatic whiff of hashish.

                some kinda vague thot abt kroetsch as a kinda kanuch e/g,
                naïve NABOKOV makin' out with a WASPish LOLITA . . .
                scums up my sleepin' mind. for CHRIST SAKE!—Let's not
                compare Mythologies.

16th/11/'83/6 pm

Dear Dale & Jim on Mayne Island:

    . . . the difference between early morning, mid-day & eventide ain't much more than a faint smear of grey. talk about lotsa rain & abysmal skies—my god, we're sure getting our fair share. why, it's all a body can put up with without dreaming of heading South. our local corner grocery store man named Benny just got back from Palm Beach with his wife. . . . my, they both lookt tanned & healthy. anyhow, i'm sending along a cassette tape of 'bird heart.' Dale—you did ask about its existence a long while ago & only recently i got a hold of it from among the heap of tapes i have scattered all over the place. needless to say, i've listened to it several times & it has its lovely moments. the whole tape, including the conversation/s of our interpolations concerning the music we were about to make, is very listenable. these days i'm making music by myself first of all, then once a week with Howard Broomfield (percussionist) & Trudi R. (voice). we've been getting together once every Friday for most of the year & where we shall go from here is anybody's guess. each day follows & i a mere child-of-time abide. . . . this is my winter of an overreaching solitude, one which goes on day after day without the telephone ringing with the least expectant caller. i am, shall we say, collared by my own ethnocentric obsessions & find nowhere to turn to but inwards. tho i haven't said a thing about our abysmal politics, both the local and the worldly, i'm sure 'it' seeps into these very words. anyhow, 'bird heart' should soothe the tedium of island existence: if not, try coming into town more often. or head South.—if we don't for whatever reason get together soon, i'll make sure i come by over the ol' Xmas holidays. p/s already the Xmas flack is accumulating at my front door. already the 1000 models of the latest shiny toy computers are hitting the department stores. my my, how timely it'll help all of us keep a tally on our happenstance. i wunder if Santa keeps track of all the kids who want him to bring them their favorite present by hiring a computer expert to make sure they haven't grown up.

                                                  yr petroglyph friend

17th/11/'83

Dear Lora:

      as you might have gathered i don't care if A.A. at the Harbourfront has anything to do with a show of mine. photographs or otherwise. bugger the ubiquitous 'historical perspective/s.' like almost anything else these days *photographs* can be a wallow of mindless images taken by anybody's aunt or uncle or that new breed of image-makers who graduate from Ryerson and think it neat that a million bucks were spent on a kotex ad. i'm, if you will, a child of a dying 'capitalism' and no doubt have had my share of brain washing—but given my predilections i'll never make images to sell anything: the artist in me long ago made a pledge to use whatever medium that came to hand to divine the callit sacral ground of all our image-making. everyone has something particular to do for the sake of life and i intend to go on spending my utmost energy for the sake of an unremorseful death. anyhow, i've finally completed my basement darkroom and am into printing photo-glyphs for a sustained period of time.—if you'd like to have a small show of them come March, i'll send them to you (FREE). otherwise, it's been incessant gloom and much rain. as for our provincial politics, ask the Fraser Institute what price a nuclear future bears. p/s do you think the 6th generation of thinking/acting computer robots will be capable of buggering each other/////

      your pear tree man

23rd/ 11th/ '83/ midnight

dear mariko (o m to be)   to be
             uthur   & john o (father   come)

i'm skinnin' the rind of my psyche to find out what it means to become a grandfather (at 58). i'll not know the exactitude of those kinds of feelings till the kid bites the air. i mean i had no way of knowing how i'd feel as a father till i was right in the thick of it (3 times—)

& even then didn't feel the real squeeze, the godawful emotional tease, till years later. *right now, say*. it's a bloody wunder that the cycles of our lives continue yielding their cupful of amazements. it's what i'd call our real plunder. ah the ineluctable, peerless, passage/s of t-i-m-e within which every THING imaginable rimes—if you want it to. i'm one of those old-fashioned kinda men who is, to say the least, grateful to all the bellies of all the women i've been able to put my ear to. i'm bombed enough this a.m. to even say 'it' surpasses all the philosophy i've read in my life when it comes to that understanding that surpasses mere knowledge. anyhow, this is just to say that the two of you have been on my mind (rites-of-passage & all that) & i shall get up to see you right after i get back from visiting Harry & Katie in Calgary, & mother & the rest of the family in Edmonton this coming week. i'm going now rather than at Xmas time. take good care of all the small things that occur one after the other daily & the days will one way or another take care of you. at least that's been your father's motto these days & by gum it does work tho, god help me, i still have all my thwarts tho i am beginning to feel comfortably at home inside of them. . . . like some cartographer's intricate detail of an imagined terrain somewhere in the High Andes, i see my life as a myriad unfolding of path-ways. o which way will my predilections, my migrant ways, lead me as 'we' CAPRICORNS veer into another rainforestwinter.

take care of the 3 of you

Dec. 4th, '83, midnight

Dear Mariko & John

since i wrote the enclosed letter to you I've been to Edmonton to visit my family. Whata terrible tug it gave me to see how all of us are getting older & older. What a wrench to feel that blaze of solitude that has always held us together. The years pass and 'we' barely communicate with each other and yet we are beholden to one another deeply. I spent most of the time with Mother and took note of her faltering ways. She spoke of how even knitting was becoming difficult and how those things she was knitting would probably be her last. All my life she has knitted things for me and as I was about to leave she gave me two pairs of hand-knitted socks to take with me. As I put them in among the things I had with me I thought this is the last things my old mother will ever knit for me and the child in me held back a sob. Mariko, Mariko, your grandmother is a remarkable old woman in more ways than I can account for and because you're a chip off the ol' block I think you ought to take time to be in touch with her. Your becoming a mother means an awful lot to her. Drop her a line now and then, will you? p/s She was 87 in August. I didn't say this to her but I could plainly see that it'll all be up to the strength of her will whether she lasts a few more years. I didn't say it to her because I knew she knew. Otherwise, your pa is very much alone these days and thinks about the three of you fondly. As usual he has a lot to do. Otherwise, he would go out of his mind. Your making me a grandpa ought to restore some semblance of the familial again—something I sorely miss. Take care of yourself and I'll get up to see you before Xmas.   Love,

Dec. 7th, '83, noon

Dear Nobby/Noburo:

        I zipped thru Toronto (—was it last fall?) on my way back from Monreale and needless to say I misst a lot of folks including you & Victor. What can you do in 3 days? The Laurentians were more beautiful than I had remembered. But then again I tend only to hold on to those occasions, tho the 'uglinesses' go on apace, to wit, the now half-century old hydra-headed missile race. When I think of my old Mother coming here when even automobiles were as scarce as the proverbial hen's teeth and how she has been able to live intact right into the nuclear/computer age, I have to think to myself that I too owe myself a future, whatever its bizarre or sublime shape. Anyhow, my old Mother & her 57 yr old middle son went back to Shikoku together this summer with our bag full of gifts, cartons full of old hauntings & rice field memories. Unimaginable that she will have the time or the pulse to go to Shikoku again tho, having sd that, it's equally true that some essential part of her never left at all. The point of all this seems to be that Kanada, its vast sprawl, never took on kindred relevances for her, whereas by the time she came here at 20, Kochi City & Shikoku had been emblazoned on her very psyche. Me, I'm more Japanese than Indian, more Indian than WASP &, despite myself, more WASP than I care to dissemble after all these Union Jack/Maple Leaf years. O Nobby, has Toronto the Good been good to you & yours? *A few words abt my kinda m-u-s-i-c.* I got into music a decade ago when I was visiting old friends in Monreale. When I was abt to take my leave of their company, one of them gave me a child's toy (ZIPPY) zither. I taught myself to play it driving back & forth from U.B.C. with the darn thing sitting on the car seat beside me. I got really good at driving with my left hand and strumming simple melodies with my right hand. I did this for a coupla years before I let the strum out of the car space (which incidentally became the most intimate acoustic space I know) and got my 1st tingle, hearing that strum in the wide world. Since then I've gone on to 'dulcimers' and 'harps.' Together with a thump or two of drumming and a tingling of assorted bells. Anyhow, give a listen and let me *hear* from you. p/s The tapes ought to tell where I'm coming from and where I'm pat.

                                        yr fallow nip friend

Dear Mike & Linda:

                how is it, i ask myself, that i am so much alone in the wide world at this time of my life. how account for the fact that the beast in me has nowhere to call home except in the pelt of an ofttimes cold self. it feels like i deserve to be there, in the pith of an abominable winter solitude, for all the lesions such solitude bears. it feels like Daphne & I, our coming apart, has undone all the familiar ties. O i've tried tying another knot but, as you both know, it takes the tacit consent of the Other to make the whole knot hold & that was not forthcoming. meanwhile, the days pass from grey to shifting layers of grey and i spend my paltry days panhandling old images in divers ways. there's a fathomless mine shaft running thru the very pith of cal-lit 'self' and i suppose i am given, despite myself, to attend to it, as memorably as i can in my present estate. love seems to have abandoned me. i haven't toucht a woman since i was out east. my fingers are becoming those curved claws winter birds grip a frozen branch with. hangdog days. a dearth & a miasmic drift of the mind's endless reams of trivia. if it weren't for the music, such as it be, i'd probably be fingering, albeit nervously, the old hangman's noose. Ah, i see i've slid over into fiction—i mean the ol' lonesome blues can get thru to you but i just get stoned and chuckle my way thru it till i'm down on all 4s on the other side of the railway tracks where i can hear the auburn dawn light up another brilliant mid-December day. i am putting my days together in some such way. just call me a born-again phenomenologist. these days, even the least (unintended) gesture counts for something. . . . which, for whatever reason, insists upon remaining utterly obscure.

13th, Dec., '83/ 12.45 am

Dear Greg:

      you might have heard by now that the V.A.G. has entered a new phase by moving into the ol' Grecian portico C.H. smack in the glass & concrete heart of a ceaselessly mindlessly changing (multi-national corporation dominated) Vancouver. anyhow, the prevalent thot around town is that 'it sure gives Art some needed class,' etc. a bunch of local Indians dresst in quasi-native garb opened the gallery with a chant & a volley of drums. it was nice to have them on hand, tho it felt like a bit of cultural tokenism. i mean, except thru Emily Carr's early work, they're barely represented. in a league, all onto themselves, and thriving, thank you. at least, as artificers. & doesn't it say something abt us on the west coast—i mean the ipso fact totem that Emily Carr is to—all intents & purposes—the Mother of us all: that civilized Art begins so recently on the bloody frontier. i am, goddamnit, burdened by the probities of such a measly History. i simply mean that as i go on testing the marrow of art in and thru my own making, i can clearly see that my own lineage as an artificer is as old as the shaman and as circumnavigating as the salmon. the art market place is a heap of disabused fetish objects i often find no more interesting than the heapt up trifles in any Woolworth store. i don't know abt you, Greg, but i don't find much comfort in recent aesthetics to return me to the easel, tho return i will in my own good time. anyhow, i'm going to be out thata way come March, and if you can slot me into a London performance of divers sorts it would give us a way (at least) to see each other again. i'm into lotsa music these days via harp & dulcimer, etc. and would like to bemuse those London ears.

my gawd i say to myself, these December days are, to all intents & purposes, a continuous twilight zone.

                                                                     yours truly,

dear Linney:

Mona came up to me during intermission at a big poetry reading at the Western Front just after i got home with tears in her lovely eyes and told me that her beloved father died of a heart attack while i was out east and hadn't i heard thru the local grapevine which i hadn't because i've been travelling incognito despite my gregarious self.
              despite the way we gave of ourselves to one another, George Fertig was 67—just 10 years older than yours truly, tho we were never close friends (George, I suspect, only had women as closer than close friends—again, like me), we always saluted each other across the chasm of years fondly. in the early days we used to talk up Karl Jung and existentialism. we both had our young brood underfoot and the hallelujah vision of the '60s kept us idealistic. George was as i knew him a quietly passionate man who spent his life divining the sacramental in art/life without any public to speak to, or for. he was/is, a natural, albeit naïve, painter, almost, but not quite, one of your modern primitives à la Rousseau, who painted a small but haunting number of paintings. it's been yrs since i've seen his work, but i do remember . . . the eerie light enveloping even the least leaf. Mona sd she didn't understand what death & dying were all abt, even tho it was all around her. i wasn't much help there—tho the thot did pass thru my mind that, more than ever, i am inexorably on my way there. we parted after i promist to write Evelyn a letter which i haven't been able to do yet. this belated letter to you will help me work up the courage.

she spoke fondly of how the two of you went dancing together and what cutouts and capers both of you made. i got the unsaid feeling from her that you were otherwise too much for her, particularly your raucous laughter, the way you threw it in the face of your vulnerability. Linney, the way we fell into each other's arms (like we've always been able to), the way our lives seem to have been divined, will tell us what's in store for us a continent apart. take care of yourself & watch out for those good lookin' middle age shysters who would sweep you off your feet, then pull the rug out from under you. Linney, we all die a little death every day of our lives, but i'm not abt to let that stop me from living as intensely as i'm able. you understand that.

>don't hang onto the memories of us any longer than you need to or want. i'm all for how we get together 'tomorrow,' if tomorrow ever comes. i hear the murmurings of my 'past.'. . . they aggrieve me, they give me whatever joy i have at the moment, but leave me feeling barren. one way or another, i'll be in Monreale come March. chant a sutra for the divinity of those arctic winds that assail us at this time of the year. let them scour us.

14th, Dec. '83, 5.30 pm

Dear Evelyn Fertig:

        . . . I've been living alone since Daphne & I fell apart a year & a half ago. . . . . sans family and familial affections. Mired, yes, inside an intense, ofttimes forbidding, solitude. It's not at all a comfort to discover what a bleak, obsessed man I am . . . despite myself, my shaggy laughter &, according to my Chinese oracle, a big 'earth' man with an inadequate, call it, bonfire. thus . . . I hadn't heard of George's death till Mona told me with tears in her eyes (during the intermission of the big poetry reading awhile back) that her beloved father had quite suddenly died of a heart attack. . . . Ever since then I've meant to write to you but I kept putting it off 'cause I didn't know what to say after the awful fact. . . . I don't imagine George & I met more than a dozen times over the past 20 years since we first got together thru the kind auspices of Jock Hearn, Fred Douglas & Others. but each occasion, however oblique, had some twist of circumstance, some bait of an idea to knot it to some future, unforeseeable occasion. & always, tho it went unspoken, we had our daughters growing up around us to turn our heads and keep our attentions riveted. George's ofttimes haunting paintings remain memorable in my mind's eye— for the incalculable silver-light that silvered everything he put into a landscape or a still life. As i sit here dwelling upon him, it occurs to me that the last few times I saw him I had had the thot that his very countenance was a suffusion of that translucent light. An ineffable skim of silver & grey. Despite the belligerent politics of our time and all the furor of the fame/ game that characterizes our mass media, I would like to think (indeed act) as if the world is made a wee bit more humane, thus habitable, by quietly obsessed people like George, who went thru life dwelling in the mind's own paradiso and had a skim of time to paint it (I would like to think) for its own sake. For what it's worth, my mother and I spent a month together in Japan: a wholesome month during which I spent a good deal of time attending to my mother while she attended to what will be, to all intents and purposes, her final human obligations. Needless to say, it had an awful lot to do with death & dying, not to mention the ongoing responsibilities of those 'who,' for whatever reason or season, go on living out their quota of breath. The Lawes of the Karmic wheel move us, thru love and kinship, and we are, from moment to moment, the whole harbinger of its thraldoms. Its myriad instances of breath. And, not the least, its extinction. I won't say a thing about all the ways we die a little bit every day of our lives: I know I don't have to tell you.

since you had asked me when you were here—
to take off my mask i have done so and
i found myself staring at the face you sd
i kept hiding behind the 'other' one you
thot you once recognized but couldn't place.
when has the mirror stripped away what is
after all only a presence in another's eyes?

since you left it's not the same face, twice

Ev: I wanted to finish this letter with something appropriate. back in '67 I published a wee book of pomes titled *Nevertheless These Eyes*. That wee book was dedicated to the English painter Stanley Spencer. I had thot at the time that, without him, these pomes would have never been sired. Anyhow, looking at the pomes again (since this letter to you began), it could as easily have been a collaboration between George and me, tho the thot of it never occurred to me before this very moment. the above pome from this selfsame book itself wears a double mask. i mean, it does depend on 'who' takes which part and where their living/dying breath is coming from. coming out of the maw of the dying year, these words salute you and your memories of a fine man. p/s I'm sure he wouldn't have you mourn any longer than, say, the life you have ahead of you will allow you to.

One way or another, we'll keep in touch thru Mona.

———————

love,

14th, Dec., '83/ 6 pm

Dear Victor:

fell by Gerry's place on my Chinatown walk. we haven't been seeing much of each other lately: it would seem, we haven't wanted to. the years have bruised us and, like an old married couple who can read each other's thots before they say them, we've got bored with the probity of our very thots. anyhow, we toked up & kickt words around without scuffing up the old sod. moments before Lara came home from school and moments before i got up to go, Gerry, sensing my leave-taking, sd, have a listen to this before you cut out. and so i listened to both of you via the music Gallery performance. nobody knows how to rave better than Gerry these days. and, as you know, very few poets in this country can cut words out of the air to fit the old respiratory system as well as he can, but i do miss that 'other' more intimately-voiced bard. what i really mean is that i haven't got an ear these days for rant. which is just another way of saying that my music is the sole measure of the range of sounds my own bod can & wants to dangle. like any true BLUES man or woman, i want those ah handful-of-chords to make the ol' bod thrum. there are no Messengers left but the last of us who go on entuning the old psyche. anyhow, Victor, the Last Night at The Blue Mule, March '82 cassette tape should inform you where i'm a comin' from. have a listen.

> yours, till our literacy exceeds
> our G.N.P.

15th, 12th month, '83/ 1.30 pm

Dear Kit:

     . . . an ever diminishing 'me' sees 'you' getting bigger & bigger. any day now, you're gonna burst into callit the size of your manhood and look me straight in the eye. or so these words lead me to believe. anyhow, i've been telling myself that it's abt time for me to sit down and write Kit a long letter and that's what i'm going to do. how are you? i mean, despite the hassles you have with your school work, not to mention your ongoing sexual reveries & whatever ups & downs they provoke in you, . . . how are you really doing and, if i may be so bold to ask, are you happy within yourself? meaning, you're a unique bird with a huge draft of wind to careen upon. it doesn't depend on how vigorously you flap your wings so much as how they cup the open air currents and move you (almost effortlessly) along. how you were first a small guy getting bigger every day in my mind's eye and then you became a bird riding the air is, my gosh, where these words have brought me to. as far as this letter goes, everything sd therein will have to be brand new 'cause i never wrote them before in this order, this rank and file, etc. you know what i mean. . . . it's almost like i am daydreaming at my typewriter. these otherwise scant words fell soundlessly out of my mouth onto the white paper to become my thots for you. scold   hold   bear   hug, not to mention all the mugging & cutting up, all the sense of isolateness 'u,' even at your tender age, bear the brunt of, will help you stave off all that's blunt and evil. learn to handle them well. meaning, let your feelings speak out. for what it's worth, all the above goes on applying to yours truly. i thot for a long while after we came apart that i had (again) made a hell of a mess of things. . . . but something in me sez it had to be for the sake of all that is 'unbound' in each of the three of us. & furthermore, i know where my affections lie and have no intention of cheating myself of their warmth. Kit, may '84 be a bonanza year for you. turning 15 was/is wholly worthwhile .

23rd/ 12th/ '83

Dear Daphne:

in so far as i've been into letter writing lately, i thot yes i must write Daphne a letter too. callit a Xmas letter. or better still the letter i owe you for all your fecund letters thru the years. as i sit this cold clear morning with the brief but bright sun glancing off my cheek, i'm listening to the cassette tape i made when we were together on the Queen Charlottes a light year ago. i can hear the surf pounding the sounds of our footsteps along the wet pebbled shore, the incessant hiss of wind, the salutary mantra of my zither and, although all of this has probably become mere datum in your momentums, i go on assiduously attending to all such evocations. i mean, despite the intricate ways we came awry and yes despite the sullen moments when we travelled afar together and never quite made out—i go on being all ears, all nose, all mouth & all eyes. i don't know if i ever told you, but 'this,' callit, a porosity-of-being, i was told in a peyote vision (back/forward in the late '50s) is the very abdomen of any artist, irrespective of time/place. this Friday morning i thot i had better get my photo supplies for the holiday ahead and i went out to start the old Toyota and, tho it wheezed & groaned, not being used to frigid temperatures, it started up. whereupon i went back into the house to finish my cupa coffee and let it warm up. then when i came out a few minutes later i found it steaming from under the hood. well, to make a long story really short, i had blown a rubber gasket and the antifreeze etc. poured out! so much for gadding about over the holidays . . . unless i get it fixt. i keep on peering over my shoulder to see if Jim has come to work yet. as you can imagine, the severity of the cold has kept him at home. me too. me be, as usual, all alone at home. . . . this my so-called 'sabbatical year' goes right on being utterly amazing in all its winter solstice humdrum. & if i may be ironic, so does the rest of the hurdy-gurdy world with its awesome solar dynamics. & as i sit here wondering what will fall onto this page, next i am thinking that this brief solstice sun spins an untellable warmth and that perhaps has a lot to do with abiding the very absence of intentionality. given the levity of the above, i am , to all intents and purposes, utterly emptied of, callit, the prerogatives of hustling language into the shapelinesses of mind's own thots. if there's such a discrete but knowable entity as a 'will,' I, for one, don't know where to place it in the structure of my being. if it's anything to me, it's something like these thin bones and how many layers of cloth i swathe them in these days. tell that to the erstwhile determinists and their dramaturgy of gross conflicts.

We made a Pledge at La Push to act in/upon the world as if our very lives were an utter Gift . We as much as sd to each other and the tumultuous sea outside our cabin window that we would Praise the whole extant world as it impinged upon our daily lives. Or so i thot thinking abt that long ago afternoon. You had gone off on a meditative walk while i prepared myself to 'mind' the mushroom's potent inscape. It was after you returned from your perambulatory walk at the marge of the sea and i had sat thru the afternoon stript of my usual visors: we spent the twilight hours gathering the mantle of night around ourselves and barely spoke of the Gift of our lives. Now, you are stooping at the foamy edge of that wild sea with its insistent heave while i click the shutter. Cupt in my ear i can hear its distant resonances, and the lilt of our ofttimes droll laughter draws the very breath out of me. It's going to take all the fervor i've got left in me to go on praising our own time given the manifold embodiments of callit the monstrous that beset our politics. It's going to bear down heavily on our most private selves and, like it or not, the pledge we made at La Push will (for myself) stand for all that is yet-to-be-born-within- us. All that makes us a 'you,' a 'me' and an 'us.' If you ever need me (wholly unconditionally) i am as close as your oh fallow ear. Love to all 3 of you from the goat-footed hermit of Keefer Street. Dear Betsy: these words don't have any real privacy in a permeable world. Nobody I know owns the language. Look! I say to myself—you've put a small net out and look at what you've caught. Season it: eat it: shit it out, but never think to own it. If it's in the New Year pack of cards I'm abt to shuffle, we'll get to talk to each other soon. Ah, Language, how it mothers all of us mercifully .

23rd, Dec, '83/ 1 am

Dear Endre:

     . . . it could be somethin' like the eternal dream of callit a nascent spring that prods my fingers. more likely it'll simply be the mind's stammerings along with the chattering teeth and hoary breath of the arse-end of December together with the virtues and viruses of living all by myself. if there's anything my old bod misses these wintry nights, it's another bod to curl up against. Carol, i mean that old hot water bottle just ain't doing the job. . . . i want to say that ever since Daphne & i fell apart i've had a recurring image of, callit, the interchangeability of coffin and bed: how the absolute aloneness in the former begins as a surmise in the latter. impossible to say how even a forlorn body lying under the same covers as another equally forlorn body had nonetheless the heat of their bodies for warmth. and furthermore, i am not elated by the fact that i can use my wits to construct a barometer to measure the humidity and warmth of a fictive woman that i can take to bed with me and be at all warmed by such lugubrious fantasies. anyhow, i'm not telling the two of you anything you don't know. and, now, baby makes a triad, another warm pod to snuggle up to, in everywhichway that tenders the hearth. here's to another fist thrown against the sky of the military mind. here's to another blisst out poet or the mother of us all. scratch a middle-age wage-earning hashish dreamer and you'll find an ordinary man with a body to keep fueled. o my cauldron of dreams! you too need a fire to distill everything into the keenest kind of, i want to callit, erotic tabulating. unbeknownst to the pulse of these words as they fall on the page . . . there's periods of both long and short hiatuses during which i listen a bit more attentively to the surge of the Pacific on the west coast of the Queen Charlotte Islands. it's my way of getting down to the sea and cup my ears to its diurnal rhythm. some thing like that. despite, despite the fact of an ongoing urge to write, i often think that my true autobiography is utterly embedded in the 100s of tapes i've made thru-out the years. it's the notion that a narrative of a life cannot fully exist, removed from the total embodiment of sound. it's callit a throw in the direction of a post-literate, wholly aural, personification. *anyhow, i'm counting on a gig there on the 21st of March.* find you then.

love,

the last 3 days with
hiro mayumi and rei together
with all their friends on denman island . january '84

friendships
and leave-takings
love-affairs
and growing children
all cared for
all held in awe

holding all
your feelings in mind:
holding in
my own feelings for
the sake of a
beneficently light-
hearted occasion
'i' click the
shutter. i am blesst
by the lilt
& tilt of a fine spring light

i am my camera and
my camera is 'me' . were both
skilful at playing
deaf and dumb for the sake of
a leave-taking. i click
the shutter . . . let the light
in and Presto! there
you are. there where you'll
never be again. . . . was
there ever such an invention:
as our all too human eye
to enthral our sense of the
poignancy of things. . . .

things
bought things borrowed
things built
things seen and un-
disclosed

things dream things cry
things lie things
think

these snapshots of
the 3 of you: these so-called
'candid moments' preview
all the unborn movements
yet to come. hold my
hands we are the 4 corners of
a perfect square inside
a perfect circle

permit me to say
i thot that all 3 of you were
much loved on denman
island and your bright faces
will surely be misst.

'i' was the pie-eyed Stranger
who took the snapshots.
i too (for my own unreasons)
wanted/ all of you close.
hear me, hiro. hold me, mayumi.

hi there, 'zero'

if you ever need me . . .
you know where i dwell. if i
ever need you i know
where to get in touch with you.
some migratory birds have a
way of flying both ways all
the rest of their days.
praise be all those sad and
happy days on denman.

o praise a poignant friendship!

mayumi:

kono hosoi koei wa
unata no uta no munnaka
ni yorokondoru. *kino*
wa umi no nagare kumo. *asu*
wa sora no utsu kumori.
unata no marukoi kawo wa
watashi no shiwa-kawo
ni tashika ni utsuteiru.
kanshin no kagame.
kanshin no itchigatsu.

reichun:

unata wa komei hana no kodomo
unata wa toki-doki yancha-bo
shikashi unata wa nanishitaji
hige no naka ni kakureitoru o-
jisan wa unata wa ichibun desu

hiro:

watashi wa nandemo
kokoro no tamei (shikatanashi)
sum hito desu. watashi
no inochi wa shiro to kuroi kato
oya ga undei ku reita mon
de shikari shibatoru.
watashi no iki ka kireita ——
kono hosoi hako wa jibun
de tsubureiru. hiro:
yaki mon no ana no naka ni inochi
mitsukeiru hito mo mukashi
kara nihon ni sudoru.

Mayumi:

your small voice
in the midst of your song
makes me happy. yesterday
there were clouds over the ocean. tomorrow
the sky will become overcast

Reichun:

you're just a nosy kid
and sometimes a naughty one
but all the same
to your hidden-behind-his-beard uncle
you're Number One

Hiro:

I am a man who lives
according to my own lights (regardless)
my life was bound
by the scolding of parents
who drew a clear distinction
between black and white.
in such a tiny box
was I crashed
that I could hardly breathe. Hiro:
people whose lives were conditioned in a small
hole like that
could often be found in the old days
coming from Japan.

(Free translation of the poems in spoken
Japanese and written down in Romaji
provided by David Aylword)

February 6th, '84

Dear Jim Caswell:

                  just a note to say that I'm doing well: that is to say, all my days are full of both the sobriety and mirth of ongoing work. and, yes, already half of my sabbatical year has passed into the mire of my divers thoughts and out thru my music, writing and photography. what else is there, I ask myself, but having all the love I can hold to help my life/work along? anyhow, I thought I ought to tell you what's coming up for the rest of (my life) as it can be pinpointed thru till September. all thru the livelong winter I've been making music (harp and dulcimer) with others and come the 26th of February we're going to put on a miniature concert at the Coburg Gallery of Photography to help old BFA graduate Bill Jefferies meet his monthly incurments. an aside to all this is the ongoing weekly sessions which have enabled us to tape our music and pass it on for other ears to hear. then there's all the ongoing writing (perhaps the most obdurate of all my obsessions) which includes several works-in-progress. including an untitled book of photographs and words about my trip to Japan this past summer with my 87 year old mother. (a book-to-be that'll be the complement of the book of my father titled WHEELS which Coach House Press in Toronto will be issuing this summer, I hope.) I also have a 100-page mss. titled 'Tom Thomson and The Company He Keeps' that will probably take another long winter to complete. And to top it all off, I've just completed a mid-winter ('all ending month,' as the Japanese say) parable titled 'Struck from the Heat of a Cold December Sun' which is about the dearth of love and a plenum of hostilities in the midst of a common-place nativity. and so it goes on. further to all this, I'll be making my spring trip out east come mid-March during which I'll be reading and making music on a number of occasions. Jim, this didn't want to simply be yet another 'progress report' to the boss, but uncannily it seems to have turned out thus. will you keep me informed concerning all matters that bear on my return this fall? appalled by the callit provocations of paging a brief note, I've gone on too long. Jim, 'we' all seem to be living amidst a thronging-of-voices that want to grab our years and cause a tumult therein. I take it that our ongoing politics is simply part and parcel of that purview. sincerely, mid-nite, 7th of Feb. '84

Dear Lora:

       it looks like i'll be in Toronto between the 12th and 17th of March and i'm wondering if i could do something for you and your students out in the boonies. if anything's possible, let me know pronto. i don't really need it but, as they say, a few extra bucks can make a holiday out east heftier. etc. now that i've got that off my back, the rest of these words can smile if they want to. already we've had an imitation of spring, albeit a false one. i took off my winter underwear and walkt outdoors in my summer whites and felt the chill in the air, tho it was warmer than anyday we've had this brief new year. nothing like talking abt the weather if you can't get a hold of anything better. old friend G.G. sd 'politics' and 'love' are inseparably twinned, or words to that effect. that thot borne out of his own obsessions tallied with my own apprehensions as 'i' too have had a stomach full of both and what i'm left with is a meager thot that goes like this: without *rapport* in the former and *intimacy* in the latter neither can procreate an earthen Vision. it seems to me to be obvious that nuclear fission is our Armageddon and living with it will go on being the biblical inferno that scours even our most intimate self. as we both know, neither 'rationalism' or 'rage' can bale us out—if we've forfeited an intimate self conjunct with all of the other intimate selves without number. Lora, let me praise both of you and your heartfelt confidence in hopefully something more beatific than our ongoing turmoils by having a child. like when it comes right down to it, we've got nothing but the ordinary 'present' to fuck the inordinate 'future' into existence. p/s i'm goin' to become a real life grandfather any day now. how's that for having lost my cool momentarily way back in the mid-50s? looking forward to it now, i'm more than glad i did. nothin' quite like havin' 3 beautiful daughters in an ofttimes hostile world to put a shine on an ol' beatnik's grimace.

anyday now the 1st purple-tipt crocus is goin' to stick its head out.

Feb. 28th, '84/ noon

dear Linney:

       got your note, your gladfull i've survived the long Montreal winter note. glad you're into your throat/ via chanting. i'm sure it had something to do with keeping you warm this so recent winter. and now you're heading south to San Diego to shout up a sutra: hurrah! for you. 'me' is going to be headin' your way abt the 18/19th of March thru till the 25th (gotta a coupla gigs in ol' Montreale). me of course wants to be with you a bit if that's in the works for us. i, too, survived winter, intact, if not, actually, wiser. the ol' gates of wisdom seemed to be getting both narrower and taller: pretty soon it'll turn into the proverbial 'eye' in the needle only a song or chant will whistle thru. for what it's worth, my 58th year began with music and clamor which augurs well for the post-Orwellian '80s. will be more than specific after you get back from S.D.: i'll phone direct! keep a bit of your heart for you-know-who. love

2nd, 28, '84

Mike: any chance in reading at Glendon and/or York U?
Daphne keeps me in touch with both of you.

Dear Mike/ Linda:

thus far the new year the Orwellian '84s, the Chinese year of the rat, has flipt me into and out of a seismic winter solitude: 1/ I'm to say the least grateful 'cause I toucht levels of myself I didn't know much about and I toucht (again—) the pulse of whatever I have to give and its name, for want of a better one, is nothing if not a plenary bite of old-fashioned, coruscating 'love.' but I'm not telling the 2 of you anything you haven't brewed yourselves, you haven't become both twinned and unhinged by.

anyhow, this is just to announce my forthcoming spring trip East and to say I'll be in Toronto at 4:25 pm, March 11th, for a week of tripping about. then it's Montreal till the 25th, then home for a coupla weeks before I fly to Nippon. anywhichway the fallow days approaching spring are beginning to open out a lovely summer of all sorts of surmises and all I really want to say is—pushing 60 ain't that bad just as long as an occasional song brushes my lips. i mean there ain't no creature-comforts left in academia, let alone our friable body/politics, not to mention that big DaDa better known in the guise of digital numerology. n-o-n-e for slant-eyed plebs like me. like, these days, there's nowhere to reach (deep down into) but 'psyche' with all its morass, all its injudicious mire of unfathomability . anyhow, I tell myself these days that your real work lies ahead of you. . . . and given the way I feel these days, I say, so it does. so it will in turn belie your willfulness as you turn into salt.

for what it's worth, I've put a Book-of-Rhetoric together titled 'struck from the heat of a cold december sun.' it's a follow-up of 'of seasonal pleasures/and small hindrances.' it's, if you want, my winter divining/s. small change and yet full of everything I've been, shall we say, into.
p/s how's 'wheels' and/or 'the pear tree pomes' coming . . . ?   take care.

2nd/ 28th/ '84/ midnight

Dear Sarah:

   I'll be in your town March 11th, 4.25 pm for a whole week of whatever happens and it's nice to be able to simply tell you this with its anticipatory purview of a forthcoming spring and yes another deciduous summer with one foot in the Orient and the other foot here in Rainforest County, B.C. For whatever it's worth, it's my year for knockin' around, tho god knows what there is to be found that way. Finding anything anywhichway these unenlightened days is more than politics can teach and, if I may interpolate, more than the reach of our gratuitous abuses of language: hence, leaping cultural fences and playing deaf/ dumb/ and mute can open up a canister of nettle, myrrh or migraine visions of something incomparably obscene or, at least, unintelligible in its manifestations. etc. . . . The thot is that I'm utterly at home (in my very self) everywhere I go. Or, like my friend Chung sd, it doesn't matter where I live 'cause wherever I am I am a guest in the House of Life. Something in me keeps moving just to test the psyche's parameters. I hate being a god-damned tourist anywhere! Anyhow, all this just a preamble to my/ your Japan of the Mind with all its prolixities and ofttimes palpable ero/exoticisms. All this and more will be up-for-grabs-in-the-coming-spring/summer. Hang in thar. 2 bites of biz: 1st, what's happening with my WHEELS and my 'Pear Tree Pomes'—are they hangin'/ a' danglin' in mid-air? 2nd, I seem to have misplaced a bunch of (ah precious!) negatives of my STONEDGLOVES and I'm wonderin' if they're among your heapt-up mss. and other datum, somewhere in an attic or closet? and whether you can ask Stan abt them? p/s I want to reprint them, for the sake of their Omen . . . (and ominously I can't place them anywhere at home). Otherwise, let's get vext together!

dearest Mayumi:

        at last night's going away party for Yuchun I played the tape we made together so that your voice rang the changes in everybody's playful party ears and, hearing us that afternoon, mingled in a typical Japanese mad-hatter's party of an umpteen number of dialects, hearing 'us' even as the leap year's added day disappeared into the hours before you left for Yokohama, listening to it over and over, i had sd to myself: if this poignant January afternoon duet is the last thing we ever do together . . . i'll nonetheless have 45 whole minutes of your breath-taking enchantments and like 'who' do you know that would want more than that if it ain't yours truly. b-r-e-a-t-h is where all the medieval airs of the genjian/ troubadour love (distraught) *love airs* come from like pollen wafted invisibly on a current of wind—millennial wind/s to wind up particularized in a Frankie Sinatra or a Leonard Cohen's romantic throat. listening to *ourselves* engaged in an ancient form of a lover's discourse—my ears my whole body trembles in the delight of being tongued by your, tremulously held, breath-taking notes, callit modalities of the heart's ancient disquiet.

        guess 'who' has flown across the Pacific to appear with big sheepish California-tanned smile creasing his face at the other Mitsuro's but the auto-body cum shakuhachi man who lives in a Burnaby house with his smiling side-kick, Takeo Yamashiro? guess what his name is?

anyhow, the two of them ate and talkt and toked up, then to the perfect delight of all the assembled guests they took up their shakuhachis and laid into a subtle duet wherein they enthralled each other and in the twinning of their breath enthralled us. but the counterpoint i most delighted in included a precisely heard kitchen-table talk between three women who delighted in seeing each other and added their voices to the two musicians heralding the ides of March.

Minoru, like any number of Japanese who have spent some time here, finds it difficult to wholly abide tiny Nomi Island or for that matter Lilliputian Japan. he's been spoilt by the ease of the actual spaces between people here as i have, tho i tend to take it for granted and in fact often feel the emptiness of all vast spaces as the wind-blown husk of myself.

Feb. 29th. '84/ midnight

Dear Isamu / Kazuko / Others:

    . . . i won't go into why i didn't make it down to Obama last summer—it's already out-of-date as news, let alone gossip. my, my, how time, sodden time flies and how both unaccountable and ineluctable it seems to be, if it be anything. every year there's so much datum flowing out of my throat into the mouth of an ocean, i'll never live long enough to have the time to dwell on that. i'm seriously thinking of taking up Japanese and becoming a haiku poet. anyhow, the real news of the moment has to do with my going to Nippon (again) this April: and as Hiro, Mayumi and Rei have returned to Yokohama recently, all 4 of us intend to visit the 2 of you sometime late April/ early May (if that suits you). one way or another i do seem to be veering, or is it inclining, towards the Orient more and more and this coming spring/ summer promises to be (i'm keeping my fingers crosst) plentiful. it almost seems that, deep down inside me, there's a fierce nut of an ancient Nip who keeps sayin' to the would-be North American, you gotta pay your dues before you can bear your grandfather's crest of honor and, one way or another, that's what i seem to be about these days. old homo/north/ameri/chicano/nip is lonesome these days for an oriental woman with all her robust/ utterly feminine ways. anyhow, i've gone 2 years without another voice in the house (let alone another body in my bed) and i'm going to keep myself wide open for . . . what's her name. 58 ain't too late to want to go on getting a gladful hard-on . Kazuko: I want to get a wee book of love-pomes translated from my kind of English into an equivalent (modern) Japanese and get it publisht in a modest way over there. Isamu: the cassette tape/s i made during the typhoon on Obama got played on co-op radio and oji playing his jamisen was a big hit. see you complete with sun-tan oil in abt 6 weeks!

March 6th, '84, 5 pm

Dear Mariko and John:

well i'll be darned if i haven't become a grandfather: one i'm sure like no other yet the same as all of them . i'm all for kith and kin of every sort these days and that my oldest daughter has had a son speaks of all the small hum-drum things that really matter to this hi-diddle-diddle middle-age man these balmy spring days . i didn't come up with any name for him and a part of me didn't want to 'cause i figure it's your responsibility—after all there's a lot of calling to be done in the years ahead and whatever you call him had better be well-meant . plant a tree in the rain forest and watch it grow . shoot an arrow into the blue and watch it arc . in my next life i think i'd like to be a woman just to feel it all taking shape within oneself . otherwise, a man is a man when he's got something (like a child) by the tail and hangs on to life's travails by his tattered shirttails . Mariko: your pa's got to be proud of a daughter like you . and John: an erstwhile father-in-law sez, 'well done sir.' see all 3 of you when i get back from the wintry east with a packet of good intentions to initiate my grandfatherly fealties .

odd the way we go on populating our hearth as if it had to be the paradigmatic way of paying gratitude to our becoming .

odd and yet somehow utterly commonplace becoming a grandfather: one who hasn't given up the notion of siring a child himself. . . .

love to my favorite Sechelt trio

March 7th, 1984

Dear Scott:

  A Mr. Arnaud Maggs came by yesterday to take my portrait. I had been out walking in the neighborhood as I usually do at least once a day and when I returned he was standing on the front steps ringing my door bell. The 1st thing he sd was 'I believe you were born in '26— when is your birthday?' I told him and he sd, 'that makes you 4 months older than me.' Arnaud apparently had a big show of his recent work at the Emily Carr Gallery which I misst tho I did catch a sidelong glance of his characteristic new-portraiture stance in the recent issue of *Vanguard*. (100 B. and W. subtly-nuanced portraits of none other than Sir Joseph Beuys.) Anyhow, it turned out to be a typically wet-grey February afternoon and Arnaud seemed much concerned about the low level of light that pervaded and after taking a number of light-readings he shook his head and suggested that we go for a walk which we did. And as we walkt and talkt our way down the street and across MacLean Park he would ask me to stop where I happened to be and—click! —he would shoot me, as it were, from the hip. Tho granted that's hard to do with a 6 x 7 Makina. It's one thing taking a picture of an innocent thing and another taking a portrait, particularly if the portrait-to-be is of another so-called photographer: one who in this case has spent a long-long time dwelling upon what remains hidden, despite the most arduous scrutiny. I mean that I felt neither more or less naked in front of his lens tho I know that I wanted to keep a part of myself (via my face) hidden from him 'cause I sensed a too-too avid professional/photographer and there's something in me that doesn't take too kindly to them as a credence. Tho I didn't want to be part of his ploy I went off with him and got him down to Ballantyne Pier and that was worth all of it.

Any day now I'll see my mug-shot in some slick magazine and I'm sure that what I withheld will be more than compensated for by what Arnaud caught of me and held onto that I won't have seen in silver bromide before. I loved the picture of Trudeau snapt in mid-stride on the parliamentary staircase with a rose in his lapel and an insouciant/ joyous grin after announcing his (I'm still in my prime) leave-taking. That picture alone makes up for the mean-looking ones the media parleyed trying to de-face him. That old Trojan horse the Liberal party won't see the likes of him (his continental/ provincial elan) for a long time. Not that I want him to hang in thar—no, it is time for P.E.T. to bow out tho only Pope John or The Queen knows what lout will take over to salvage the ol' flim-flam ekonomics we are all (unwittingly) the pall bearers if not the blue-chip share-holders thereof. Any day now the magisterial cosmetic surgeons in Dallas will have so upgraded Comrade Bennett's tense profile we'll mistake it for the biggest smile this side of the Rio Grande. There's a video of, callit, the rhetoric of political smiles, not to mention the equivalent rhetoric of Yankee Fundamentalists, which deserves to be researcht. Like, I say, some guys have a patent on it and others have to cough it up. Photography, its myriad images and all the wily trips-of-the-trade/ not to mention the high-price of Capitalist image-making, is both a distraught / unwrought bag full of gleam and gloss it makes the ordinary world look like tallow and grime and that's its loss. there ain't any special moment of an image unless we will it to be that way—to highlight the credibility of our sight. So be it. So what . . .

Any day now somebody is going to come along and write a small book of 'portraits of the self' that have their occasion in all the snapshots he/she occurs in in the old family album. Any day now the son of Karsh, or is it going to be the daughter of Barth, will cast a cool eye on their respective daddies and say, hey, let's begin with our baby pictures and trace the lineaments of our selves thru the everyday divinity of light and shadow, snapshot by snapshot, till we're right up to date: let's see if we can recreate our several selves and uncover a brand new/ old as the last ice-age psyche and live to tell about it. Describe it, in the old acceptable ways. De-construct it in all the fallibly new ways. But, and here's the rub, let's not palm our portraits off as depictions of an epicene Greek God or Goddess (like, larger than mere life), let's cut the crap about the importance of some people's ordinary faces and how utterly boring other types are. Lookt at intently as an infinitely subtle moving object, the least imaginable things have a decisive aura. To my way of thinking (at least now) photography is, almost to spite our remorselessly categorical selves, the purest instrument we have for the divination of phenomena. All of which makes me an old-fashioned 'phenomenologist,' a veritable Tu Fu or Basho.

—If Photo-Glyphs have anything in common with say Painting and/or Music, both of which I know thru the intense practice of, it must have something to do with the fact that 'I' am, if you will, their psychic pool table, speaking of Joe's Portuguese Place on Commercial, their mathematically imbued wind and weather Nuancer . And last but not least—their veritable scapegoat . Like the least of Walt Whitman's illegitimate kin—a slant-eyed 'me' feels beholden to A True Democratic Vista, one undetachable from 'The Song of Myself' as I sit here punching these keys, 15 minutes away from Main and Hastings . To wit: anybody's ritual moment of picture-taking and its concomitant snapshot, intently regarded, have an ingrained topology which, like my own snaps, have an actual credence larger than the moment of taking .

—If I *know* anything these halcyon days and, needless to say, there are days and days when 'knowledge' is (whatever it be, in substance if not in fact) the most dubious—no, nothing—*thing*, a profound kind of, callit, statistical mindlessness, if I make a gesture towards the least notion of a 'fine art' these days, it's within hailing distance of my neighborhood . I am sick onto death of disembodied art, by which I mean an art without an actual community except one's remorseless peer-group . Marx could have been wrong-headed—it isn't Religion that is the opium of the people . It's that old succubus, History . For what it's worth, 'I' a 2nd generation Asian immigrant's beloved son wants to write a hitherto unwritten chapter of The Big Book of Native Voices of The Pacific Rim Nation/s by writing/ chanting/ harping and snapping pictures of the Here and Now, Where I live and feel at home . There are after all these 'other' faces, 'other' voices and 'other' concordances I have to be attentive to : to be sure—I'm moved to respond because RESPONDEZ is its own becoming .

To wit, did you get to see KOYAANISQUATSI?—that appalling view of the last days in America seen thru a roving fish-eye's lens. ('Fantastic cinematography,' a young friend who had seen it down South sd.) Ah, it's surely had an overwrought elliptical, stop-frame / slow-motion, sweep and naturally they used the most expensive optics of the pre-eminently Hollywood-manufactured Holocaust Industry . None like a satanic visual feast of imploding/ exploding things to keep the mind reeling: I mean, back in the '30s when Griffith and C.B. de Mille re-manufactured the homilies of EPICS—'a star was born every minute' and a havoc was always just around the next kiosk hiding a cast of thousands of, I was going to say, minions. Ah the bitter pill of a bleak house, one so unmitigatedly craven—not even a wily desert dune mouse shows his head till the endlessly shuffled pack-of-images begins to go flat and turn in its resonances: do we get an eyeful of a wasted urban homunculi/americanos with unspeakably creast and lined faces? The worn-out, corroded faces of the last Romans on earth. I had the thot during the endlessly falling silver shrapnel of some esoteric piece of telecom that this post-Biblical brew of a veritable D-O-O-M-S-D-A-Y had something to do with venture capitalism and Hallucinations of Lethal Weaponry cum Power of all the so-called advanced nations of the world, not the least of whom included tiny Japan. Having sd pundit-wise these things concerning the high price we pay for nurturing the mind's craven need for images, I simply want to add that Coppola's haptic Hopi 'take' of the end-of-things is the Siamese twin of none other than Al Razutis's *America*, an equally hypnogogic vision and that the former is, despite the big money, no better. Both being homo-americanos of much the same period, they like the explosions and fireworks, not to mention the mental havoc of oblique angles and clamorous juxtapositions. For myself I'll say this, that I do deplore being trivialized by all the cinematic versions of a post-Biblical Wrath-of-GodDOOM.

days later:

I've been waylaid by sundry appeals for formal letters of protest to the S.C. Govt. viz the range of their so-called edicts, emendations, and legislations concerning our oh (sickly) educational system, and all the ways it's being undermined by a veritable 'Depression' economics, not to add a lack of a substantive Vision . In short, I've been penning a number of letters, besides this one for you, tho all are addresst to much the same issues, e/g., 'ideological' issues .

Back on the track this morning, I've got little or nothing to add to the ongoing fluxus concerning our pet toy: our asst. means of copycatting anything visible via the camera and all its light and lens variants that haplessly abound in an information-privileged world of dubious concepts, litigations, pronouncements and all the paraphernalia of our electronic media, our computer databanks with their veritable cornucopia of images-for-sale: images for hire: images to placate, the awful state of ungrace in a world always up for grabs . Finders / keepers / losers / weepers . I really don't want to add to all the lip service concerning sd 'instrumentations'—except to say that a part of 'me' wants to be strictly anonymous, an amateur who takes snapshots of Life's little ritual moments: like a gathering of faces, a marriage, birth or death . Not to mention the untaken snapshot of a loved one who left for a distant country . I don't have much of an appetite for the notion of a photographer as some kind of weird voyeur, one who uses a view-finder instead of a key-hole . I haven't much of an appetite for the kind of portraits, say, that issue from the sd photographer's prerogative to stage an event for the sake of some pre-conceived stratagem of image/s . For myself, I do like the notion of being simply present in a fully accountable way as a member of the family, or intimate friend, household guest, and go about taking snaps, where they live and breathe .

Moments after you left after our convivial talk: It occurred to me that my own insistences via my working out a real mythology of self here, at this time, on these Pacific shores, in and thru all the art I want to go on making, are for me the *real politics* of this time and place. I am tired finally of the arrogance of those who have written and those who go on writing the History of N.A. as if it had little or no veracity without the European Conquest/s and all the extravagance of its turbulent Histories to build an otherwise 'savage'/'wilderness' into one final Epilogue: one last triumphal Conquest of a Mindless Nature: one last Media as The Narrative of a False History fall from grace. Given the remorseless quantification of all such histories, it becomes perfectly obvious that it's-all-up-for-grabs, all a belated venue of touting, or is it tattooing, the garb of learnedness / razor sharp discriminations/ even/ ideology on another generation in quest of an unconditional, if not blamelessly/namelessly, manifest God. . . . 'Me' has a yearning, a veritable thirst for the actual voice of my ofttimes bewildered psyche and it seems that 'I' have had to go thru, callit, this 'false' history in order to see the true alignments of my often rebuffed 'oriental' self: the veritable 'Pacific man' I am, and all the myriad things that means to the likes of me.

Even in photography I seem to be beholden to a Karshian View of A Veritable Race of White Geniuses none of whom I could model myself after. As for the 'faces' of our ubiquitous ENTERTAINMENT INDUSTRIES, their 'mind over matter' preempting of a real, I want to callit, topology of humanity's faces, not to mention farces, is, to say the least, lamentable. Having sd my piece, I would simply add that my photography wants to speak itself.

Put another way, my eye uses a wholly mundane ground-glass thru which an ofttimes fetching world of things dream themselves into existence. My immediate thought is this: that 'things' do not need to be elevated, or put in their places (in a fateful hierarchy-of-things, more or less relevant). My thoughts propose that they'll trace their fate on my view-finder . . . if I give them a chance to dwell in a sphere-of-light. The earnest amateur in me sez, once you are utterly conscious of all the wiles of light indoors or out, you can toss your light meter into the nearest bush and begin to really trust in your eye's aperture. I love dwelling inside a snapshot like I love dwelling inside a slice of melody on a harp. Neither really needs all this writing, this literature to be literate. And I want to add that the politics of our mass media, our museum without walls, our educational system with its outrageous clamor for a badly misshapen 'dialectical materialism,' needs the likes of folks like me to redeem the veracity of our 'logos' as well as our 'mundus.' Exponential, yes, but not exploitable.

All the additional materials included in this packet belongs in the concentric circles of one man's take. Hava look. Have a care.

p/s Relevant datum concerning the works
you've pickt for the show, forthcoming .
I'll draft all of it out east
rather than hustle it now . Ah the torpors of
another green spring! The torques, too.

an afternoon in an ancient park in nara

---

cradles alongside the thick stone and mud wall opening out on an esplanade of ancient parklands: this unintentionally nameless garden with its roundabout walk prefiguring unexpected vistas these closely cropt heraldic groves of trees these hedges shrubs and seasonal flowers together with these still pools seem altogether familiar tho truth to tell i can't name a single one of them in my rudimentary japanese. they impinge upon me. curve towards and away from me. indeed they exfoliate right in front of my lens without the least bit of wind. if i had had the thot of taking the perfect color snapshot of a garden such as this one i'm almost certain they would look just as plausible as these. snip! snip! snip!   the unseen hands of the invisible hedge-trimmers groom another subtle curve in the bough of callit a civilized wanderlust. redolent with the virtues of hand-crafted attention this small garden could be said to possess a subtle, altogether human, elegance in its unobtrusive scale. these snapshots take their place in among the myriad-images prefiguring an ancient feat of shaping lattices of light with circumspect ardour. decanter'd they'll risk pure invisibility for the sake of a prisma-of-radiant colours. given the breadth of a 21MM lens—what i can see peripherally is no more than a mote of sand in the great bronze buddha's ten-story tall vision. i clip my fingernails have a cup of tea while listening to the invisible gardeners gleam a bag full of green leavings before the two women pass on by and out the opening.

march 28th, '84, midnight

March 29th, noon, '84

dear Nobby:

       got back after a hectic week in Montreal the night of the 25th. got back thoroughly winded and plumb tucker'd out till today and this letter. i had meant to phone you the following day but i had to catch the late morning train to Montreal and decided not to—thinking you might have been worn out and slept in late. we didn't have much of a chance to exchange views afterwards 'cause the performance had run on far too long and everybody seemed to be in a hurry to clear out. i did have the sinking feeling that you didn't want to have to talk about it 'cause you were pisst off tho i'm not at all sure if any of the above is true 'cause i also felt we'd put our hearts into it for whatever it was worth. . . . i kept listening for/to you and almost always knew exactly where you happened to be standing and believe it or not listened as intently as i could whilst reading my text to your subtle accompaniment. i found myself lifted upon a palpitation of sound that carried me on into the omens of a poetry as a performance . i know i was driven to the completion-of-the-whole-poem despite the prolonged discomfitures and incipient aural deafness of our so-called audience and that the momentum thus generated pusht the limits of a collaboration (between us and our audience) to the so-called limits but i'm not about to apologize for that 'cause that's precisely 'where' i want to be/am working at whatever i do these days. anyhow, i've listened to the c.t. of our performance a number of times and i for one simply say i'm sure gladful 'we' did it. i simply assumed we had enough going on in the day-to-day throngings of our life and whatever it is that this myriadness teaches us to put our multifarious sounds together and come up with at least an utterly unique occasion. Nobby, listening to us on tape again i think we did do that. love/

dear Victor:

      the lost glove plus your letter arrived today. i wasn't put off or dismayed by your strong words 'cause i had long ago come to certain conclusions about *that* evening and among them was the awful thot that 'i' had indeed been callous if not lacking in sympathy and felt hangdog about my caper. till i got to Montreal where i listened to the cassette tape on several distinct occasions and felt Nobby's music as a quite persistent pulse, one which was the equal of my uttered insistences. thus, there are these 2 overlapping, distinct experiences: one, the *actual* performance and the subtle drives in/around/ and behind *it* and how two men get it on. two, the act of attention brought to the act of listening to the performance on tape and what such hearing tells. i simply want to say that on both counts something was missing but much less so on the tape. i only wisht i had ript the Text wide open to let in more of Nobby's soundings but, driven by my desire to tell what was actually present to my mind, i seemed to have overreacht and hence breacht the unsaid terms of all such collaborations. believe me when i say that Nobby and i couldn't reach across all the years we've both gone our separate ways to become who we are and get that into the collaboration without working longer at it. i don't know if your *response* incorporates your talking to him later but he didn't leave me with the impression i had co-opted him. in fact i had the distinct impression the evening had been as much as it could be given the briefness of our interface. like i say the cassette tape tells me the occasion had its own kind of fineness and that counts for something special. for what it's worth i got the uncanny feeling that *you* and *i* have veered away from all the things that held us together and the curve of our paths will take us even further apart till we come into our utter selves. meanwhile, i am moved by the alacrity of your words and heed them to taunt the remainder'd ego out of myself. take good care of your haunts.

march 30th/ '84

for victor: herewith, a response to your letter.
as for sarah and you, viz your paranoia,
i suggest you work it out with her—
i'm not the middle-man cum broker when it
comes to the 2 of you. hang in thar

how to stay in alignment
with one's true sentiments . how to be
entuned with a host of other
ofttimes ambient, altogether efficacious
soundings without sounding
the ol' beat . how to both listen and hear
each small note of sound as
an aural sound . how to collaborate
without the least coercion .
how engage a disquieted listener intent
upon his own vowels ? what's
the architectonics of a musical dialogue
and does every sound have to
scour a waxen ear to score an epiphany ?
i, too, detest my own ofttimes
rampant ego and all its forlorn cacophony
but, believe me, i/we put all
of our heart into that performance and
your letter hollows me out .
i would cup my hands for whatever alms i
might get from my judicious friends
but i can't be scape-goated into
thinking myself an avaricious musical\
monstrosity simply because i didn't
fit my words into a stream of sounds you
would have liked to hear . believe
me, these words hold onto your criticism
grievously 'cause it's right on .

a small harbour on nomi island one hot afternoon in may

---

i kept putting a hand or a foot into the view-finder to see 'how' one or the other conferred a signification on the landscape and quite unintentionally i found myself creating a syllabary of gestures as if a deeper, darker instinct had etcht an ideogram-of-wonder upon this ancient may day sky long before these words hatcht in the tidings of their own diurnal rounds flounder 'd into view on a white page. i found myself walking about in the low tide much sighting along barnacled grids towards the far horizon. i stumbled upon a small block of hewn granite and held it poised at arm's length: intensely aware of its compact weight, i took measure of both the far off mountain of precipitous rock and the brute grey concrete sea wall that shored up an eroding foreshore. by the simple act of thrusting a hand or a foot into the frame, my very appendages turned into one more faceless, unconstrained mute thing. thus i unwittingly underlined the enigma of silences at the very heart of the photo-glyphic act. such as they are, these words/ their captions have been embosst for the fingertips of the blind. o feel their brine summertime wind tousle the sea's green hair. it's my conviction that a true amateur photographer is a wind and weather man in more ways than one. being a bit like basho and a host of other perennial 'on the roadsters,' i use a camera instead of a sumi brush to brush in the details of an altogether salutary moment. 'these snaps, me thinks, have callit, their own forebearers,' their seeking .

march 31st, '84, noon

April 1st/ '84, noon

letter to myself on the 1st day of April, '84
_____

dear 'me'

the fulsome days of springtime open out: gladfully, i sit here with the noon-day sun caressing my left shoulder. these small words want to begin daydreaming. they, too, have been laved by this bright April sun. they, too, are finding themselves humming an old tune. downstairs, mother keeps one eye on the teley while the other eye spies each loop of her knitting needle. outside, in the back alley, Jim and his buddy are gearing up for another day of good old shop-talk with their drinking buddies while the bent old Chinese lady from the apartment at the end of the alley walks by minding all the small pitfalls, and just yesterday i held my grandchild in my arms while his mother talkt about the many details of child-care with her family and friends, and it was the first time in a long-long time there was the sound of a crying babe in my bachelor house and something in me was both bemused and stirred. something in me said only if the politics of the family were at the heart of the politics of a society we'd be better off than we are . tho it wouldn't necessarily preclude the wretched or the despotic. so he wrote the day after they all left to return to their homes, and the very thots he had had when he held his grandson on his lap lapt up all the conviviality . in 5 short days i'll be flying off to Nippon again. . . . i wonder what'll be in store for me this time and what will be signified. . . .

her last trip up to the family grave on top of mt. hitsudan

THEY had a number of good reasons for returning to shikoku again: after all it was the seat of their families from ages past and they had both discovered long ago what it meant to have an uncommon family name one unlisted in any telephone directory in north america outside of british columbia and alberta canada and that 'here' it was common enough tho largely confined to this paradigmatic pacific island this petite but voracious mother lode. 'we are if anything the very "figures" of those Myths that would sustain us . . . ,' i thot as i let them pass and took a sighting from the brow of mt. hitsudan. but it was after all 'she' who had kept the legend of a fierce but full-hearted samurai alive for the sake of her godless children in the new world and their numerous offspring. she had been the chosen one the one who accompanied him on the eve of her leave-taking up the steep slope to the chosen grave-site with its sweep of their beloved kochi and the inner harbour. here, he told her, he would keep an eye out for the ship that would bring her home after she had made a niche for herself across the pacific. now he's underneath her petite feet but she intent upon each vexatious week never looks up. from the very day she set sail from shikoku she lookt out of her acute bird eyes upon the daily store of humble-pie and never lookt back 'cause her beloved kochi, circa the 1st W.W., had already calcified in her mind's eye. it would always be there for her as it was when she was seventeen. even as she chatted with her grandnephew whilst dividing up the assorted flowers she wove another look in the many-coloured lore of a legendary native son and what he had indeed bestowed upon her small bent back. then with the incense lit she knelt in front of each stone and claspt her hands offering up a heartfelt prayer. while her sturdy grandnephew carried her piggy back up a number of rubble slopes on the winding path back . . . i a dutiful son hung back and clickt the shutter one last time. these snapshots divine, mundane, mother, time .

april 1st, '84, 4 p.m.

Tuesday, April 3rd, '84, noon

dear Trudi:

listening to 'us,' the 2, 3, 4 of us, again before i fly across the Pacific . thinking about all of our, it must be, intense ardor while listening to our heart's thrum . on the verge of going to Japan, i'm asking myself, how come? what ties you over there as well as here? what's the shape of all of this, this running around, this poignant music? barb'd by the thorns of my own ego. caught up in callit the thraldoms of, is it by now, a wholly imagined love, i listen to us doing our thing and find a soulful answer : i'll not achieve a more fulsome collaboration than all these occasions we got together and made a heartfelt music together . i'll not find myself speaking quite so agilely as i did with you, Howard, and Mayumi . crossroad . i'm standing at some X road i can't read the sign telling me its name but this thronging—this petite increasingly deaf mother, this canticle of song, this grandson, Esko Anton, these my 3 daughters, and all my Toronto/ Montreal friends, not to mention those over in the orient—all, all overwhelm me and i find myself taking refuge in an abominable silence . Trudi: let's get together when i return and, yes, let's invoke yet another Sumeric summer . palpable as this grass i'm smoking, the music stretches being . going off to Japan again, i'll gleam what i can and let all the rest be . Vicki T. and i—our dance/music performance at Concordia U toucht the veritable ground of 'eros' in the improvised art . Nobby and i got there too tho more stressfully . eastern Kanada ain't going to see the likes of me till i regenerate my locus . truth to tell, we barely have need of each other . as for 'us' and 'blue mule live,' i'm all for us going onwards to wherever the music takes us . have yourself a good summer and i'll listen to us on tape over there . i'll unravel a score for the sake of all those things that can break our hearts . i'd never think of breaking up a family . . .

Wed. April 4th, '84, 3 pm

Dear Jim Caswell:

thot i'd better give you a fill-up of what i've been doing and i'm abt for the rest of my—gawd it's almost over already—sabbatical year. 1st, i've got a rough draft of the letter i intended to submit to the review committee that was here to assess us a short while ago. i worked hard on it for a week or so but didn't get it straight for all the obvious reasons, particularly getting a head on just what we're abt as erstwhile educators in the domain of 'art' these days. i have also to deal with callit my own 'politics' in the relationship to the predominantly English est. and its ubiquities and haven't got it straight yet, tho i have to admit i'm quite as disenchanted with their scam as i was when it got ignominiously implemented. anyhow, if i get around to writing it clearly i'll send a copy to you just so that you'll know where i take my stand. i clearly won't get it straight till later in the summer after i return from my trip to Japan (leaving April 7th am/ returning end of May, early June). i was in Toronto/ Montreal for 2 weeks in March and among a host of things i did the following things which may or may not be consequential viz my curriculum vitae. read a long portion of my new writing titled 'struck from the heat of a cold winter sun' at the Music Gallery on St. Patrick's Street on March 15th with live music created by Nobby Kubota percussionist extraordinaire. 2/ gave a reading of 'the pear tree pomes' and a talk on the relationship of art to language as practised by an insider to a bunch of bright kids at the Ontario College of Art. in Montreal: 3/ Vicki Tansey, well known avant-garde dancer (protegé of John Cage and Merce Cunningham in the late '60s) and i improvised a dance/music duet at Concordia U, my old art factory. i'll tell you abt trying to rent a harp for the occasion sometime. anyhow, we got a handle on one eventually and that's what i played and she danced to. 4/ gave a reading to a bunch of nice dull suburban kids at John Abbott College, talkt to them abt 'poetry' which they had hardly ever heard before, unless it's the order of a tribal rock lyric with all its hype and linguistic naiveté. came away with the feeling that the 'arts' were, despite their apartness on campuses, definitely on the doldrums, like nothing got taught that provoked a recognition. 5/ showed my current photography and talkt abt it and photography to another bunch of similar kids the next day at J.A.C. and that occasion didn't feel much better. the colleges in our fair province, the ones in Quebec, particularly the anglo ones, are having a hard time keeping the ol' ED FACTORY from going off the skids. i mean i was left with the feeling that Pedagogy (like Politics) ain't got a Vision these days and without one we're at the mercy of a mendacious Ekonomics, one that appalls even as it hands over a false affluence. 6/ S.W. has probably mentioned the big PHOTO SHOW together for the coming summer at the V.A.G. well, i'm in it and my portion of the show will consist in 3 series of colour photographs taken last summer in Japan, together with texts. for what it's worth, this series of photographs is simply a small part of the photos i've taken in Japan thru-out the years and i'm going to work up a big show of them in the next coupla years. so, it all goes on and so will the teaching this fall. have yourself a good summer and i intend to be as effective as i possibly can when i return. count on it.

yours sincerely,

wed., april 4th, '84, 11 pm

Letter to Myself 2 Days before Leaving for Japan

―――――――――――――――――――――――――――

'i'm gonna take a slow boat to China . . .' on the juke box at the Chinese cafe in Sunnyside, Calgary, late '40s. had discovered Arthur Waley's Chinese/Japanese translations but not Ezra Pound's. in fact, given all my grammatical hang-me-ups, i didn't think i could/would. apart from whatever i learned from my parents and their asst. friends in Calgary before and after the war, almost all of what i came to know about Japan came thru translations of one sort and another, and so it is that my Japan is, among other things, an altogether habitable place in my mind: my callit duplicitous, ofttimes errant, mind. i take it that mind is itself grounded in language/s. anyhow, that's where these thots are coming from and, wherever they get to under their own volitions is as much as i can deal with. shaped by English and, despite the awesome geography of the plains, its cultural assumptions, i have had to work my way thru to callit a mode of articulation of which this self-addresst letter could be said to be an example. the impulse to shape a viable world, one which i find voided in our political life, has driven me inside the labyrinth of a language to gain for myself an articulation that could be said to include both strands, or is it strains, of my Asian/American heritage and now, more than ever, i simply want to proclaim its pan-Pacific resonances.

'i'd walk a mile for one of your smiles but don't fence me in' combines 2 half-remembered old ditties to suggest a 3rd. viz, i just want to come into an ease of simply being myself and go on being open to wherever heart bids me to. such is the gist of this letter to myself.

Apr. 6/ '84, noon

. . . it's been a kinda soulful coupla weeks being both a grandfather and a petulant but dutiful son. it's been a big window on 4 generations of 'us.' and it's clearer to me than it ever was that i do have my life-work cut out for me and all of you are part of the weave. ask Kit and Daphne over if you feel like it. and do ask your friends by.

Dear Fumi/Pete and Kiyo:

    Thot i'd better leave the 3 of you a note on the eve of my taking off for Japan. Do, do make yourselves at home till at least the 31st of May.—If i intend to stay longer i'll let you know well ahead of time but it won't be later than the end of June. My, my, how time flies. i mean that mother has been here almost 2 weeks and she'll be staying on at least another week after i'm gone and it'll be up to the 3 of you to do what you can for her. now there are 2 things she wants to do before going back to Edmonton. 1st/ *getting out to Clearbrook* to be with Cliff and Julie and their three kids and getting back to Keefer Street this weekend. then, there's the matter of *putting her on the plane to Edmonton* when her time is up and telling Irene and/or Joyce when to pick her up. in between, she'll want to be taken to some friend's house and that's abt it. you know how she likes to inquire and talk and you know that it's all abt 'whoever' happens to be that crosses her mind right then and if you feel like it give a listen but otherwise she can still take care of herself and that includes going to Chinatown or even down to Powell Street for a daily walk, tho she isn't half as sprite as she was a few years back. i'm not saying anything you don't know something abt. as for the house: like i say, do be at home completely but please observe the following. 1 / that all of the many things in/abt the house have a certain order and in so far as possible please don't mess around with it. or, if you do, restore to some semblance of the way it was. simply put, i've spent quite a lot of time placing things in something more than a random order and i want them to be there that way. simply good house keeping, ain't it? i'm leaving 6 (signed) cheques—use them only for paying the UTILITIES like telephone, hydro, taxes. all other expenses incurred will have to wait till i come back. Don't leave the house at night without pulling the back drapes and be sure the house is lockt up at all times when you're out. put all the correspondence i get somewhere conspicuous, and tell whoever calls where i've gone to, but don't say a thing abt how long. would you believe me if i sd that on the eve of my leaving for Japan i'm not at all sure why i'm going, apart from finding out where i left my 3 super-8 films and their sound-track plus pieces of other art-projects. still, something has me by the tail and there's no going back, piece meal. . . . i've never felt more like the very weather itself. love 'pa.'

last sweltering tropic afternoon at
the minshiku on the beach in kohama listening un-
intendedly to the long straggly haired
tokyo kid on the 1 am surrounded by cassette tapes
and empty kirin beer cans singing quiet-
ly to himself in the manner of a johnny avalon
listening to the distant murmurings of
the incoming tide tied to this over-arching sky
this mid-day / mid-may these words hold
up a chalice of radiant light to an unfettered
pagany. wreathed in sea weed coral and
tidal leavings my own burnished throat sings all by
itself   these okinawan throngings reek

4.40 pm / may 16th

wave———
o   i too crest
with
the full moon
already
my 10 days here
a tidal
thronging
o   un—
spent tropic
sunne

listening to kochi-ben mingei high above the kagamigawa

watching the sunday afternoon fishermen in high rubber waders
trolling for their supper   watching pleasure boats
tilt in the down-draft   the young lovers floating in lazy circles
watching the solitary river-bank walker stop and stoop
to some small thing lodged in the tidal muck   watching an endless processional of people   river's paraphernalia   pigeons
and gulls   while the wide river empties out   leaving
muddy embankments along the foot of tall grey concrete retain-
ment walls   listening to   a plangency of river voices i
hear mother's voice . . . like a familiar scold lifted un-
harried on the torpid summer air and i could also tune-in
on brother george / sister mariko . . . whereas my own un-taught
vernacular got plangently shaped along the bends of the
elbow river just below the brow bramble and chokecherries of
scotchman's hill in a long forsaken foothill city in a
vast dominion i'll never quite call home watching / listening
simply intent on being inside a round of summer days   my
self, my heart's clock but a tic-toc entuned to a vast diurnal
tidal clock   i, i seem to have always stood at, at that
confluence where the river and the land continuously lave and
lap the emblazon'd air : you, you can't step twice in the
same slip-stream no matter how many times you step or even lunge
into a familiar body of water. still water an entrancement
mirror. lo the kagamigawa never sleeps it simply seeps down in
to the bottomless black well in everybody's lorn psyche . . .

home: again . alone, again
keefer street silences a balm after the incessant clamour
of tokyo & its awful array of 'bed cities.'
'nothing like putting the vast pacific between us . . . ,'
i thot, thinking of hiro, rae & mayumi
in totsuka, the four of us sleeping side by side aswarm
the throng of traffic in a 2nd storey 6 tatami room .
nothing quite like being home at last
all alone: the inexplicable distances driving the
hundred small intimacies of totsuka, gotenyama, kochi
and kohama into a, nonetheless, heartfelt
emptiness .

'sabushiku naru'

'zuibun sabushi kimochi munei ni motoru'

June 2nd, '84, 648 Keefer Street, Vancouver, B.C.

Dear George B:

      phoned Ang before I left for Nippon for C.C.'s address. she gave me his address as of the 1st place he resided in Kyoto a quarter of a century ago. it turned out to be a lovely part of town, one i hadn't visited before, but nobody in the neighbourhood knew C.C., not even those at the local post office around the corner. as things workt out, i found him in his tiny coffee & cake shop a few days later and within moments i knew nothing had changed between us. i listened to his news for 3 hours and barely had a chance to ring in a want-ad. as for seeing C.C. abt local news—that is current news of Nippon—one might as well ask the local constabulary sitting in their pews at a busy intersection. for what it's worth, i learned 2 things. 1/ he's at work on 3000 pages of explicating L. Z.'s A. 2/ that K.R.'s translations of Marichiko's *Love Poems* are sheer invention. that no such poet exists except in R.'s imagination. . . . it seems to come down to this—that obsessed men have little time for another man's obsessions unless their obsessions coincide. unless the spirit cries out. need i add that these are cranky times and i'm feeling them in my very bones.

      . . . ain't it amazing how the media throw up these handsome middle-age w.a.s.p. faces for our political edification? i mean how all the turners, mulroneys, mondales, bennetts & their ilk, unrepentant Capitalists to a man, enact our miasmic ekonomics. p.s. like the light step in your tread thru *Kerrisdale Elegies*.

                              Yours

1st day of autumn, midnight, '84

Dear Luke:

    . . . Wasn't it 'just the day before yesterday' we met on 4th & Burrard and you askt me if I needed a lift and I (astonisht to meet you on the West Coast) askt what you happened to be doing out here and you replied, 'why, it's been a dream of mine for a long time. I'm glad I made it'? Or words to that effect. Anyhow, I hear thru the Can/Art wire service that your moving on and among the things you're abt has something to do with the 'art' to be gathered together & shown at EXPO '86—is that so? I of course don't know if I can get a small piece of the action but I would be curious to know what you think of the following proposal, one whc I intend to carry out, one way or another, as a small gift to callit the 'Japanese' in myself for my 60th year (January 18th, '86). I have in mind a *big fat book* of *colour snaps* with an *ongoing narrative* plus an *exhibition* of 11x14 colour prints (much like those in the V.A.G. Photo Show) . It'll be all abt *'my' Japan* (which won't look anything like the stereotypical glosst-over images that abound in our literate world). 'It' ought to be a *visual/verbal* 'autobiographical' odyssey of my comings & goings over a lifetime at the intersection of 2 kulturs/ 2 languages: it ought to be (ideally) in 2 if not 3 languages, synchronistically aligned with the colour snaps. For what it's worth, the 3 sequences you had on show this past summer together with their 'texts' are a preview of sorts. If you are at all interested in all of this give me a call and I can fill in the peculiarities as well as I'm able.

yours truly,

Here, for what it's worth, is an outline of my proposal:

A big fat book of colour snaps taken over the past 20 odd years and the 7 occasions i have spent time in Nippon. These snaps fall into sequences: the individual snap, whatever its intrinsic qualities, is, simply & inevitably, a part of the whole scan. i envisage each sequence as a discrete chapter with its own text, tho each text will join the preceding one & the following one to form, callit, a *disjunct narrative*, albeit an *autobiographical narrative* of origins, friendships, celebrations & landscapes. Further (if practical & auspicious), there'll be a black & white sequence of my childhood in both Alberta & Japan at the start of the book, and 'stonedgloves' somewhere in the middle, capt by a discrete series (again black & white) of my father & mother's birth places in & around Kochi City on the island of Shikoku where I always return to whenever i'm over there. Like i've already sd, 'it' ought to be a visual/verbal celebration of my comings & goings at the oceanic intersection of 2 cultures/ 2 languages over a lifetime. i have a faded snapshot of myself at abt age 4 standing beside my cousin Kenjiro on the family farm in Umagi: i seem to be squinting due to the sun and with some discomfiture hiking up my woolly drawers. . . . i only know i was there 55 yrs ago because this snapshot, plus the stories i still hear from my country relatives abt the way i was then, tells me so. Another part of me will never reclaim the complex feelings i must have had having crosst an ocean on a slow boat to arrive in my father's childhood yard. etc.

Anyhow, this as-yet-to-be-titled picture book has to find its own way of being born into the throes of this politicized, media-ridden world and i am, if you will, its agent-at-large. i'll do anything to get the wherewithal to midwife it. 'Art' as i know it is bound to the very depth of *one's autobiocraphical self* and all the heedless images/words that can reify it. 'Erotic mundi' for 'love of the world' begins and ends in the throes of each man/woman's psyche. For, you see, the artist in me doesn't want a mastery of things, events, or people that doesn't proceed from that constantly thwarted attempt at a mastery of one's originally undivided self. Like any artifact truly worth shaping, this unborn book will bear the imprimatura of a life time's quest for, callit, the divinity of images haplessly traced on my very epidermis. As for an exhibition of the aforementioned sequences of colour snaps (together with the 'texts'), they ought to be at least 11x14, ideally 16x20 thru-out, with the most telling parts of said text interwoven thruout. And again, ideally, i would like to see a simultaneous exhibition in both Kanada & Nippon. All, if possible, to occur in '86 (my 60th yr!). Need i say that i'm more than willing to put all my energies towards actualizing this ambitious proposal and that furthermore i have spent untold hours working towards this very moment of writing to you abt it. If it fits into your scheme-of-things, let me know. If it doesn't, it'll seek out other ways of its coming into being. i mean everything i've made has been that way anyhow.

Nov 6th, '84, noon

some thoughts concerning your end-of-semester project
_____

bear in mind what i keep on stressing:
your photographs should bear the imprint of 'engagement.'

the thrust is towards an actual involvement
without which your pics will be (despite the image) empty.

on each occasion of such involvement 'you'
are as much the 'subject' of the pic as the thing pictured.

the trick is the rapt ability to think
visually .

.

if it is possible to speak of the modes of
the eye's attentivenesses: one of the modes would be
a multi-form visual-field awareness by which
i simply mean   seeing everything in the view-finder as
necessary, therefore congruent, especially
from corner to corner/ diagonally. & with a 35 MM camera
we're talking here abt *seeing* instantly .

.

bearing in mind my admonitions: bearing in mind
the ongoing rush-of-phenomena. not to mention
the mundane ground of our being. all the ritual
moments between birth and dying: PUT TOGETHER A
SMALL ALBUM OF YOUR PHOTO-GLYPHS TAKEN BETWEEN
SEPTEMBER & THE END OF THIS YEAR. MAKE IT INTO
AN ALTOGETHER AUTHENTIC SLICE OF THESE MOMENTS
OF YOUR LIFE. (i'd like to remind you that all
of the moments of our lives are equally precious.
& that you can't photograph the 'future' without
abiding all the 'presentiments' of NOW.

.

photography like poetry and music celebrates
the etheric earthbound body.

Nov. 22nd, '84, noon

Mike:

      ol' Monreale days/ eastern township poet D.J. in town to read at the W.F. he read in his inimitable way from some new work which toucht the uplifted skirt of one or another of Balthus's nymphets . he sd they toucht on the erotic if not the pornographic imagination . D.J. has, to say the least, wit to spare . i thot of him speaking, as it were, thru D. Milne earlier and how a landscape, albeit an essentially civilized one, spoke thru him . now in fervid middle-age he seems to be taking a peak thru Balthus's eyes at a congress of entablatur'd young women caught up in the thraldom of their own obsessions. anyhow, i did get off on him again . we're a like age and all that rages in us keeps rattling the lip of the ol' id . it strikes me that D.J. & our Lady of Words, P.W., have something in common—can't finger it but it's got something to do with their old-fashion'd lyrical tone, their subtle, verbal machinations . callit their erudite aplomb . . . there's a lot going on locally tho most of it is a storm in an English teacup at best . —the thraldom of what used to be called the 'avant-garde' with all its quixotic fixes has been vanquisht to the hinterlands . almost all poetry has returned to the clasp of a now belated modern tradition . in short—i'm failing i suppose to keep up with the latest scam and i really can't feel i'm missing a hellofalot . i mean—keeping up with 'self' is about all the energy i've got these besodden solstice days . Mike: the callit great challenge continues to be an unutterable open-endedness .—wouldn't you agree? p.s. perhaps next week i'll be sending *the m.s.s. off to you for keeps* . Linda: i'd be pleasd to receive a xerox of your review of my show at Scarborough and, yes, let's keep a handle on every day 'cause each day passes altogether soon enough. . . . my 59th coming up January 18th . HA!

Nov. 23rd/ '84

dear Stan Dragland:

    . . . like ghostly presences we've passt each other in the midst of our ofttimes fouled-up lives and haven't really toucht each other . for what it's worth, i'd like to say that *Journeys Through Bookland* is an exceptional read . i pickt up a copy at the Coach House the last time i was there and read it complete on the flight back . it seems that you (Stan D.) & i share, at least, a prairie childhood but you're the one who has shaped it, inimitably . i, for my part, have wanted to but haven't finger'd the chords of its immensity—tho the prairie kid i was is still very much a-live in me, however cadaverous he's become . Ha!

    . . . sittin' here i'm thinkin' of my T.T. & The Company\ He Keeps text and know it's germane to the above . other matters have willy-nilly taken preference and i haven't got back to it but i do have that sense it'll have to be re-shaped to include more of my prairie-self if it's to become accountable . J.T.B. among other writings tells me so .

    i am writing these days at an intersection bereft of women except for my daughters, and the writing is an attempt to account for such bereftment—is in fact shaped by all the old-fashioned notions of 'love' and its reticulations, albeit at the interface of 2 kulturs/ 2 oceans and an impoverisht language scoured by both . as an act of balm for one's own derelictions, 'writing' is a hazardous game and i would throw all caution to the wind if i thot i could truly finger, however ruefully, my own heart's bent .

    being an erstwhile canuck i'm more interested in how my own psyche happens to be embedded in layers of divers kulturs, not the least of which is my Japanese . i am intent these days on sounding both the perplexities of politics and the politics of self as inexorably twinned . what's the shape of that as prosody . . . ? may you gain heart thru all that has happened to you lately .

                                                                      regards,

Nov. 23rd, 10 am, '84

dear Stan B./ Mike O.

here's a xerox of W H E E L S showing 'where' each of the snapshots should go——
i've had to shift the TEXT to accommodate them——which means the whole book will
be several pages longer than the m.s.s. of your previous printout . i have of course dipt
into K.M.'s DESCANT several times & think that the way she scored snaps & pomes
terrific——in fact, if you have in mind a similar format you could simply ask her if you
could use her spread as is . thata way the hind part of the book is already complete and
all the rest has its shape given, as it were . not incidentally, the snaps as she's
reproduced them are exactly the right scale for the surrounding text——neither too large
or too small but themselves the size (if not the heft) of the pomes. at any rate, i see the
snaps as an exact visual counterpoint to the *text* and not a mere adjunct and whoever is in
charge of the layout ought to keep it on their mind . (for what it's worth, the snaps were
taken on the trip and exist in my mind's eye as integral with what i kept as discrete notes
in an ongoing journal.) anyhow, it's your baby from here on in .

December 12th/ '84, 3 am

Dear Sarah:

      as i sit thru this long wet winter night daydreaming of Nippon i am including a 'you' i alone am given to know 'cause you also have your part to play in callit an Orient of the Mind. like somebody (unnameable) has to all intents and purposes stackt the deck.—i don't know about you, but i often feel these days that i'm inexorably 'fated' to do/ be 'me.' furthermore, the most 'telling' form of communication occurs when a 'we' finds ourselves talking from the pith of that undivided self. i go on being amazed at how utterly specified the gist of 'i' and 'thou' is. . . . am i making any sense? anyhow, these drear winter nights stir all the dormant rapture in me, and need i say how un-becalming that can be—given the end of another year's entropy. p/s my 59th comin' up . . . & as i sit here the thot occurs to me that nonetheless the pith of one's erotic ground is both endless and seamless. i would 'act' in/upon the world from *that* place always if i had sufficient courage and humility to do so. as for the rhetoric of our 'body politic'—its mired, calcified, ofttimes barren, ground—i think to myself that 'it' must be the drowned voice of our once undivided self. i hate the ofttimes loathsome materialism it bespeaks.—not to mention the implacable 'bureaucracies' ad nauseam. as you probably know by now—Joy has been here. we saw a bit of each other, a bit more than we have to date: i gave her *In the Shade of Spring Leaves: The Life and Writings of Higuchi Ichiyo, a woman of letters in Meiji Japan*—to give to you. ask our dear friend Maya about her. then . . . if you feel like it, pass it on to Anne Ireland whose own efforts to become a writer are also echo'd. all of this simply says that i am barely interested in 'writing' of whatever *gender* that isn't, in its intent, thru and thru, heartfelt. it's the 'ground of our common fealties' that gives me a rush—everything else is almost pitilessly news. or is it 'fiction'? . . . 'i don't want to set the world on fire . i just want to stop the flame in your heart . . .' the Ink Spots croon on late night radio and so . . . it's off to my Spartan bed. . . . above my head the vaporous dream of your trip to Nippon last spring : mine it well 'cause you'll be felling trees . love to D/Y and Others. may the onslaught of winter astonish you with its zeal.

                                . . . LATE AS USUAL

Late winter 1984

Dear David & Candice / somewhere in Portugal

  Old friend Dennis Reid was in Vancouver. He sd you and yours have got a house in Portugal and after Paris had moved there. I remember that Candice had a family there and my second daughter had travelled thru Portugal & sd that it was a lovely country and comparatively cheap. Anyhow, I've been to Nippon for the 3rd summer in a row. And I've been sorting out what all the comings & goings are about, if they're about anything but endless brine. I did get your postcard from Paris and I did think of you but didn't get around to writing. Lately I've got into the awful habit of not writing anything down unless I sit to a typewriter and/or speaking into a tape recorder. I mean anything that I would have to write by hand (like a postcard) or a letter written while on the road has become vext.

  Anyhow, I've been in Toronto lately (weekend of Nov. 1st) and among other things I spent an afternoon at the Coach House with Stan. B. & Company. They've gone thru what D.Y. calls a 'cash flow' problem and their activities have for the time being been diminisht. Nonetheless, Stan assured me that the Pear Tree Pomes were definitely on the books and to tell David B. to get the 'illustrations' to D.R. or himself pronto. I for my part have been writing yet another, hopefully final, draft of them and will send you a copy along with the up-dated one for M.O. & S.B. along with whatever ideas merge (with yours) concerning layout and typos. So much for biz.

  Besodden winter and lugubrious politics have taken over B.C. Place with their unappeasable thirst for upstaging almost everything but the endless rain. It's impossible to laugh much these drear days. It's impossible to go anywhere without going lean 'cause our children's children's future is at stake and it's become hateful to me the way our demo/techno/petro/multi-national/system goes on plundering the world for its own puft-up estate of human achievement. For what it's worth, just got back from a concert at the east end Cultural Centre where I heard a quartet of violins & a nifty cello . They (Kronos Quartet) played what sounded like a difficult piece by John Cage, the old I Ching cum Zen composer of, among other timbres, the eloquence of silences. It was a piece that sounded as much if not a whole lot more like 'silences' than actual soundings . In fact, I thot whilst listening that it sounded a lot like a traditional 'renga' (linkt haiku) with its single heave of sound surrounded by the echoes of the dying verse merging into tonal silences . The piece was titled Thirty Pieces for String Quartet (1983). Tho born in 1912, Cage is to all intents and purposes simply 'ageless'—I want to say like any first rate artist ought to be . What got thru to me via Kronos is how their exactitude matcht their musicality and hatch'd those vibrant 'silences' that is for me one of the hall-marks of the divers music I care to listen to . Being to all intents and purposes musically illiterate, e.g. don't know how to read musical scores of any sort, I am all the more compelled by, callit, the mathematics of a notation system that enables the music to be present for any number of ears providing you can read it . That puts me in with the 'bardic' tradition of carrying the song around in your heart . Or not at all, not at all, linear . It seems to be in the intricate 'interweavings' of lapping sounds that a score as such provides a mode of musical discourse . Otherwise, you simply pitch it to the varied timbres of the wind . and let it move in and thru you . One day I'll have to play a tape of my 'recent' music which includes my version of singing—just so the whole paraphernalia of language dissolves into song .

I've got an MFA student who has spent time there. She tells me that within the compass of a small area the landscape is spectacularly varied and the people accessible . She also mentioned that 'living' is comparatively cheap there . Shades of Mexico circa mid-fifties when I lived a year in and around San Miguel on a couple of thou with lotsa of rum, 1st class Jamaican rum, to spare . It was the only time I really hallucinated on booze and lived to tell how topsy-turvy everything in sight became . As later, with Daphne in Yucatan, I photographed the pyramids stoned : stoned on high-grade Mexican pot . Not that any of these indulgences ever shapes insight into anything but an absorption with whatever happened to be present . Or, at least, seemed that way . And furthermore, there's at least the faint traces of how the Portuguese way back in the 16/17th century were among the most powerful ocean-going people of the world . Why, they've given the largest group of Japanese outside of the islands their speaking tongue . I remember meeting South American Portuguese-speaking Japanese and I was blown away by the cultural ambiences . Like we literally had no common tongue to speak to each other thru! Anyhow, this letter is about the 'pear tree pomes' and what your share of their making has come to in Portugal .

~

David in Portugal:

i've been going over the P.T.P. literally letter by silence by letter to pull the whole works together the past month and the enclosed xerox of them ought to tell the changes subtle & otherwise they've gone thru. i think the most relevant issue for you is the change in the order (chronology) of the pomes : i mean i have shifted them around again—always with the keen intent each pome might inflect the one before it and the one after it relevantly—tho i needn't tell you such shiftings don't always work . thus, the placing of your *illustrations* has been affected, tho i hope it won't be too disconcerting . anyhow, have another look at the overall layout and reconsider 'where' each illustration ought to be and get the specifics off to coach house: like i mentioned, they're still gung-ho, tho given the thick layers of conservatism plus cutbacks of all sorts, particularly in our case and their govt. grants, it would be smart if we got the whole thing together and into S.B.'s hands soon . M.O. is going to be in charge of it for the press and D.R. has also sd he would look in on it for us .

Jan. 4, '85

Mike & Linda:

    nothin' quite as subversive as an unsuspected bout of malignant (mucous) flu to mar the Xmas holidays and put all the well intentioned 'work' to route: almost ten days in which the least sensation, itch, phlegm or snow-drift thought had my complete undivided attention. & now it's the 4th of January and i'm on my feet again and would say thanks to whomever for such winter riddlements and the sheer small pleasure of this morning vigil beside the window overlooking all the peaked slopped-snow covered roofs of my neighborhood, etc.
    Daphne & Kit came by last night to spend an evening with me. we went off to the Punjab on Main for a hot meal to warm our fog-bound bodies and it was a comfort to know we three still dig each other and, mindful of all the small scars, indulged each other's petite nostalgias. later, she phoned to say that she had talkt with you, and that you were coming out this way towards the end of the month and would stay with her & Betsy on the 23rd & 24th and stay with me on the 26th and this is just a note to say please fall by and share a day or a night or both of this my 59th January. yes do that.

January 5th, '85

Isamu, Kazuko & assorted children:

some days go by almost changeless
each daylight hour bleakly shading into bleak night
snow-bound deep winter nights without sun
nor, i might add, a woman—might incline you to believe
i am utterly desolate . . . but it ain't
altogether true tho my body inclines me to believe
that the cycles of the seasons all the,
callit, diurnal rounds, and the seasons of 'eros' are
metaphysical mirrors held up to each other
anyhow, all i have to do these days to charm the vile
winter spirits out of my system is to tune in
on 'Kohama air waves' and presto! my sullen body re-
trieves a long-lost (acquired last summer) tan and
readily warms itself up from the tip of the toes.
why, there's some wee voice in me that keeps whispering
'well, why not Kohama next summer?' 'why not choose
"hot" instead of this inscrutable "cold"?'
some days i think i sit down and write the same words
over and over again and because i shifted a 'but'
from one place to another and mixt-up what fell between
i must therefore have a new thought if not exactly
a new feeling and am therefore goaded to write. other
days the language fell crisply onto the snow-white
unleavened page as if it always knew exactly where it was
heading and despite the picayune pleasure in all that
i was simply bored with playing footsy . i spend
a lot of time talking (as it were) to myself and i suppose
this is another 'i and thou' instant of it—the self-
ventriloquist. tho i hope not. KOHAMA has a radiance
no thick pelt of cold winter fog can dispel.

January 5th, '85

Claudia :

        housecleaning . . .
come across 'honey' with yr luvly note
plus comely mug-shot   dipt
into its comely eros   the beguiling
shade of your copious blonde
o you impossible blondes!
nettle of hair those gone awry
tilted eyes. all all an
abundant surmise. . . . 'i'   was at
the peak of my ego those days:
i really did believe in
a revolutionary politics centered
within the erotic body : i
remembered believing in the intrinsic
holiness at the heart of art/
love making : and yes i was craven
when it came to women, particularly a woman like you . . . . the
day we shopt for an 'off to Paris' hat
for you the night after you read
me Heinrich Heine . . . i knew would be
callit our cut-off point . & yet
down thru the years you've persisted
an agate touchstone i often shine.
Daphne & i parted (amicably) 3 yrs ago.
i suppose i played a real role in
helping her son grow up. we all love
each other to this day and i'm sure
like you & me   we always will.

tenderest outpourings to you dear Claudia

mid-January '85

Sarah / David :

      we're into our winter   lotsa cold and snow   i've just come thru my mid-winter snivel my week-long bout of an unnamed Asian flu   so much for the work i was going to get into during the Xmas holidays   the dope around town got as much buzz as Sanka coffee   nothin' could lift me up to the o' numinous sphere unless it's a good sweet fuck and where it might come from is unstakt territory   not that i've had much of an appetite for making out   memory alone aswarm with tits cunts undefiled female minds   their names legion their proximity equidistant their manifold smiles and grimaces leaven these crusty snow-bound words   Daphne and Kit came by over the holiday inn salutations   she greyer impeccable as ever he an erstwhile Johnny Travolta cum black leather greasy hair pink cheekt fast talkin' punk   we'll always get off on each other we're each other's staunchest witness thus far   otherwise i don't know what's goin' on round town   no part of the writing crowd if there is one   no part of the photography/paintings crowd if such groupings continue to exist   music continues to enthrall as almost nothing else can   makin' my own music as if it were a long sustained croon of a winter bird who forgot to fly south and misst being hen peckt takes away from the gout   periods are conventions   songs are nothin' but breath and a little moon-dust   i'd trade all my wit for callit the distemper of lust stiffened by permafrost i might be able to get it up   who woulda thought this incomparably soft appendage could have caused such oblique havoc   who would have ever thought it could be talkt into being instantly stiff as a ram-rod   how stroke a pussy with flaccid comb   these early mornings before i surface i am a persona non gratis in a series of tableaus which feels so close so very close to the acts of my waking hours—night and day are barely distinguishable   almost as if both personages and acts are consonant   needless to say these words are trying their damnest to finger an already desiccated woe-be-gone moment   they flay the air descending they'll fail 'sometimes i wonder, "did i write this? how did i do it?" "do it while you're young, Mr. Pinckney. put all of your passion in it." she smiled.'   Djuna Barnes in *Sweet Evening Breeze* by Darryl Pinckney in the *New York Review*, Dec. 20 '84, sez it—almost like Sheila Watson also did when young   i could be bonkers but the i/me i happen to be proposes that at 59 i'm really just a wizened beginner and have my best book ahead of me   i don't know its shape but i would surmise it'll have to have equal parts of 'heart' and 'wit' and be able to turn a hairlip to N.F.'s kinda exegesis of can/lit   fuck the authorial god   is the father the prophetic son and the holy ghost mortgage on an Asian Canuck's otherwise divined life   i seem to heave towards abstract patterns of thought whenever the words are unwrought by an actual love   i seem that way to be a child grown into absurd manhood who likes to take up as much space as he can by a fusillade of geometrics   'i cried for you' were the last true words he said. . . .

Jan. 16th '85

Mike: . . . it all started with that *consternation of impulses* surrounding a couple of would-be books of poetry: the intent to present to C/H a definitive manual-script for the *P.T.P.* and *WHEELS* together with other matter, not to mention the simple thought of writing to you—all, all of it got displaced after the initial burst of working old hobby-horse texts etc. 'cause i contracted a virulent Asiatic virus which knockt me off my feet for a coupla weeks and put the screws to my winter fantasies in Hawaii (where i of course intended to hustle the work—Ha!) then when i got up the Xmas holidays were over and i lookt again at the undone work and i almost puked—sincerely, your would-be plangent poet your numbskull author .

dawn: Jan. 18th '85, my 59th year

my umei:

    these 'Komei' words see
    themselves in the oval mirror you
    hold up to them: their
    spectral-feelings a Prism of your
    Ongaku.   i, i have often
    played our Capricorn Duet . . . your
    breath ruffles the drafty
    feathers of an Old Bird clutching
    a bare winter Verb. dumb-
    founded 'they' hang upside down in
    a new year cave.

    hold me in your dream one night
    and i'll feel the warmth
    of your breath . . . hover over me

    give my love, such as it be
    to Hiro & Rae, equally, we '4' be
    a perfect 'square' & then sum . . .

Jan. 21st, '85

My Dear Fuku:

      My musician friend Minoru Sumimoto came by and I had him read your *Spring Calligraphy* .

To my lifelong chagrin I cannot read or write Japanese and from here it looks like I never will . How many Languages does an Artist speak without saying anything ? Your *Spring Calligraphy* makes my head turn cartwheels . And, to top it off, your card arrived just in time for my 59th Birthday . Thank you .

. . . Would you believe me if I told you that I'm already planning on a trip to Nippon this summer ? I don't really know 'why' I'm drawn there but drawn I am and I'd be a fool if I didn't follow my predilections . So—don't be surprised if you find me standing at your door. Kohama's Sun haunts these Northern English Words . . .

. . . Allen Ginsberg & his friends were in India when you were first there and though he hasn't gone back as you often have he kept a Journal which I'm enclosing. If you can't get into it pass it on to Isamu who knows about it. And of course knows Allen & his friends 'cause they are all part of the '60s Mythologies. As I am.

May 'haru' in Shuzan be a sprightly green.

Jan. 21st, '85 midnight

Dear Michun:

I came across this long ago slide, and I thought 'Ah, there we are the six of us including *little Yoko* who isn't at all interested in having her picture taken like we adults seem to be.' I left Kohama last summer with a Gift for the two of you from her. She was getting off on her new-found freedom and everybody, including the old men, got off on her presence. I'd say that she entranced the very tide there.

The slide also presides over the weekend Trip the four men in the picture took to the Japan Sea: with 'you' at the wheel—burning rubber on hairpin curves—while we three hung on for dear life. Isamu your big brother is at this moment (the actual moment of looking intently at the slide) in Kohama with his young family—but back 'then' he was in North America with his first family. Neither Syuzo or Dansun had any children then . . . and your daughter Yoko is all of eighteen now. My, my, how Time flies and in its flight bears us along. Thronged . . .

(Michun:—I'm already planning to be in Nippon this summer: among other things I would like to find a *woman* to live with and the two of you would be doing me a big favor keeping 'her' in mind.—if you see her tell her I'm already a heady 59—but physically & mentally sound and yes has a future ahead.)

yours faithfully,

February '85

dear Fee:

—took these back in spring '79
i declined to tell you 'everything' that's happened since i too

am inclined to put it into a story nothin'
like a twice old Tale with or without 'love' & 'gore'

sometimes i feel it's only 'dialect' that bears witness to
the keel of my feelings for the site of the 'real'

haven't been in N.Y. since—
haven't thirsted for its pinnacles of commerce & high kultur

my ambitions these days seem to be closer to an archaeologist's
the founding of N.Y. is too recent to be anything but

the ongoing news of the day with or without Walter Kronkite
all that glitz and sweet mayhem

barely dents the weather of this other millennium this
scallopt sea coast with its latent animism

i never got off on the brusque we stood to one another
something in each of us got the other's goad

i had my drunken after-opening party at Max's Kansas City
i had my weekend of instant stardom

what has opened out since then is buried in the pit of self
my ignorances go on being abysmal

pushin' 60 is some kinda prod like Aaron's rod
nothin' left to be done without probity

Fee (& Susan): let these slides be my gift for the gift of
your writing   let the stackt deck fall. . . .

Sunday, Feb. 3rd, '85

<u>*pelting my ear with the music i want to hear*</u>
<u>*proposes at least two things*</u> . 1/ keeping my ears open
to all sounds (noxious & otherwise) canned, or
alive, but continuing thru-out all that's heard to sound
the <u>*actual body*</u> of my own acoustics—to tap
all the tremulous sounds stored up in my own psyche with
and without other musicians, in equal time .
2/ that in & thru an intent act-of-listening in the very
act of playing an instrument and, equally, inside—
the very hive of listening to oneself make music instantly
(played back and even collaged together in time) enables <u>*the feeling ear*</u> to incubate as well as resonate
psyche's own sweet & sour songs . in so far as i know music
i think i know it best as <u>*the body's unencumbered*</u>
<u>*song*</u> . it is not impossible for me to think of 'the body'
as the complete musical instrument of which all of
other divers instruments in time are simply sonic extensions
of our fingertips, mouth, and throat-speaking for all
of, is it 4 or 5, senses . <u>*blood pulse heart-beat*</u> measure
the pitch as well as the timbre of our cadences .
and for what it's worth these days i'd like to add that the
closer it stays to a <u>*conversational acoustic-space*</u> the
best i like the music i make : hopefully 'it,' that is <u>*the music*</u>,
pitches a tent under the stars where we can lie together
and listen to the heart's own murmurings . for myself &
my sense of song: there's nobody listening to this tape but us .

someone at a party read somewhere that so and so had sd—
in disparaging Rock 'n Roll Muzak that it was nothin' but the
unholy marriage of the blackman's rhythm & blues with a
whiteman's electro-magnetic instrumentation and that it was
the 2nd half of the 20th century N.A. middle-class & all—
most all white urban tribal music. <u>*Jimmie Hendrix/Janis Joplin*</u>
you name them   their fames are legion   their music an ear-bend.

songs from a Suite of Love Songs titled *The-Ace-of-Hearts* with Mayumi, Honda & i being voice
& harp (on a tape) & i singing & strumming a poignant Blues at the Western Front, Oct. '84.
Buddy Bolden's wrackt psyche is also (imperturbably) my own. needless to say, yours too .

the artist ain't nothin' but a network of inchoate soundings making a momentary sense: everything feeds back into the Maw of the Real .
                                      Love

Feb. 3rd, '85 (2 pm

my dear Stan: & Others who'll have a hand in it:

   Sarah Sheard told me via long distance that C.H. has W H E E L S in the works and / i thought MY GAWD it's really beginning to turn into a long-awaited book but I hope not without me—not after coming this far underailed.

   for what it's worth—here's how 'it' looks to me from here: to begin with we already have the *1st third in print* in Gerry Shikatani's anthology *Paper Doors* and let's say C.H. could simply pick it up from there. (i mean that it's more than adequate without *the snapshots* i'm leading up to as an integral part of the whole Text.—which leads me to the *last third* as printed in Karen Mulhallen's *Descant* 44/45, spring & summer '84, which i liked on sight & still do.—i mean if you go for words/images you couldn't do better than pick up where she left off. (ask Karen for a copy if you haven't had a look.)

. . . the snaps & the words both have *their sightings* of the *same* or *another* occasion of this tripartite trip. they do belong together and furthermore it's an opportunity for me to update/reanimate the word/image format i first put together with *Stonedgloves* (one of the C.H.'s early publications).— O tell me you want to can afford to incorporate my snaps and i'll show you where they should be tipt in to the body of the text.—i keep coming back to the layout in the aforementioned issue of *Descant*, for visual clues and i'm passing the word on for what i think my book is worth.—why, i would gladly chip in and pay for the cost of the reproductions if i thot you could be prevailed upon. . . . glad it's in the works i'm of course looking forward to the proof pages. and a spring Trip east .

. . . tell me what sort of paper beast you have in mind for a cover . . . tell me your inclinations Stan and i'll lean one way or another.

Feb 15th, '85

Dear Sarah:

D.Y.'s play ('For Pin Heads') opened at the Arts Club: The Court—the everlasting mayhem—of Love as well attended by all manner & sorts of post-60s derelicts and media nabobs. someone i overheard sd (after the show in the Arts Club bar) that 'it had lotsa eastern glitz tho the content was "nothing" but another cream puff.' entertainment is better elixir than television, i thot to myself as i sat in the front row watching the beads of sweat fall off the heroine's damp brow as she leaned into another song & the would-be hero found himself thronged.

   compact kaleidoscopic with perhaps an excess of comic gestures & retorts—the addlepated middle-age Love (latent in me) got off on all the ambiences. after all it ain't everyday i can get off on knowing i don't know nothing about play writing and find myself love's lout.

*

my oldest daughter (Mariko), her carpenter husband & 10 month-old son have been living with me the past month. we make one weird family watching the days go by and 'Esko/Anton' become daily more agile. i forget myself, tho my age shows. i play the part of grandfather daily and i forget the hairy young lover i used to be. that middle-age prairie hick who fell in love with Anne Murray didn't know what was good for him: he didn't know he had to love himself before he could really be something more than a forlorn troubadour. but—then again—who am i to say, given my own derelictions, my own throngings?

*   **LOVE,**

ask D.Y. about the lovely walk we took down to the water front on a perfectly clear false spring afternoon . . .

spring up in Georgian Bay sounds like sheer bliss but i'm already thinking i'd love to go to Nippon (once) again tho i haven't had my mind made up for me. i'll keep it in mind Ha!

Fri. Feb. 22nd, '85

Mike

      D.Y. been here in his fluorescent green bulky knit sweater which turned a lot of heads brought forth a farthing of astonisht gasps . his play or at least the way it was staged this time around had perhaps too much glitz and overplayed what is—afterall—a homely tale of love's purple travails. it had to be as it were elevated to the status of show-biz—which it clearly and enjoyably was. nothin' like a northern tale of a forlorn snow-bird to put the torch to the tourniquets of love. we all know it's often no more than a gleam in the 'i' and yet we want to leap over its ramparts even if it's only for the sake of another pratfall. o i've been known to fall in love with a siren or a shady lady's voice like 'who' hasn't in this kultur or any other i know of but i seem to have come to a time in my life when i can pleasure myself as well as others by becoming my own sweet & sour song-smith: i'll even yodel if i thot it would assuage all my erotic hindrances. Mike: you know what i mean and so does Linda, D.Y. & of course Sarah. Mike, here's the last draft of the P.T.P. we have scoured each other thoroughly. if you on the other hand have any cogent suggestions, let me in on it. for what it's worth they've been implanted in 'me' and will in their turn feed another sapling. keep the top humming and the spin off will be a momentarily poised equilibrium. for what it's worth i've been studying tai-chi to keep an altogether too sedentary body supple. Mike, 60 is still a handful tho of an unaccountable frequency.

Fri. Feb. 22nd, '85

Dear David:

  Dennis sez you're in Toronto for a bit and that you brought the illustrations for the P.T.P. with you and intend to put the finishing touches to them for the P.T.P. Book. (What LUCK!—) i've been working away at a final Draft of 'em and tho they're not all as shapely as i would wish them i feel they're on their own.—if for instance 'you' who've probably read them more often than anybody but me have any clarifications, do 'write' them out and i'll commend them or not. others, particularly D.R., likewise. after all, this is a co-operative book—even tho the outpourings could be said to be 'mine' which brings up the following thot that 'you' and 'i' could have equal billing—be, as it were, the co-authors of the P.T.P. &—i might add—the more so if S.B. intends the deluxe hardback he talkt about bringing out. anyhow, i've struggled with callit their rank & file order and what i'm sending is (again) as shapely a sequence as i can make them while all along 'they' made themselves. David:—i could fly to Toronto on the spur of a day if we need to have a consultation. otherwise, phone me (collect) when you have a moment before you return to Portugal .

  'it would be nice to be able to birth the P.T.P. this year with my 59th birthday behind me and 60 coming up . . .'

  . . . any day now i'll be let off the hook of an incessant writing and i'll be able to 'do' other less myopic things. ha!

March 17th, '85 : midnight

dear Sarah :

      first it was Mihao Sawada : then Maya Koizumi and now (rather, yesterday) it was Joy Kogawa : all sterling middle-age ladies with lotsa true grit and each their share of wit & irony . as one of the reigning nits of this nogoodnik lotus land, i get to take each one of them to Kochi's for a splendid sushi dinner and we both get to exercise our wits without anything as complicated as 'goin' to bed' to vex the good-will & idle chatter . have all the wellsprings of our mutual elan vital begun to slowly dry up or is it simply put in abeyance? aw gee whiz! don't tell me they've all had their true hearts crumpled a number of times and don't want to play in bed anymore . i still think of an actual body beside me now & again just to keep the old bod riddled until its fancy gets tickled again . otherwise, my lust would seem to have been tableau'd till the ol' stone cutter whets his chisel to begin another rondo of precise incisions to welt her febrile body . meanwhile, 'his' has long ago begun to sag imperceptibly in front of his very eyes . Sarah : there are women i love and will never sleep with 'cause it's not in the flip of the cards, and there are women i only dream of sleeping with 'cause they're in every sense of the word utterly inaccessible . and then there are those that encourage the outrageous act and they never stand still . a real warm body in hand is worth a thousand vestigial images sequestered in the mind's own labyrinth of them. . . . i might have gone to bed with each of them if our signs had been twinned and then again i suppose i never will . like the ol' birth pills of the '60s 'love' has its phases and out of phase is simply another way to praise those things that were there to be talkt abt above and beneath love's cantankerous sprawl . Daphne came by lately (too) and we had a lovely night out and both of us talkt about us & u. . . . all this just snuck in while i was getting ready to go to bed . 'hullo, how are you?'

                                              LOVE /

Mid-March '85
U.B.C. Fine Arts

Dear Page Hope-Smith:

since i was out in Richmond to see you i have been thinking about the exhibition of my colour prints which i'd like to call *I N & A R O U N D M Y J A P A N* and i've been making music with my musician friends with the intent of shaping an Opening Night Concert one that will even take 'us' by our surmise and astonish us and because i've spent most of the long winter shaping the final draft of two books of pomes (which will be publisht by Coach House Press in Toronto this year) i've of course been dwelling inside a labyrinth of words out of which the words of the-end-of-the-exhibition-Poetry Reading will of itself emerge . needless to say, there's a lot of work ahead, and it won't be consummated till all 3 Events are past-tense . meanwhile, the ongoing politics swarming all over us and inflecting our very educational system of which i am an altogether too long a member disturbs the latent poise of everything .

the V.A.G. has a large series of b/w prints of mine in their permanent collection titled S T O N E D G L O V E S—you could ask them for a loan of them as an integral part of the show: they could fill the smaller gallery and also be, as it were, a synopsis of/for the colour prints, which they truly are . (the enclosed pomes/catalogue of the initial exhibit organized by the N.G. back in the early '70s ought to clue you in.) p/s i do want all the enclosed photo material back as it's irreplaceable.

though the actual music is as yet unknown and given the way we work together and play, it'll largely be an open-ended improvisational recital. we could give some thought to how the concert might be staged . here, for what it's worth, are some ideas i've been thinking abt:

1/   the concert ought to be held in the
smaller gallery where STONEDGLOVES
will hang and there ought to be a raised dias
abt 10 ft. square and not more than 14 inches high
on which we'll sit and/or kneel facing the opening
into the larger gallery . given how clean
the gallery floors are, it would be nice to have
cushions on which to sit all around the raised dias .
we would prefer to be just a head higher
than the listeners' own ear-level .

2/   'our' music draws its sustenance from
the Japanese/Asiatic modes of classical/folkloric
music & song with its wide range of sonorities, all this wedded to what we know and practise

of all forms of Indo/European/North Americano
music : 'we' as musicians are interested
in, callit, our own brand of Pacific Rim synchronicity .
both our musical skills and repertoire are,
to say the least, variegated . the thought is that
'we' ought to be 'on stage' right from the
moment the exhibition opens (tuning up and limbering
our voices & instruments) while all along
whoever happens along can do whatever they're doing—
and if they want to sit down on a cushion
and listen for awhile they can—think of the music
as a kind of informal 'jam-session' one that
will build up into an intensity of some duration
before the evening of seeing/listening ends .

i'll get a list of the names of all musicians plus
their specialties to you, soon .

*

as for the end-of-the-exhibition *poetry reading*—
it'll be from several texts of poetry of/for/abt my Nippon .

*

(the older i get the more i am aware of the fact that
i am, after all, a 1st generation Asian immigrant's son and
all my life i've straddled an ocean . almost everything
i know abt myself is rooted in some such rumination . and
need i tell you that everything i've done in the name of
A-R-T (of which this upcoming exhibition, concert & poetry
reading are the latest venues) is in divers ways a
Pacific Rim humanoid's manifestations .
                                                  more details, later

3/
        1/   invitations
        2/   a simple catalogue
        3/   transportation to & from the exhibition
        4/   insurance   and
        5/   a silk-screen poster

        —i would like to have a say in 1/ 2/ & particularly 5/

       3/ & 4/ are altogether your business .

1/   an *invitation* specific to my show/concert/& reading
     needs an exact text which i'll be sending

2/   a simple *catalogue* of the same
     needs its concomitant 'text' which along with a repro
     if that's possible (again) needs an
     exact text & a choice of what'll be reproduced .
     (i won't be able to deal with the datum
     for the catalogue till a month or so before the show
     'cause there's both a 'printing' & a 'selection'
     process involved before a catalogue can be .

5/   a *silk screen poster* is something i want to have
     a direct hand in and if you can tell me how much you've
     allowed for the 'cost' of producing the same i'll
     see what can be done and make that a collaboration with
     one of the many printers i know in town .

i've been very taken all winter with an ongoing 'writing'
and 'teaching' in the very midst of a university politics—
the provocations of which i haven't felt since the late '60s.
all of which i'll be putting aside by the end of March—then
we'll give our whole-hearted attention to 'my Japan' & all
else for the sake of an early summer celebration . meanwhile
keep in touch, particularly with the small details .

yours sincerely   Roy K. Kiyooka

March 27th, '85

dear Mike:

tight arse type. not because i like it that way but because i've set my praxis 35 up thata way for the final draft of WHEELS and i don't want to change it till it gets done.—if you can help me get rid of all those cute truncations, not to mention the little affectations, i'm sure are scattered thruout the text i'd be more than thankful. what the P.T.P. needs now is another pair of vigilant eyes—like yours and yes Linda's. mine become more and more myopic and a part of me (the equally vigilant reader) doesn't trust the thrust of the Text any longer. it's been almost 3 yrs since Daphne and i fell apart and almost as long since the PTP pomes began their own tally. meanwhile, we do see each other (periodically) and whenever we do we seem to still get off on each other thru our talk which continues to hint at all that we lived thru and have been dismayed by. tho we've never really spoken of it, i think she would agree that our coming apart was posited in the relationship from its beginnings. meanwhile, Kit is goin' thru all the N.A. media/mythos/murk with his hair on end and his burgeoning man-body encased in black leather complete with studs. but i know he'll be his own man one day and i'm going to be around to see him be it. my own daughters are all grown up and given the trying economic times making out as well as they can. i watch them come and go and am deeply pleasured to have them praise my life. these days it almost feels like they'll be the only women in my old age tho they do encourage me to do something about it which i don't seem to be able to do. just finished reading *I LOVE: The Story of Vladimir Mayakovsky and Lili Brik* by Ann and Samuel Charters. when it came to the last chapter and Mayakovsky's suicide i was moved to tears. I CRIED. given the awesome rhetoric of ideologies these impoveristht love-lack days, i felt keenly his callit psychic loneliness. i mean here i sit nearly twice his age and, tho filled with the rage of life, feel, despite that rage, circumscribed. don't come near me. don't touch me. just give me a job and i'll be absolved of even the need to speak of love. etc. meanwhile, the days lengthen and the first cherry blossoms tip the windblown trees along Keefer Street. Mike: writing letters to you and others is about as intimate as i get these days, tho unlike Mayakovsky who it would seem had to die young, i have an old age to face up to forthrightly.
          love to both of you

i'm enclosing the missing poems and where they belong in the sequences: like the others they've been re-sculpted to chime w others.

after
there must be at least one pome to a pear tree

o dance a jig on
the pear tree's midden
heapt with divers   p/s this repeats (echoes) the 2nd
wonderments . language is   verse of the poem beginning

a fool's fruit   'these words seem to be
                                                         rehearsing—'

fool-proof pear trees bear
the laughter of

put your ear
to the pear tree's trunk
hear its sap hum

after
'the body i am is the purest instrument of desire i know'

who knows if i'll be around when
they come to chop my pear tree down to make room
for another two-bit condominium .
magpie   magpie   swayin' on a wry black branch
will you caw me when you spy the
axe-man coming down the alley 'cause i want to plea
for all the children who haven't had
their chance to climb up into its leafy hideaway
and there's a young couple who paused in
their morning walk down the alley to look up at it
and have blue-printed a nest for three

magpie   magpie   will you be our unpaid informer
our 'i' in the night sky ?

like i sd : rid the P.T.P.s of all their affectations / David Bolduc has shaped the book for its
             illustrations with the inclusion of these 4 pomes—the overall format is, to all
             intents and purposes, definitive.

April 5th, '85

palette
black
perspicacious
striations
white
shadow leaping
taper
a Bedouin
face

i thought (then
that 1 side of the tape
would be for Vicki
and the other side for
Richard: guess
which side is for whom?

now) i think that
either side is for both
of you. just as
they were—back to back
in the W.F. Concert
back in Oct. '84

—as you might guess
i am into my voice:
i am writing my own song/s.
the bird of poetry
wants to trill as well
as sway on a branch

may your own Harkenings under the brow of Pinnacle Mountain be weather   dance   and throng

. . . have i got a proverbial tin ear?
how else account for the sheer number of times i have re-animated
practically every poem i've ever found and even after
their publication—i have often had a consuming urge to mettle with
their pliant alignments. nothing as 'quotidian' as a
memorable epithet and nothing quite as indelible as an awkward image.
both, i've been told, are a matter of discreet attention
to the rise and fall of sundry syllables.
for instance: i've spent the whole of Good Friday morning mulling
over a prosaic moment introducing otamatsukuri-onsen
in the latter half of WHEELS (again . . . and
i still haven't got its labial consonants in an undefiled order.
see what i mean about possessing a tin ear?
somebody told me years ago that having a tin ear was like thrusting
an old-fashioned ear horn up to the Beloved's most
intimate whispers.—it blew me away to think of all the nuances
of her speaking i hadn't listened for.
what i want to know is —did Ludwig Beethoven possess an absolutely
perfect-ear for pitch and frequencies before he went deaf
and thereafter that perfect-pitch found its lodgings inside his
passionate mind? 'i' seem to 'hear' what i indeed
harken to from instant to instant while all along each nuance is
subsumed in an imperturbable silence. language   that
amazing Hinge on the doorway opening out onto all Phenomena.
long live all our heartfelt trifles embedded in
the Heraldic Rites of (another) Spring. Spring's Infuriations
perk this small pod of work/s.

these days i am eavesdropping at the gossamer bounds of poetry/music daily listen to my words
mock themselves/ hear their torpor on tape

Good Friday for Richard and Vicki

April 13th, '85, 9.30 am

12 SONGS : 1 for each month

    1/   *re-tune Harp pitch each octave to*
           a tonal aura (retain the same
           for the duration of the month : allowing
           for chordal decay).

    2/   *beginning with improvisations*
           let both song and music find their timbre
           write/sing/play itself into air

    3/   *be 'local' like neighbourhood/weather*
           be <u>raga ongaku blues</u> : duration
           an unfolding rather than punctilious

how April's gently sustained warmth lifts
up the bursting buds and all of a sudden the willows
along Spanish Banks emblazon a dullard sky
with a dazzling yellow/green carapace of unfolding
leaves and the bulkings of my winter body feel
a lightness it had displaced ingratiates the
surrounding air . this my habitual drive out to ubc
unfurls the cadences of the seasons. singalong

    one song/poem for each month
    each song/poem to be composed extemporaneously
    and (yes) sung on a 46 min. tape:
    each tape embodying the discovery of the
    melodic line and its harbinger
    the monthly song . each tape presenting the way
    the entire <u>song</u> got itself shaped.
    all the variables within a pre-tuned octave and
    letting the mode unravel itself .
    how to reside in the psyche's daily weather to
    chime the Gift of Seasons seem
    to be the plea for these April surmises .
    let the oncoming heat of summer meld
    all our contrarinesses . begin
    love . . . begin with the plangencies of May

                              before a class at
                              U.B.C.
                                        April 14, '85

how the first
     gently sustained warmth
lifts the bursting
     April buds and all of a sudden
the giant willow un-furls
     a dazzling carapace of tender
yellow/green leaves to
     leaven another summer . . .
as 'i' high-tail it along
     the upper reaches of Spanish
Banks sniffin' brine air
     strummin' my zippy-zither

     s-u-m-m-e-r-t-i-m-e!
     the lassitudinous air divines
     the melodic-concord
     Concordance/s . April ain't
     by a long shot the cruel-
     est month . . . he smiled
     overlooking the blue strait

April or May 1985

My Dear Wilfred & Sheila :

      . . . another semester over and thanks to last year's leave-of-absence i ain't too run down, tho the well of ideas has just about dried up . 'pedagogy' is an act of faith these maladroit days when Whitman's, not to mention Marshall MacLuhan's, *Democratic Vistas* have turned into a cancerous economics . there's a pall hanging over our whole Education system and i suspect it has something to do with more than the economic morass, the stab-in-the-back 'cutbacks' in funding at all levels—it has something to do with the surmise that 'we' as educators have been complicit in the very inequalities we are besodden with . and 'art,' the handmaiden of our earthly fealties, is once again mugged if not strait-jacketed by our pitiless materialism . these days the once highly touted wealth of the western world is, shall i say, almost a barren ground . some part of me despises the wholesale plunder of the world for the sake of our lugubrious well being . impossible to believe in the scientific mind of a kultur such as our erstwhile neighbors' who preach individuality at all costs while practising an awesome genocide . anyhow—our 'pedagogy' is a wounded beast and whatever is festive about the 'arts' is doomed to be a sacrificial offering . believe me—these drear thoughts impinge upon *the work* and it takes all the strength i've got to talk about aesthetics, let alone a painting or a pome . harrowing—the generations of us—humanoids . hapless the way our perversities work through us . as for my own work, it lies beckoning but undone . a few days rest and i'll be able to turn to it again and hopefully it will overwhelm me. who would have ever believed that a kind of obdurate patience becomes itself the requisite challenge, the very gist of speaking out . you both know what i mean . . . i wish i hadn't said it .

one of my favorite hangouts in Vancouver is a place on Commercial Drive (heart of Little Italy) called Joe's. it has snooker tables and whiz-bang computer slot machines and lots of tables with chairs and a central ordering/fixing/paying & talking bar. it's run by a bunch of Portuguese, tho you wouldn't know it except for the posters and other images that adorn the walls, plus the complete geniality that seems to pervade the place. like overnight it became one of the haunts of the literary/artistic, peppered with feminists, professional union workers and ardent European/Asian immigrant guys and gals. tho Vancouver doesn't have a patch on Toronto, it's come a long way in terms of a diversity of ethnic communities with a particular kind of emphasis towards the Asian-at-large. the Chinese in all their dialects here will have real political clout a generation or two down the line 'cause their numbers will continue to increase, whereas the more typical W.A.S.P.s have reacht 'zero' replacement (always excepting the Bolducs of course). as for us Japanese Canucks (all 50,000 of us thru-out the breadth of Canada) we've taken up with the rest of you and with almost 75% intermarriage we're going to be utterly assimilated according to David Suzuki in a recent forum concerning all the grievances born out of the 2nd WW. he literally sd that we were a dying species. i heard him say my thots even as i would strenuously deny such prognostications.

Late April '85

watching the afternoon dwindle
goaded on by these lengthening spring days i tell myself
you owe it to the erstwhile Viewer to
write an Introduction to your Canadian/Japanese festival
show at the Richmond Art Gallery. . . .
but then 'who' am i kidding? what i really seem to be about
is simply showing you some of the faces
in all sorts of places i've been and they're all around you
'cause i thought you might be interested in
what a Canadian/Japanese artist who has spent most of
his time abroad in his parents' homeland
has taken time to look at and be in the presence of.
to be a photographer is to be engaged in
callit the ongoing ritual act of looking intently at
the world and let its radiant light inflect
everything within the scope of a view-finder . nothing is
boring to the mirror the light glances off:
everything of substance leaves its imprimatura on the film
the world inside a cast shadow thrown on a wall
induces its own verifiable hallucination.
the photograph as 'nature morte' is to the modern age
the very embodiment of ritualistic effigies.
ask the great stone sphinx about the durability of hewn
stone tablets / the fibrous translucency of papyrus.
ask Prince Genji about tissue-thin sentiments.
everything on earth has its moment of testimony: its valorous
presence as a witness to mutability. 'i' am no
different, i tell myself, bent over another vinyl sleeve
of hitherto un-printed negatives. Viewer: if you
just happen to glance at a face that is recognizably your own
you'll know (wordlessly) what a photographer is
all in all about.

                        time to get back to the darkroom. . . .
                        time to conjure up another silver breviary

                        memory re-tracing its perilous steps. . . .
                        all moments got their own lucidity : these

                        i shudder to call my very own retrace
                        amazing moments of never-to-be-repeated grace

some midnight thoughts concerning the shaping of
in and around my Nippon

in so far as i think i am a photographer
as when i agreed to gather 'these' colour prints
together for your Canadian/Japanese show
i am a photographer of callit the ahistorical
'commonplace.' for every action-packt emotion
riddled photoglyph (taken as if by stealth
by avid documentary photographers) i would click
the shutter on the least eventful thing:
like a fabled 'yukioe' woodcut artist i would
inscribe the whole panoply of this our ofttimes unruly (floating world) on your eyeballs.
such as they be these colour prints have quite
literally become the actual moment portrayed. i really want to say that 'everything' has
its way of surpassing our intellectual proclivities. photography is nothing much if
not a compassionate (celebratory) eye .

. . . one has to open themselves up to the imago mundis
and disappear into it. one ideally wants to reify
all their waking/sleeping moments without a dire inter-
locutor. . . . if only that were possible it would
be, to say the least, monstrous. unimaginable that omni-
vorous, never sleeping eye. all the myriad frames
of this our fair earth under the surveillances of untold
satellites add up to the purest notion of what could
be called <u>latent</u> <u>content</u> without the intervention
of human fealties. almost <u>everything</u> has had its snap
shot taken and according to the Warhol rubric been
famous for 15 minutes : the whole biosphere parleyed into a scientifically authorized commodity of quanti-
tatively ascertainable value. now, i'd be a fool indeed
if i wasn't in my way an accomplice to these vituper-
ations but i think i can say that these colour prints simply
celebrate the earth as i have come to dwell in it.
nothing i know, even as i know that such knowing dwindles
in the face of my daily un-knowing, tells me i'll be
around another time (in this guise) to behold this
litany of people / places / and all the ordinary things

*that fill sight, again. i am, if you will, only interested
in taking pictures to embody the poignancy distilled
in the very silver of paradigmatic phenomena .*

*there is an actual Text that ought to accompany
these colour prints. there are if you will
all the interstices between each frame and as often
as not there's a whole sky that could be filled
with a cloud-text. . . . i keep telling myself even as
i know that in the very act of typing these words
i cannot be in the darkroom printing pictures
let alone be outside taking more of them . it's always
one thing at a time, time and time again: one
small word following another as time passes and the
bright afternoon slowly dwindles down and all
the slant shadows on the clapboard houses on
Georgia Street shift and the setting sun spins a
lavender twilight above the church rooftop.*

*there is an actual Text that automatically wrote itself
into the colour print, in the very moment of its
actual taking. embossed upon the very texture of the
things portrayed: the colour print is their pal-
impsest. anyhow, i had resolutely thought that i could
get into the daily rhythm of selecting/printing/
and writing an accompanying text but needless to say
i was kidding myself (again). thus it is that these
colour prints got no text, let alone an identification
label . . . tho it's my hunch they'll make themselves
apparent if they're lookt at intently. like anything
that would unconceal itself—— these colour prints
bear the burden of an onlooker's undivided attention.*

*whether the myriad things take notice of our presence
or we in our passages take note of them: all things
are rooted in the lucidity of a ceaseless collaboration.
crossing varied thresholds with unattenuated ease
has been one of the pleasures of growing older and
as such i think i can say that these photographs do not
beg for familiarity. in their own way these prints
are nothing more or less (given the aggrandizement)
than the typical family album. like the familiar snap-*

shot they capture a pixilated moment and put a number
of such moments together to tell a discrete narrative.
'i' am, if you will, both the watcher and the person
being lookt at. there are the myriad ways light graces
any place on the face of the earth. there are mirrors
in space gathering up cones of silver star dust.
moving out from Keefer Street—into the vast Pacific
Rim world—i am, if you will, a gimlet-eye borne out
of all that's celebratory in a brine edged swirl .

. . . i want these words to tell me what it is i'm
thinking about: i want them to stand up beside each
other, but only long enough to release the image
into the eye's own acuity. these colour prints contain
their own nomenclature: they are as common as each
thing's fate. if ineffableness be one of photography
's attributes, it's ok with them and me. breath
held long enough leads to suffocation. the virtual
absence of light can swallow up an object. history
permits the nightmare to flaunt and flourish.
these prints already constitute a hermetic archaeology.
the past i care about is enfolded in their present-
tense .

. . . i had, to all intents and purposes, forgotten how arduous it is putting a big exhibition together. all these weeks sorting through hundreds of negatives after checking their contact sheet imprint under a magnifying glass and tentatively deciding which frame/s to print. then the hours spent in a toxic darkroom, testing, printing, discarding, and printing again. and as always, it's the first emerging of an image that excites one to go on doing it. now i think i am a fastidious dark room technician but that doesn't save me from the awful days when every print looks drab and badly composed. some days i got a handful of prints that embodied the moment of their taking completely: that is, they became the utter image of an otherwise fleeting moment. other days (working with the same premises) i ended up with unmitigated dullness and a poverty of colours. and, in and thru this darkroom ritual tracing a hieroglyph of silver across my retina, i somehow know that these bright colour prints are nothing but a fleet glimpse of this our floating world. laying them out on a clean floor to find their most telling alignments, i read and re-read the whole series like a complex mosaic of scintillant shapes and colours. some series have (given the particular occasion) an exact numerical order. others seem to be variously interchangeable without compromising their tale. . . . the ardour of getting a big exhibition together consists to a large extent on both the promiscuity and, yes, the strictness of our habitual 'memory-traces' and the portents they unconceal. every brush with thought / every image conceivable of a whatnot / every salvaged epitaph glosses the unquiet surfaces of these colourful prints. behind the labour put into their public appearances, behind the masquerade of earnest words, these images cast a dearth of enchantment unbound by rime or reason.

late April, '85
In and A Round my Nippon

a post-Introduction to
the peregrine eye blinking at the marge
of a feckless High-Tech
while looking out for the indisputable place
each of us hails from .
In and A Round my Nippon has its roots
in a unredeemed vernacular
just under my skin

May '85

my dear *Stan* & *others* at the *Coach House Press* at the rear of Huron Street:
_____

sustained days of a hot summer keep getting blown away by ocean squalls and other vicissitudes of callit the weather. and, despite myself, so does the work on the manuscripts of W H E E L S and T H E P E A R T R E E P O M E S: 'poetry' rides the air currents better than most things, being as it were 'light as air, etc.' anyhow, this is just to tell you that i'm about to get back into both of them & if summer's torpors don't set in will have them to you by the end of June. first there was the end of another (politically activist) academic year at U.B.C.— then the getting together of a large colour print exhibition for the Richmond Art Gallery together with an opening-the-show concert and an end-of-show poetry reading. all this followed by a concert (music & poetry) and the premiere of my daughter and her boy friend's film titled 'clouds' for which there was an endless amount of work. thank goodness it's all over and like i say i'll be able to get down to work on shaping up the aforementioned book of poems. why, if i'm lucky i should still be able to take off on a holiday sometime this summer though i don't have plans.

thinking about the work remaining to be accomplished on W H E E L S, i should think it'll take a week to ten days to pull the whole together. the major work consists in placing/spacing the snapshots within the body of the text and, though i have most of the snaps to hand, i'll still have to print others up. this, plus a last scrutiny of the text and some final revisions. as of this moment i can say that the end of W H E E L S has its definitive form in D E S C A N T and with that in mind the rest of the book ought to fall into shape readily enough. (for what it's worth, i do prefer the 'typos' in 'D' better than the too plain, or is it brute, typos of the mss. copy you sent sometime ago. i have no idea of 'format' but (again) if it's about the size of 'D' all the snapshots will have to be scaled down and i do feel that they're the right scale (in relation to the text) therein.—like the snaps shouldn't be so large that they overwhelm the traceries of typos and nor too small that they look simply like a phrase or paragraph, say. anyhow, it'll all take shape i'm sure when i get the damn thing to you . . . soon. and that's i hope not a heedless promise!!!

June 3rd, '85

dear Ann Ireland:
    and Tim Deverell:

    well, i'll be damned—if it ain't one sitcom it's another bit of cannon fodder. will success congeal around Ann Ireland's fleet heels? or will it be merely a palliative, another goad to excel at oneself? given that SEAL BOOKS along with Kellog's Corn Flakes and glossy vignettes of a Yuppie's Heaven happen to be among the most exemplary commodities of our maladroit CAPITALISM, will a certain Mister Takahashi lay down his magical baton and take a humble-pie bow? and will a certain Maestro we all know get an autographed leather-bound copy to read on the plane between intercontinental gigs, and will he frown before he nods off? time zones change. Beethoven is a multi-million dollar musical industry. fleet days go by. chapter upon chapter of half-read books lie face up, unread. the long dead authors unfurl their copyrights to cover their heads. pennies from heaven rain down upon them. '. . . never has the naked collective will of capitalism been so apparent as it is today': money not only talks, it laughs all the way to the bank. funny to think of how some guys get a buck a word and other guys (using those same words) can't fetch themselves a penny. funny to think of 'words' themselves as the equivalent of 'currencies.' when i think these days of 'Faustian compacts' i think of our national deficit as being quite literally an inverted mountain of disabused words, a spinning like a child's top on the soft spot on the top of my head and all i want to do is lie down and play dead. play deaf/dumb/& blind. have, as it were, no mind at all. like shadow/no substance. reach out! reach out! touch the silken cuff of fame and fan the flames of your yet to be born unravished psyche, quotidian verities. solace &/or balm for all that remains, for whatever reason, unborn within us. those months you spent here on the Pacific Rim: the colourful tent on the escarpment overlooking the sound and all the music and, yes, even playfulness will be part of the content of your book to me . . . even if i never get around to reading it. Toby and Alister float into view as our separate lives momentarily collide, yes, even capsize, before we drift onwards to wherever the current takes us. love the allotment of my crazed days. will a certain Tim Deverell also take a bow? love,

June 7th, '85

dear Mike & Linda:

Summertime & the livin' is queasy in Lotusland sums up the adamant Politics of B.C. Bennett & his Proletarians. Like, how come the Multi-Nationals keep trashing the core of the city to erect those glistening towers while B.C. Place entertains the Masses with the likes of Billy Graham and the Biggest Trailer Show on Earth, and Pat McGeer plays footsy with the Curriculum Vitae of U.B.C. and, whether he knows it or not, there's a profound malaise, if not an inherent contradiction, in the whole sweep of our Educational Edifices: to wit, the '80s seem to have buried every kind of truly (ofttimes unruly) radical thought—i say this with all the hub-bub of Post-Modernistic Art held in mind like a sitcom.

Have you seen the latest issue of ESQUIRE inappropriately titled The Soul of America? 'Because what people actually say is usually too incoherent to print at any length, Manso has *edited* their testimony so that everyone speaks in the same tone of voice: two of Mailer's wives, his secretaries, lofty New York critics, a boxer and a cop who once arrested Mailer, all sound exactly alike. Not one is the least bit reticent, etc.' (*Mailer: His Life and Times* in NEWSWEEK, June 10, '85). Which came to mind after i dipt into 'E' every night for a week.—i mean all the perspective, personages and places the assorted authors quarried had the whole burden of Yankee Doodle Dandy 'know-how' 'spit & polish,' not to mention 'glitter'—& of course those intricate greast-lightning 'deals' that are the stock & trade of an errant scientifically-endorsed PRAGMATISM. All these authors, be it said, are indubitably AMERICUN. 'the average word, like your ordinary turd, costs more per inch in the U.S.A. than anywhere else in the universe.' 'i' as a mere Canuck have ofttimes thought to myself that it's certainly a perverse world that touts such an expensive, albeit democratic, abuse of language. Pour a vile sauce on it and make it hurt. Cut it up into paraphrases and let it pump adrenalin. Someone sd 'History has to go to bed with News 'cause both stand together in the same New World fundamentalist Pews.'

My 89 year old mother is with me for a month. She, of course, can't read a word of this. i mean, after nearly 70 years in this country her actual English is, to say the least, rudimentary. And yet, we both know that she is more the actual pivot of my own psyche than any huge America can ever be. 'Home is where the heart can dwell without compulsive speech.' We—my mother & i—have spoken to each other all of our lives through a vernacular compounded of a rudimentary English laced with a rudimentary Japanese . . . though we can each speak an impeccable 'Japanese' and an 'English.' i seem to have written for 'her' as much as anyone, including myself. i think i have done so because we have always known that true-words can't ever cost a penny and when they do they shouldn't cost more than anybody alive can afford. Words, at least all the homely words, are—we have always known this in our daily *usage* and our daily *keeping*.—All this meander just to tell you i'm fit and waiting (like everybody else) for S-U-M-M-E-R T-I-M-E and all the easy livin'. Hang on to dear life and toll the knell of these our Halcyon Days of the End of another damned Century. . . . do you two think that my Pear Tree Pomes will grow into its own book this year?   love

June 7th, '85/ noon

My Dear Mayumi:

Let the enclosed 'billings' tell you how busy I have been—at least since you so unexpectedly phoned me. Let all the days since Totsuka be at least partially acknowledged by the enclosed cassette tapes. Let it be known that I have sung thee, over and over again, and that I have been quite thoroughly wrung out. 'I' seem to no longer know 'how' I stand to a woman, whether it be my mother (who is visiting with me) or 'you' among a host of others who remain in my life. Let these cassette tapes tell you how I have felt and why there isn't any other way of telling you. I'll never be able to say my feelings to you in Japanese and that's part of my chagrin. I'll never be able to speak a plain enough English for you to grasp. All I can think tells me to be glad that 'we' did sing together. And that was quite enough. Anyhow, I have been thinking about Nippon and the possibility of my going there again this summer. If I do, it'll be in July/August and would certainly include a stop-over in Totsuka, as well as Kyoto/Gotenyama, and of course Kohama/Okinawa. Meanwhile, have a *listen* and be assured that I'll let you know of my whereabouts one way or another. Love to Hiro and Rae.

p/s   my so-called singing
        accompanied by your real singing
        of a piece titled The
        Ace of Hearts occurred at
        the Western Front

        Sarah Vaughn singing
        'Thanks for the Memories . . .'
        courtesy Co-op Radio

        on the other tape
        a reading/chanting of k-u-m-o
        and other soundings
        (see the enclosed billings)

        have you been tuning your voice to
        the sounds of Totsuka . . . ?

                                                                 love

June 12th, '85, noon

Claudia stoppt off for a few days after attending an astrology conference and before she flew back to Pennsylvania. Daphne and Kit will be coming by this afternoon before Kit flies off to Hawaii and Australia with his step-brother Colin to join his real father and step-mother down under. from whence they'll go on to other parts of Asia and then to parts of Europe before flying home in the early fall. meanwhile, Daphne and Betsy will be moving to Edmonton where Daphne will be the recumbent poet in residence at the U. of A. ceaseless criss-crossing would seem to characterize my wayward summer days. and to top it all off, my aged (89) mother is with me for most of June, and need i tell you how our days together reenact an earlier mother and child rite of passage? blitz'd, i mind each moment as if it contained all moments whatsoever, and so the day's entrance in my errant psyche. hallowed be thy name. let thy kingdom be built under the beneficence of Pinnacle Mountain. this lout would invoke all things archaic for the sake of infusing the least movement of my mother's thin arm lifting to stir her cup of morning tea. the least sound begets a fundament of feelings. though i do not know the shape of the coming summer days, i can safely say that they include the thought of coming out to Quebec to spend a week or so with you . . . all this will surely crystallize sooner than ever. have a listen: have a read.

June 15, '85

Bart:

Got yr Boston letter with its copious notes.
I suppose you are wondering what's become of your erstwhile collaborator.
To tell the truth, I'm up to my neck revising WHEELS
And looking after my 89 year old Mother who is visiting with me.
After all the Performance and Exhibitions after
All the abysmal Politics of another Academic Year and the Poverty of
Our current callit Post-modern Pedagogy I haven't had
A single worthwhile thought for us : thus the
Incontinent Letter-Writer is no good for anything but lame excuses
Ad nauseam. For what it's worth—I'm still thinking
Of flying off to Nippon & Kohama Island come July—I'm thinking of
How I might rejuvenate my scoured psyche. Meanwhile . . .
The Summer Solstice awaits us and the 1st of August will soon be with us.
Bart: There are lotsa musicians & dancers of all sorts
In the local J/C community who I'm more than certain would take part
In the 'outlined' Performance Pieces. All you have to do
Is (1) tell Masio 'what' and 'whom' you want. & (2) be on hand early
Enough to get acquainted with the Scene: the rest will happen.
If I seem to be leaving the Occasion open-ended, it's because
Of my wanting to escape the city and thus escape all prior commitments.
It's because I'm in need of Replenishment. Meanwhile, have a listen
Have a read and I don't know if Masio mentioned it to you, but
You're more than Welcome to stay in my Powell Street Studio (adjacent to
Oppenheimer Park 'where' the festival takes place): the Offer
Holds whether I collaborate (one way or another) or not.
I like your 'ideas' of Planks in Equilibrium with concomitant poetry
&/or cacophonous sounds. I can envisage a taut balancing act.
Bart: the Festival Crowd is both 'local' and otherwise. ——it can take
All you have to put out. Keep in touch. I'll let you know
What I'm up to within a couple of weeks at most. I remember visiting
The Isabella Stewart Gardner Museum in Boston years ago before
Busing down to N.Y. for the Premier of Marat/Sade. Ah! The Flaming '60s!
B.C. Bennett notwithstanding. Heartfelt Regards,

June 16th, '85

Bart:

It's already the eve of the long summer solstice and i do remind myself that you will be here in a short month for the Powell Street Festival. At this very moment the only thought I have for you is this—— that I will certainly do everything I can with/for you for the P.S.F. even if I happen to be 'elsewhere.' Mother is still with me. Need I tell you that the toll of these long summer days will grace whatever you/we do? Bart: if you want to get the Air of late summer/ early autumn into a Performance, you could think of an outdoor piece in amongst the Festive Folk in the Park. That, plus an Indoor on-stage piece at the Fire Hall Theatre: Like 2 Tilts on a See-saw. Speaking of 'see-saws'—how about 2 of them —parallel to each other and parallel to the front of the stage—(big sculptural ones) on which 4 Performers slowly teeter-totter while chanting/ declaiming/ singing/ playing instruments/ etc. Bart: you can shape it just so far in your mind: giving an actual Performance calls upon our most lively intuitions aided and abetted by the talent around. Like I say, the Vancouver J/C Community has lots of it: musicians, poets, speakers, singers, & dancers aplenty to tap into. Open mind / Open doors. Lattices of Summer.

June 18th, '85

Dear Sonja:

Summer's here at last. Here it is a few scant days till the Summer Solstice, and all my body can say is Ah it's here at last O let it burn away all the accumulated spring mildew. Let it be a moveable feast or better still a fistful of fire to alloy this my 59th summer. Mother has been with me throughout June. She'll be 89 soon. Like your own Mother, tough as nails. And brimful of the family and all its sundry gossip. Why—it was just the other day she asked about your once crazy husband, what's his name. She wondered aloud if Sam's gimpy walk had straightened out. She never mentions 'us' anymore in the same breath. She hasn't any reason left to. Down the years I have often been unforgiving when I had to listen to her chatter—but these mid-June days we have spent together simply prove to me that she is the authentic oral historian of our family and will go right on talking till the end because there is no other way of telling the real truth of how her consciousness shapes time. And need I tell you that time seems to be of the essence when it comes to telling the tales of a clan or tribe. Like 'who' married whom, when, and how did so and so turn out to be a real arse hole and 'why' do some people die before their time while others seem to outlive their pulse and on and on. Anyhow, we'll never lock horns again 'cause we both know the roots of all those frailties each of us has been born with and we both know what sheer perseverance means. I'm sending you a couple of Nippon books I've recently read and thoroughly enjoyed. I couldn't think of another *person* who might get off on them as 'they' are also part of that huge fiction Nippon has become as the foremost exponent of Western-Style Technology or, like the lies of us, a habitable corner of our very consciousness. If you can't get into them, you could hand them on.

Ah now I remember why I sat down to write you a letter: would you believe me if I told you that I am still haunted by the loss of my 3 canisters of super-eight film— the film, together with the cassette sound tracks—I misplaced that summer? No sooner had Mother arrived, she tells me that she too had been re-tracing all of our steps and that the only possible place left in her head as the likely place was the very first place we stayed at in Yokohama before we went on up to Maya's place and hence on to Osaka and Kochi City. Now, Mother doesn't have the least notion of that Inn's proper name because she never remembers hearing it. I, for my part, remember 'you' in the Yokohama Bus Terminal looking in the local telephone book for an inexpensive place to stay. And it was you who got us there that night, and didn't we stay another night after that? Anyhow, Sonja—scratch your noodle and see if you can come up with that working-class Inn's proper name, if not its actual address. I can then get my friends Mayumi & Hiro to ask about it, though I know it's belated. Then & only then I'll let it go, go for good. Hope you're having a bright prairie summer and may your garden thrive. Sam, likewise.

your ex-officio
lover

June 24th, '85

Dear Stan and Others at the Coach House Press:

. . . It doesn't look as if I'll get to Nippon this summer unless I go late. It doesn't feel that way this the day after the longest day of the year here in Vancouver B/C. O I know I could simply take-off and leave the work undone till i got back but the truth of the matter is that I have already put it off too long and it's reached a point 'where' it can no longer wait. I am, of course, speaking about WHEELS and the final ineluctable text. Almost 15 years down the line and shit!— it's still perplexed! still vext!

. . . Anyhow, I'm going to go to work on it and, come what may, I shall hang in with *it* till it's completely present-intense. I do have all the snapshots ready to be enfolded in the body of the text. Now, all I have to do is sit here till the very text straightens itself out, word by word, and then I'll get it away to you. My god, how, how I do want it out from under my delinquent fingers! Then there's the additional goad—the desire to be on the road. The desire to meet a handsome Lady, which, given my hermetic life, isn't very likely unless I let myself go out into the big wide world. One thing seems certain this summer and that's how fraught air travel has become. Ah, perhaps 'travel' has become, to all intents and purposes, mordant, if not moribund. Only 'air' permits that unspeakable fall-from-grace: that terrifying free-fall. I'll take WHEELS almost any day despite its frictive momentums, its linear ways. So, hang in thar.

. . . All through the live long summer day I have sat at my desk working on WHEELS and I have barely completed another 3 or 4 pages. All through the years that *these* and other wheels turned, I have let the better part of my life be enfolded in an unending series of discrete words by which a simple story might be told. But the real truth of the matter has had to do with the ardor of finding my own voice and its proper apparel. Thus, it is that WHEELS is a re-engagement with what I would call an immersion inside the whole body of an erratic, sometimes antic, syntax, not to mention all the hype of an ancient grammar. All of my life I seem to have to discover the root/s of the arts I practise within myself. Thus an almost incessant trial-and-error dogs my work habits completely—if someone had told me years ago how arduous the act of art is, I wouldn't have kept it up all these lunar years: I wouldn't have spent my life thus. Or would I? 'Repetition'— though never the same nuances twice—seems to be part of the way we are in the world, singly, or together. How many ways are there—seems inflecting even the word 'the,' let alone the world/s of, say, the word 'mother'—let alone the 'father' of this cargo of platitudes riding these rumbling iron wheels.

. . . For what it's worth, I've leased a 'canon' copier that both enlarges and reduces along with all the other characteristics of most copiers and I intend to try to reproduce both snapshots and text the actual size of the book we want. I'm into it as a project that will, hopefully, enable you to follow through with our book. And, yes, I'm going to get into 'it' as a way of printing up small editions of all the abbreviated texts I have on hand which nobody in their right minds would want to have much to do with. I'm quite looking forward to callit the immediacy of turning out a wee book without all the usual hindrances of going through the whole book publishing system with its quirks and delays. I'll certainly let you in on my canon copier adventures. Meanwhile, my DEADLINE for WHEELS is July 16th. Stand by—there'll be a spiffy manuscript arriving at the Coach House shortly. . .

Circa July '85

Dear Linda:

at Kaya Kaya, Toronto

a letter to read over tea and biscuits at Kaya Kaya

my 89 year old mother spent a whole month with me: she had had a hard winter in Edmonton and caught an infection which led to a gradual debilitation and a lack of hunger—thus, she arrived, grey, wizened and without the least appetite. i was quite appalled upon seeing her. the long days of a west coast summer passed. i for the most part simply went about my work and she for her part crocheted and watched her favorite television soaps when she didn't get visiting, or had a caller. my three daughters all came by regularly to pay court. at one time one weekend i had 4 generations staying with me including Esko Anton, my year-and-a-half old grandson. need i say that each of our days had a poignancy? yesterday, in the awful aftermath of that Air India flight and the explosion in Narita airport, i saw her off at the airport where hundreds of overseas passengers were all having their baggage scrupulously searched. older than the century itself, mother hasn't the least fear of flying: she even said she would like to go to Nippon once more if one of her children had the time and would be willing. she was six years old and already going to school when the Wright brothers flew one of the 1st planes. now a mere seventy odd pounds, she never talks of the end but I know that she has spent whole days, weeks and months alone with her thoughts and at her age they would include her own mortality. it was only after i got home from the airport that i noticed she had left a gift behind. it consisted of the lace doily she spent the past month crocheting: she had placed it under my bowl full of assorted shells from the island of Kohama in Okinawa which sat in the center of my tatami table. i looked at it. took it up from under the bowl and really looked at it and marveled at its interlacings. i thought of how she had either knitted, sown, or crocheted all the live long days of her life and all the untold blessings each shaped thing bestowed. i thought of the brevity of the days she had left . . . i thought of my own share of breath as that bounty she had bestowed . i almost cried. love to Mike and all

August 9th, '85, 7 pm

d'ear Rhoda
      and Trudi if she wants to

i'm booked to return on the 26th just a few days before UBC sessions and all that begins. i've succeeded in driving myself out of the house at last—now i can begin to do nothing but live it up without letting either 'will' or 'intentionality' intervene: at least for 2 weeks. got nothing in particular planned but Toronto, and if i'm lucky Monreale, with or without my friends: summer has taken a bunch of them away to other parts of earth.

—if you and you come by to do any printing or otherwise, you could throw the back patio door open and if you want the front door too (while you're printing or simply present) just to freshen the air in the house, and, yes, water and spray my three, no four, plants. (the big jade out on the back porch is quite a water gobbler. the medicinal cacti beside it should be sprayed regularly but infrequently watered. as for the big leafy avocado in the print room, it too gets real thirsty and needs a pint or more water every few days. not to mention a tonic spray job. the small bristling cacti in the middle of the living room window facing Heatley make a tablespoon of water go a long way. it's been a wondrous bloomin' as it has now bloom'd seven times.) don't worry about the back garden: the best view of it is from my study/bedroom window. you'll find that the house is as quiet and secure as a house can be and do 'be'/be at home. Kiyo knows you're goin' to be around. Jan and Scott haven't got back from Quebec City and Mariko might phone, tho it's unlikely—just tell'em who you are and get on with whatever you're doin'.

(. . . i have been into cleaning up my act: i seem to have been articulating the completion of the 2nd Cycle on the threshold of the irrevocable 3rd Cycle comin' up. 'give your whiff of a life the fulsome shape it deserves' has been the injunction. 'tan reiki' they name 60 in Nippon: a time to be re-birthed.

Rhoda: by all means let's share some laughter when i'm back.

Nov. 1st, '85

My Dear Fuku & Michun :

My 2nd daughter Fumiko (Jan) will be coming to Nippon to attend a showing of her movie. You will probably hear from her via Syuzo Fujimoto & Family with whom she will be visiting. Let her tell you about 'herself' and yours truly. It is astonishing to see my 3 daughters (now grown women) making their way in the world, albeit an ofttimes trying world: like—only 'yesterday' they were children and myself a gullible grown man with nothing but paint, music & words to glue a life together. I have read the letter that Nora your granddaughter wrote on your behalf at the time of your 'exhibitions.' It has moved me many times by its lucid telling. And need I tell you that I have looked through the catalogue of your paintings & drawings many times and many a time since I have sat down to write to you but somehow I couldn't bear with it. The catalogue has been passed around in the community I am a part of and much appreciated. If I ever get to INDIA it'll be in part because of your haunting paintings. Chances are it'll never happen but there's no telling what's in store as far as the so-called future goes:—I know it opens onto death . . . but the rest of what's left of breathing is hopefully open-ended. Nippon is a 'burrow' in my conscienceness I sometimes lie in & other times I simply fall into. I'll never be 'Japanese' 'cause I'll never be at home in your language. This I know with chagrin and it's something I've felt the twinges of all my life. This face bears the mark of one whose 'mother-tongue,' despite all appearances, is English (shikata-ne). The Book of Colour Photographs will tell you something about the vast & varied landscape of Canada. Both Isamu & Kazuko will know some of it. As does Syuzo & others. The other hand-made book 'October Terrain' has been compiled with all of my Japanese friends in mind. Think of it as a kind of mirror held up to the world that you can (also) read your faces in. Sitting here on the far side of the Pacific during a typical October squall and thinking of all of you living your equally fervent lives—I feel your friendship as intimately as those friendships I have here. If Nora is still in Nippon have her interpret this letter for you. The days pass. . . . Each day ravishes me: I'm ofttimes left speechless. Caught up utterly in the palpableness of the world, I am sometimes its sere witness. Sometimes an empty vessel. To leave a grace-note in the air of our times seems presumptuous. I am nothing but water, air, wood, earth & metal: an aggregate of base elements with an urge to 'ongaku.' I didn't get to Nippon this past summer. My work kept me close to home and before I knew it was the end of summer. But I am already telling myself that I shall have to spend next summer over there—if I keep telling myself it's bound to happen. It is such a moisture-laden grey day I tell myself, 'you' too are being nurtured, and yet the chill in the air reminds me of both 'death' & Kohama's hot sand beaches. Revery & heat.

November '85

vegetable being
veritable inclinations: posited

by the earth's gyrations
an instinct to lean towards the sun

indistinct thrum of all the
un-sounded music-of-the-spheres

a radiant rain-drop rolling
off the serrated tip of a downward curving leaf

that 'plop' you hear
is not the rain drop's actual sound

'language' often creaks
when it can't sing a song of frankincense

bend your pitiless inclinations
into a pretzel . watch—

the tear drop rolling down my cheek—
hear its silent madrigal

accentuate the ridiculous and the sublime
vegetable/beings

veritable inclinations climb the wall
fall down and crack up

(try putting a crackt egg together with bond-fast

<u>V E G E T A B L E / B E I N G / S</u>

Being a Suite of unhurried Poems
To Complement Richard Turner's Monotypes
To Speak 'of' 'for' 'with' & 'to'
Them—as We Speak over a coffee, ofttimes
stoned, to each other. Being, to
all intents & purposes, A Desire to Dwell

within the Palette of a Monotype
and Deciphering its Paradigmatic Colours
show forth a pensive wisdom. Being
among myriad things, at least one part
'vegetable,' these words sprout their
very own waxen-wings. Vegetable-Mind i
also be betoken an image's nurture.
Let the lion and the lamb lie down together
in the mind's own cage and let them
roar and bleat till these poems turn green.

he thought that each man and woman who cares for domesticated animals like dogs and cats probably cared for them within the bounds of their intrinsic nature and in no wise act differently towards their pets than their human relatives or friends. he thought of all the assorted cats that played an intrinsic part in his friends' daily habits and how they all tended to be mostly black and how they seemed at all times to be as integral to his living/working space as, say, his heapt up foam egg cartons and all the paraphernalia of painting and printmaking, plus all the finished and unfinished work hanging from all four walls, and it seemed inevitable that one or another of his many and varied cats got into a painting, print or monotype and almost invariably (excepting those occasions he really let loose and toppled over into an utter fantasy) they took the place within the frame of the monotype and looked as if they utterly belonged. it seemed to him that the seemingly casual way cats stayed in his life bespoke a willingness to let the cat or cats live on the verge of an instinctive wildness and let them be inalterably steadfast to their own natures. it was the way the 'beast' in him prowled through the miasmic hues he could conjure up on a small sheet of glass and, without once showing his sharp teeth, allow a vegetable being to seem real: it takes a special nature to divine a cat's soul and perhaps that is what accounts for the fact that there aren't that many fabled if not famous cat paintings.

for want of the perfect word to describe these
'transformed' mask/s or are they face/s for want of a precisely
relevant precursor of the transformed face/s i might
extravagantly cite 'so and so' the eccentric vegetable-face painter
or closer to our own modality of a berserk madness Francis
Bacon or again Peter Peter the pumpkin eater, etc.
in that sense of citations these transmogrified faces are neither
delinquent or especially daring. nonetheless, i am
startled by how a thin viscous swatch of colour can suddenly
jerk into a mendacious leer and simply by blinking
my eyes that same swatch together with all the other dabs and runnels
of colour funnel through my mind's eye and turn into
a cavernous critter with gloating epidermis. these small monotypes
of transmogrified faces flatter our tatterdemalion psyches.

i, for instance, have looked intently at them and, though
i thought often enough that my own face lay embedded within them, i
also felt the steadfast gaze of an alien race of once glorified
but now largely nullified Aryan Gods and that pinnacle
they in their madness ascended to got fused into each and every
seam and runnel of these, these perdurable grimaces.

it was almost as it he had turned away from painting to get into poetry and getting into poetry enabled him to get into his friend's paintings in all those ways 'talking it up' never seem to enable. it was almost as if his friend forsook sculpture to get into painting and, having got himself embedded there, he buried his literacy in the sparkle and murk of his palette only to enable this act of extrication. these words retrace the etymology of all vegetable/beings back to a primal clasp of air. all paintings breathe an unleavened act of grace. these monotypes are leaves from a Braille textbook of un-named beasts. these words are their beast of burden: they'll never surmise the meaning of the aura that surrounds and enfolds each pristine hue. death is an un-named blossom that stains the upraised hand.

vegetable/being
veritable inclinations posited by
the earth's gyrations
an instinct to lean towards the sun
indistinct thrum of
all the music of the spheres
a raindrop rolling
off a downward curving leaf

the plop you hear
is not the rain drop's plop
language often creaks
when it can't sing. sing
a song of frankincense . . .
bend your inclinations
into pretzel. watch
the tear drop roll down my cheek
listen to its silent
descent. accentuate the
ridiculous and the sublime
vegetable beings
veritable inclinations

imagine an arm length away

tv set with both utterly static-images
interfaced with quick-dissolves
& a kaleidoscope of images . imagine
yourself sitting at a table
littered with the evening meal & a heap
of butts watching an untitled
Tableau. . . . minutes may seem to be
ticking by but nothing moves . . .
till you reach out to tap a tiny button
and another indissoluble image
does its silent caper on your retina.
imagine all this while you light
up another cigarette and nothing seems
to be happening, nothing will move
the image ahead 'cause you have
pickt up your ballpoint pen and begin
to write *the conversation* you have
all along been having with *it*.

i have stared at this or that image
startled by it i have sometimes found a
phrase on which it can escalate into
a riddled moment   these words have been
shifted through the same trance that
continues to adhere to his entranced 'i'
surmising a daub of un-named colour

all the tropes of a formal speech lie
embedded in the runnels and shifting
planes of colour, all the silences too.

Isamu/ Kazuko & others:

  listening to some of my 'Kohama' tapes lying awake in the middle of a winter night : hearing, like a lover's whisper'd murmur, the distant outgoing tide behind Oji's jamisen and Okinawan songs, i warm my thin body by the remember'd warmth of all of you and your conviviality. more and more i tend to surround myself with either music of my own making or the music of my friends wherever they be . less and less am i taken by callit the symphony of ambitious soundings, the stock-in-trade of so-called great orchestral music with all its intricate sonorities, its ability to move a musical elite i feel no part of . it becomes clearer as i grow older that it's the simple heartfelt kinds of music/song that make me glow, tap my feet and cry . toss a song into the tropic air . shape a pithy legend and let it drown in somebody's ear . sometimes i think that all of our silences hug a small song . i'm sorry i didn't get these books off to you sooner but my intentions are well meant : i've been keeping an eye out for the kinds of N.A. Indian/ Eskimo legends you might be interested in and here they are in one bundle . listen, listen for the wind in between the words of these stories and you'll hear the innumerable dialects of an almost dead if not withdrawn language-system : the 'English' of their re-telling is an empty chalice burnisht by the millennial winds of N.A. 'i' of course grew up with cowboys and Indian legends and have been in my own way an Indian among the motley of white men, but i have never heard or had an occasion to listen to an 'Indian' tell his own story in his native dialect . it would almost seem that 'he,' despite his ongoing actual presence among us at all times, exists as an act of judicious translation tho, as i come upon him, i would believe he embodies a lost, once sacral, ground of callit 'being' in his millennial perseverance .

Dec. '85

The Canada Council / Explorations Grants

Dear Richard Holden:

    The book of Talking (provisional title) is well underway with Gerry Gilbert, one of Vancouver's poets par excellence, acting as editor, grammarian and transcriber. We've been doing an awful lot of miscell. listing from a heap of divers cassette tapes accumulated over 20 yrs. The whole process is a bit like strip mining—yards of verbal muck to uncover a small lode of telling words, etc. Anyhow, we do intend to get on with it and complete it in this the Chinese Year of The Tiger.

    The *Pacific Rim Letters* (provisional title) is in its post-sifting and correlating phase. They cover the period from 1975 (the year my *Transcanada Letters* were publisht by Talon Books) till the very end of this (ah now) past year. In bulk, it'll be a comparable size to T.L., with a larger preponderance of letters to friends in Japan. My no. 3 daughter is undertaking the re-typing of the extant letters and this should be completed by early summer. Apropos both G.G. and my daughter Kiyo, see the last bit of my letter of application wherein I state that I intend to hire somebody in the Vancouver Writing Community to carry the work out under my supervision.

    The enclosed statements, including the receipt for the word-processor, ought to speak for themselves.

                                  Please forward the 2nd Installment so
                                  we can get on with both projects.

                                                      Yours sincerely,

AFTERWORD

for what it's worth

Special Delivery
300 letters. One sender, Roy Kenzie Kiyooka. Many addressees. Often even more than one recipient of the same letter—'Dear Isamu and Kazuko,' 'Dear Mike and Linda,' 'Dear Richard and Vicki.' Letters to friends, lovers, daughters, associates, acquaintances. Kiyooka writing to his students, the Canada Council, the National Film Board, galleries, the Governor General of Canada. Kiyooka writing to Kiyooka.

300 letters written over a period of nine years, 1976 to 1985, sent from 648 Keefer Street, Kiyooka's house, or 356 Powell Street, his studio cum Blue Mule Photo Gallery. Some never mailed. Many belonging to a chain of letters between Kiyooka and his addressees. Some re-written after they were mailed. All of them copied. Perhaps some of his correspondents didn't know, or if they did they didn't necessarily like, that he copied his letters to them; perhaps they expected the cipher always included in a letter in figural ink—*Dear X, this is just between you and me, this letter is for your eyes, and yours alone*—to be honored. Or they felt—still feel so?—that a letter should not traverse beyond the space between letter-writer and addressee. But they must have known. They must have known that RK was not a disloyal friend, but that he had a thing about copying letters, copying them in good faith and, what's more, publishing them. I imagine most of them knew that.

300 letters.[2] Written on a typewriter, carbon-copied or photocopied at home on his Canon copier. Signed 'Roy' or 'Roy K. Kiyooka'—the capital letters in clean, bold strokes—in black, often red or brown-gold, ink. An afterthought often scribbled on the spot. Typos unabashedly left intact, small cues to the urgency of the given moment, an attribute of Kiyooka's signature. Letters folded and placed into envelopes, photographs, and other inserts often slipped into them. Then taken, on foot, to the post office, most likely the post office in Chinatown, Vancouver. Perhaps after a brief pause under his much-written-about pear tree, Roy lending an ear to the chattering starlings in its bare branches, or saying hello to Jim, the ace mechanic. Stamps attached to the right hand corner of the

> i mean to go right on making carbons of [my letters]—i aint got scruples abt literary proprieties and do want to keep some sort of a record of my own thots viz letters. besides letters are the only things i write sometimes and they happen to be written out of the same concern i wld bring to bear if i were writing something else.
> Letter to Phyllis Webb,
> *Transcanada Letters*[1]

envelope—his palate must have grown accustomed to stamp gum, perhaps even fond of it—the letters were dispatched to Montreal, Toronto, Edmonton, Kohama, Yellowknife, Vancouver.... The postal technology in action.

Letters by a major artist who went to Europe only once, but who frequently traveled from Vancouver to eastern Canada, from the Canadian west coast to the Far East. His unremitting correspondence lessened those geographical distances, 'West' and 'East' becoming a möbius strip, a figure keeping in sight, yet deconstructing, their uneasy alignments.

Though most of Kiyooka's letters certainly reached their recipients a long time ago, they have remained in transit all these years, waiting for their ultimate destination, a terminus they were intended for when they were first written. Some people may burn or otherwise destroy letters they write in a moment of heat or confession, while others may destroy letters they receive—fearing they might fall into the wrong hands. Trepidation about a letter being purloined goes hand in hand with the compulsion to write letters. Letter-writers with a public profile often spell out in detail the terms under which their letters can be accessed, or have their letters sealed for years to come after their death. T.S. Eliot's 1,131 letters to Emily Hale, reportedly the largest single collection of his letters in the world, are sealed in the Firestone Library, Princeton University, until January 1, 2020. Kiyooka did not share this need to maintain the putative privacy of letters, at least not the confidentiality of the letters he wrote. His letter-writing was writing at the limits of public and private space. It is in this sense that these letters have reached now their ultimate terminus—terminus not as the end of a line, a projected place of arrival, but a space where a route ends while another one begins.

Pacific Rim Letters, a one-time delivery, lets Kiyooka post, as it were, his letters yet again, only this time they apostrophize the moniker that has been indelibly inscribed all along behind every one of his addressees. *Dear Reader...* Without their proper names being erased, his initial addressees are translated into you and me. 11 years after his death, 30 years after the original publication of *Transcanada Letters*, these letters written on the Pacific rim change hands. Their itineraries find a new destination, appropriately so, for Kiyooka's letter-writing was—is—a series of performative gestures that have always been intended to journey towards this event: the reception of his letters by his

> Usually the last things that get published—it mostly happens posthumously—are the letters. The old morality postulated that letters were of a 'personal nature'—therefore discretion, particularly as it affected one's contemporaries, was of the utmost importance, etc. What I'm doing with my letters is releasing them as contemporaneous as possible with the events they are talking about. *The psyche as muse.*
>
> Kiyooka 'Laughter'⁵

> THIS is my letter to the world,
>   That never wrote to me,—
> The simple news that Nature told,
>   With tender majesty.
>
> Emily Dickinson

> Alvin Balkind: You don't see your letters as a summing up, do you?
> Kiyooka: No I don't, though the overview would propose that as some kind of a possibility, but in actual fact it's too fragmentary. I've got a jigsaw puzzle which I don't know the extent of, which I've started piecing together, that's all.
>
> 'Laughter,' 12

imagined—imaginary yet real—readers. And though these letters remain—at least technically—the same, they are transfigured in this exchange of readers, become othered to themselves. Similarly, their original recipients may be unchanged, but our reading of the letters sent to them reveals new correspondences. The letters' publication, then, results in a different reciprocity between Kiyooka and his readers-addressees. All this in keeping with the fact that Kiyooka as sender is never wholly self-present, that letter-writing is no more authentic than fiction, that life-writing is always incomplete.

if this letter should happen to find you, you'll know why i'm not at home.[4]

It must have been about a year after Kiyooka's death in early January 1994 when, while visiting Vancouver and staying with Roy and Slavia Miki, that I first saw and browsed through 'Pacific Rim Letters,' a typescript spiral-bound in two volumes, 417 pages in total. Miki was in the process of editing the major project Kiyooka had left unfinished at the time of his death, *Pacific Windows: Collected Poems by Roy K. Kiyooka*, published in 1997. As Miki explains in his 'Afterword,' Kiyooka had decided to collaborate with him on collecting and editing the poems, but what was meant to be an '"involved" production process' (302) inevitably became 'one-sided' (310) when Kiyooka died suddenly. 'Pacific Rim Letters' was 'an indispensable resource' Miki relied on to continue with his editing (300).[5] Nevertheless, *Pacific Windows* was not the only project Kiyooka had left incomplete when he died. While Miki was clearly designated to see through the editing and publication of the collected poems, 'Pacific Rim Letters' was a typescript in search of an editor.

Be it poetry, photographs, or music, there was habitually more than one project Kiyooka worked on at any given time. Even though he had already begun to assemble the letters together, he was not necessarily engaged with the editing of 'Pacific Rim Letters' at the time of his death. A project he was without doubt at work on at that time was the interviews with his mother that Matsuki Masutani, on Kiyooka's own request, had conducted and recorded in Japanese. His daughters Mariko, Fumiko, and Kiyo invited Daphne Marlatt to edit this project. Marlatt was still in the process of editing this text when she and I got together in Victoria to talk about its publication.

Kiyooka: I've got six incomplete texts, and I pick them up every so often and I sit down to them, and if I can, I really get into them. [. . .]
I haven't established any hierarchy of writing. There are people who are really facile, and they can say, oh well I'll do this this weekend, and then I'll do this the next. I've never had any of that—never, never, never had that.
Roy Miki: Well, when do you know when a text is over with?
K: I abandon it. That's what I do, really.
M: You abandon it, then it's completed, well it's not completed, but it's over with.
K: Or it abandons me, either way.[6]

The large publishing house in Toronto that had declared an interest in publishing it was insisting, contrary to Marlatt's editorial sentiments, on editing that would result in a more accessible and, therefore, marketable text. Kiyooka would have looked right and then left, chin slightly raised, and laughed at this logic for bringing a book to life. He often lamented the impact the market economy had on the arts, a recurring motif in his work, but he did not stop publishing; he relied on 'self-publishing as a way of getting [his] words out' (RK Papers, quoted in Miki's 'Afterword' 301).[7] Indeed, he never forfeited the imperative he felt to 'hazard an audience.' 'Hazard' not in the sense that Kiyooka feared that no readers would be interested in what he had to say, nor in the sense that he felt vulnerable to any unenthusiastic response his writing might have elicited, but in the sense that, though 'beholden to the white culture,' he felt compelled to speak out about things that mattered to him, things that took to task the cultural establishment, and did so in an uncompromising fashion. As he says in 'Inter-Face,' his interview with Roy Miki, 'one has the authorial look of what gets published, but if you're like me'—'like me' referring to his Japanese Canadian identity—'you know how vulnerable you are in terms of what it costs you to be able to say what you have been able to say, and knowing that once you go through that ground you never look back. You can't, because it was sort of crawled over' (51). His unrelenting attentiveness to the world 'dictated' that he did so. Hence often assuming in his writing the part of reader, the role of listener. As he did in the case of his mother's story.

There was no doubt in my mind, when Marlatt let me read Mary Kiyoshi's telling of her life, that this was not only an 'accessible' narrative—at once as transparent and opaque as any life narrative can be—but a story that demanded and deserved an audience. An issei woman's memories about her immigrant experience in Canada, it is an archive of the domestic and the social. Bursting with nostalgia for Tosa (Kochi City)—her 'heart's true country'—it is also inexorably Canadian. Moving yet unsentimental, Mary Kiyoshi's story is inextricably related to what has shaped Kiyooka and his writing. Her story and his letters complement each other, two chapters in the long serial narrative that encompasses Kiyooka's entire work. I proposed the manuscript for publication to NeWest Press. *Mothertalk: Life Stories of Mary Kiyoshi Kiyooka* was released at the same time as *Pacific Windows* edited by Miki and published by Talonbooks.[8]

<u>this would be closer to a closet syntax if</u>

i didn't hazard an <u>audience:</u> hear me—I found myself with
a lacuna on my hands and despite my reticulations
caught myself——talking, out loud.
these words propose to be
an exact dictation, wherein every word counts as it
were for a parallel number of exact heart-beats. monitoring
my pulse with a laser stop-watch I counted out my portion of syllables
and wrote them down. [. . .] these unrepentant
lines would surely crumble into a ziggurat of formless
nonsense, un-monitored by pulse. there's both a <u>redneck</u> and a
fraudulent <u>epistemologist</u> lamenting for a nation inside
this hive of antinomies. sodomized lobotomized & c-b-c-itized
their latinate etymologies turn into perma-frost. homer's
perdurable odyssey and mao's long march, notwithstanding. [. . .] that awful
'DEFICIT' in which all the
'advanced nations of the western european/north american world'
seem to be hopelessly mired in— conflates our toxic nightmares.——
let's face it, <u>poetry</u>
won't, by a long shot, re-settle the gaza strip or even finger
aboriginal rights but—and this is my pitch—it at
the very least deserves its fair share of 'prime-time' for all
the <u>forlorn ears</u>
   March : Prose : Works n.p.

Though there was another unfinished typescript of Kiyooka's that Miki showed me on that occasion in Vancouver, it was 'Pacific Rim Letters' that posed, I felt, an 'urgency' to find an editor and see the light of publication. While I hope that 'The Artist and the Moose: A Fable to Forget,' a satiric novel about Canadian culture centering on Tom Thomson, which 'abandoned' Kiyooka in 1989, would find an editor some day,[9] I considered taking on the editing of the letters. Permission from Kiyooka's estate to edit 'Pacific Rim Letters' and publish them with NeWest Press followed soon thereafter, but I did not start working on the project right away. Other commitments and various circumstances prevented me from doing so for a few years. Moreover, the fact that this was the first time I had undertaken to edit a writer no longer alive, a writer who as a person had not been a stranger to me, made this project a challenge. The death of the author, Roland Barthes' trope of asserting that an author's life and intentions are never immanent in what she or he writes, attained a particularly poignant irony in this instance. Reading Kiyooka's unfinished texts at that time, and talking, on those and subsequent occasions, about Kiyooka's work with Miki and Marlatt, as well as with other writers and friends of Kiyooka's on the West Coast, was a continuous wake, at once remembering and celebrating his work.

The more I reread 'Pacific Rim Letters,' the more I engaged myself with Kiyooka's other texts by rereading or teaching them, the more intricate and difficult my editorial task seemed to become. While *Pacific Windows* remained an invaluable source, it was *Transcanada Letters*, the forerunner to the letters I was to edit, that served as a constant point of reference. The first resolution I reached in that preliminary stage of editing— and the only one I never wavered about—was that *Transcanada Letters*, long out of print, had to appear again. While *Pacific Windows* has offered Kiyooka's faithful readers easy access to his poetry they already knew but also to chapbooks that had not been readily available, *Mothertalk* has earned Kiyooka a new generation of readers, many of whom not familiar with his earlier work. Though *Pacific Rim Letters* can certainly be appreciated on its own terms, it calls for *Transcanada Letters* not only as a companion, but as a measure of the scope of Kiyooka's letter-writing, a benchmark of his journeys within Canada, and between Canada and Japan, a compass for his trajectories from one art form to another.

> . . been working on Tom Thomson's Secret Papers the ones found all bundled up on the topmost cupboard of an attic attic cupboard. [. ..] A bundle of papers retrieved by a young friend a student of mine who was working for the demolition firm during the summers. He sent them to on knowing that I would be interested. And I have been going through them and I thinking that T.T. had a commonsensical (therefore a——Canadian?) view-of-things. [. ..] Anyhow, I've been working on Tom's secret papers and what will come out if viz my own writing is anyone's guess.
> Letter to the Mur-muring Maiden, TCL 175

A Scene of Inheritance

Pacific Rim Letters resembles a collection of letters gathered together after the death of their author, but it differs substantially from such volumes. As I have already mentioned, even in their present tense, at the time that they were written and mailed, these letters were intended to reach a readership beyond that of Kiyooka's correspondents. Though bona fide letters, written for specific and actual addressees, they were also composed as missives to the *polis* he inhabited. Collected together in this book, they exceed the economy of the postal system, and submit (their) delivery as a trope of inheritance. Their belatedness, insofar as their new readers are concerned, is symptomatic of the larger narrative inscribed in these letters—larger than the particular circumstances and occasions Kiyooka writes about, but developed through them both overtly and obliquely.

Offered as 'a biography of self cast upon the study wall,' *Pacific Rim Letters* constitutes a major part of the artistic and intellectual legacy Kiyooka has left us. Itself 'a humble heir of' the 'endless processional of words' that make up the cultural, social, and political history of our 'covert ideological times' (PRL vi), it belongs to the Western tradition of letters while, at the same time, exposing the underlying ideological assumptions of that tradition. It speaks, then, to the profound ambivalences that characterize Kiyooka's life as a multidisciplinary artist, a cultural practitioner, a Japanese Canadian citizen, teacher in the academy, family man, friend, and lover. These roles cannot stand apart from each other. Indeed, *Pacific Rim Letters* is a text that performs the convergences of these different selves. While written separately, then, assembled together these letters become an epistolary biography written in the first person, an autobiography written in dialogue with others. But the personal and artistic history that is composed letter by letter in this book leaves a door ajar to allow us a sustained look on the world at large. In this regard, these letters can also be read as commentary, *essais* in which Kiyooka expounded on photography, pedagogy, capitalism, 'art biz' in general. The 'weaving/ wavering narrative' that comes into view not only lays bare Kiyooka's 'obsessions' and 'truculent thoughts' (PRL vi), but also shows each letter embodying—sometimes subtly, sometimes fervently—Kiyooka' witnessing the profound changes in his social and cultural landscape. So, while most of his letters are 'apropos'—one

> where 'polis' touches
> 'eros' and both touch 'art' is to
> say the least / where you find me.
> *Pacific Rim Letters*[10] vi

> Art is not separable from the I
> that wld be a family man a husband
> father and brother. How shall I
> accomplish—thru Art the very
> shapeliness I can some sometimes
> 'see' as my life, etc. remains the most
> insistent the most compelling need.
> Letter to his Mother and
> Father, TCL 208

of his favorite words—of something that is of immediate and direct concern to him, they also chronicle with great alacrity the actuality, as well as the constructedness, of the world around him. Their account of the personal—translated into that of the cultural and the social, and vice-versa—constitutes Kiyooka's bequest to his readers. As a narrative, notwithstanding how partial, of Canadian cultural history between 1976-1985, *Pacific Rim Letters* may focus primarily on the local and the regional—be it Vancouver, B.C., or Kohama, Japan—but also moves towards the nation and beyond it, shuttling between the 'West' and the 'East.'

His first 'Book-of-Letters' (TCL, 356) covers a time in Kiyooka's life, 1966-1975, that can only be called hectic— numerous cultural activities and engagements, and many trips, all within Canada except for his milestone visit to Japan in 1969. During those four months in Japan he lived in Kyoto, but commuted daily to Osaka to construct 'Abu Ben Adam's Vinyl Dream,' his commissioned sculpture for Canada's pavilion at Expo 70. His forays to Expo's construction site occasioned *StoneDGloves* (1970), but also brought about the recognition

> Kiyooka: The dilemma that I've come to in terms of art is simply that I no longer know the form of anything. There isn't a form, a container, a structure, *per se*, that at this moment I can say of, I'm going to use that as the form of what I'm going to do. In that sense I've come to a most curious place, and that is: everything I'm going to make will have to find its form.
> Balkind: But you are after all gathering your letters together and that's a form. [. . .]
> K: It's an attempt to create a form, because the intent of the letters is not simply the fact of letters. It's an attempt to create some kind of space whereby the actual occasions of one's lived life from day to day can be given a relevance at that time in one's life, rather than in the future.
>   'Laughter' 12

> . . . that it all
> has something to do with a quest for our
> 'Sources': Roots or Ground, no matter, there is
> the urgencies of travel, the places We need
> and the depth of self the place may reveal to our
> selves. During the 4 yrs spent in Quebec I
> thought many times of how easy it wld be to grab
> a plane and fly to Europe for even a week-end.
> I never did and now that I'm back on the westcoast
> again) I am beginning to wonder if I ever will.
> Whereas, the Orient (sources?) seems to be
> a necessity therefore inevitable. The more so since
> I find it hard to have purchase of the sod I
> find myself an heir to. Thus, I see my own travel-
> ling as an actual need to plumb my own back-
> ground. Or its that we are all 'nomadic' and possess
> nothing nothing but our own bodies and that for
> only a short while. . . . (TCL 78)

> when I'm most bereft, it's the nameless Jap in me who sings an unsolicited haiku in voluntary confinement. I don't want to go on moanin' the old 'yellow peril' blues the rest of my days. Gawd save us all from that fate. [...] One day I want to tell you how music forms a linguistic bridge across the endless chasm of speech. One of those days I'll come by to play my dulcimer.
>   PRL 108

The inevitability he attributes to his attachment to Japan echoes, to appropriate Edward Said's words, his 'right to return,'¹¹ a right he exercised many times in the period 1976-1985 covered by *Pacific Rim Letters*. Even though the gist of *Pacific Rim Letters*, along with that of most of his writing, is a consequence of the amalgamation of the various aspects of his self, his Japanese heritage stands out as, perhaps, the element that most determined both the course of his life and his intellectual and political world-view. The memory of finding himself, at age sixteen, an unwelcome 'Jap' at high school—the aftermath of the invasion of Pearl Harbor—is inscribed in these letters in different ways and under various guises—as it is in his other writings.¹² But it would be a gross misreading to suggest that these letters memorialize that history as a compulsive recital. There are relatively few direct references to those experiences. But this does not suggest that their traumatic effects on Kiyooka had been transcended, as though that history had been safely contained in a finished past. The 'end of history,' or, for that matter, the 'death of history,'¹³ is a grand fiction intended to assuage guilt and anxiety at best, bigotry at worst, as much about the present as about the past, a quixotic stance that breeds complacency. These letters, through what they elide, summon up Kiyooka's personal and community history not as a continuous indictment, but as an articulation of his belief that the effects of history are not transient. *Pacific Rim Letters*, then, is a living archive of the legacy Kiyooka inherited as an 'Asian North Americano,' a legacy that persists. That these letters reach his readers at a time that has produced more refugees, displaced persons, exiles, and immigrants than ever before in history grants it a special poignancy. It is a subtle, yet powerful, exhortation to be vigilant about our historical moment, a bequest we cannot afford to ignore.

Pacific Rim Letters' method is, then, that of the poetics—and politics—of outwards, qualities making this text function as a scene of inheritance. Whether he plans one of his engagements—a performance at Scarborough, a reading in Toronto, an appearance in Montreal—or one of his trips to his beloved city Kohama, or takes a stand when he is denied a study leave as a professor of Fine Arts at the University of British Columbia, or resists 'free enterprise pedagogy,' Kiyooka invariably approaches, and stages, these activities as 'probing' events. In his letters to Lorraine Monk of the National Film Board (1977), requesting support for *13 Cameras*,¹⁴ a collaborative project of Vancouver photographers, 'probing' and 'probes' (as nouns) are the words

> Letter writing . . . is truly a communication with spectres, not only with the spectre of the addressee but also with one's own phantom, which evolves underneath one's own hand in the very letter one is writing.
> Kafka, *Letters to Milena*

> *begun as a book for the G.S.W.S.*
> *in Halifax N.S. Sept. 71*
> *with the title From Under*
> *The Granville Street Bridge—*
> *Sunday after the War—Outwards*
> *it is the book of a painter*
> *poet husband father brother friend*
> *and lover 'who' found a few of*
> *the missing pieces of a life*
> *and put them together.*
> 'DEDICATION,' TCL v

> 'pedagogy' is a wounded beast and whatever is festive about the 'arts' is doomed to be a sacrifical offering.
> Letter to Wilfred and Sheila Watson, PRL 303

he uses to describe the project's goal. Be they collaborative or not, such probing events show Kiyooka being deeply engaged with his social and cultural milieu.

The poetics and politics of outwards in this text, then, is neither a one-way forward movement nor is it a gesture towards a finish line. It is in this sense that *Pacific Rim Letters* is a scene of inheritance. It offers a record of the various legacies Kiyooka accumulated, but it does so not by unquestioningly recycling inherited values. Inheritance for Kiyooka, as I read him, goes hand in hand with his relentless probing. Embodying the past, but always actualized in the present, this inheritance now becomes our own—a *lesson*, a gift.

In the Mode of Inglish

Transcanada Letters ends with a letter to Daphne Marlatt written in the same place and month—Tuesday, April 15, 1975, Qualicum Beach, B.C.—as the letter addressed to her and her son Kit that opens *Pacific Rim Letters*.[15] Similarly, while the earlier title begins with a report sent to the Canada Council in 1966, the latter ends with a letter to the Canada Council, addressed to Richard Holden and written in December 1985. This structural correspondence between the two volumes—surely no mere coincidence—reflects the seriality of Kiyooka's composition method, but also affirms the two poles that marked his life trajectory: love and family, on the one hand, and art making, along with the inescapable commerce about 'art biz,' on the other. This is only one of the many similarities between these two collections of letters. An afterword is not the right place to offer a detailed analysis of how these two books relate to or depart from each other. Even so, I would like to highlight, briefly, some of the formal elements that recur in both, elements that grant Kiyooka's writing its distinctive signature.

Probing language

Readers who encounter Kiyooka's writing for the first time will no doubt be astounded by his use of the English language. In his own words, he writes as 'a white Anglo-Saxon protestant with a cleft tongue' (PRL 107), a Japanese Canadian who, had his life 'taken a slightly different turn' when he was younger, 'could have grown up and learned to read and write Japanese as fluently as English.' Writing in this cleft tongue means writing

if i make a gesture towards the least notion of a 'fine art' these days, it's within hailing distance of my neighborhood . I am sick onto death of disembodied art, by which I mean an art without an actual community except one's remorseless peer-group. [. . .] For what it's worth, 'i' a 2nd generation Asian immigrant's beloved son wants to write a hitherto unwritten chapter of The Big Book of Native Voices of The Pacific Rim Nation/s by writing/chanting/harping and snapping pictures of the Here and Now, Where I live and feel at home . There are, after all, these 'other' faces, 'other' voices and other concordances I have to be attentive to : to be sure—I'm moved to respond because RESPONDEZ is its own becoming.

PRL 252

[He] was tremendously articulate with a lineage of language that was utterly perverse. Somewhere within him was Wallace Stevens and Stanley Spencer, Jiminy Cricket and the art of Fontainebleau. He was the only person I knew who could use the world 'demarcation' regularly. He was the only man who could stretch out the words 'phenomenal' and 'amazing' to an excessive length.

Michael Ondaatje[16]

in a language that is rampant with fissures, an inglish, he called it, that is indebted as much to the 'street language' he learned in his Calgary neighborhood—'a ghetto: Jewish, Hungarian, Chinese, East Indian, and Native Indian'—as to his self-education, and what he learned from the use of language by such poets as Charles Olson and Robert Creeley.[17] The unconventional ways in which he punctuates his sentences, abbreviates and capitalizes (or not) words and names, or uses syntax—all the consistently employed inconsistencies that mark his writing mirror the fact that he grew up 'athwarted'—'You are of it [dominant culture], and you are not, and you know that very clearly.' It may be a strict copy-editor's worst nightmare, but Kiyooka's inglish reflects his 'mode of attention,' attention to how 'the syntax of colour' in painting and the syntax of language 'interface' with each other. It is also the result of his 'quest for a language as the modality of power' that would allow him to 'be present in the world.'[18]

If his language startles and astonishes, it is, then, because he 'conjugates' his 'own vernacular,'[19] something he returns to in these letters time and time again. This is a vernacular, however, punctuated with a diction that, in Marlatt's words, 'mix[es] the common or colloquial with the erudite, even the slightly archaic.'[20] 'Baroque diction,' Scott McFarlane aptly calls it.[21]

This erudite vernacular produces a montage effect, whereby the historical is rendered as contemporary and the old becomes new. What's more, the immediacy, informality, and the accent on the personal—characteristic elements of letter-writing—are interspersed with the voices of writers, artists, critics, and philosophers, so that, even though many of Kiyooka's letters in *Pacific Rim* speak of his aloneness, he is never quite alone.

A *'cornucopia of wondrous things'*[22]

If Kiyooka's letters are a writing of action, a laboratory where writing happens through words some of which do not often make it out of the dictionary, they are also a space teeming with quotidian things. His attachment to the concrete, to the minute details of everyday life, is one of the distinct attributes of his letters, yet another element of the poetics of outwards that bespeaks his relentless attentiveness and capacious imagination. From his reports on the weather to the detailed instructions about the care of his mother when he goes out of town while she is visiting him, to the logistics of planning a book or

> The term 'baroque' is derived from the French for 'misshapen pearl.' Kiyooka's use of baroque words suggests a vocabulary that does not seem quite proper to the otherwise straightforward language of the poems [and letters]. Baroque diction arrives like a misshapen pearl and points to the other knowledge systems and other time periods grinding away and stirring up what is being observed and recorded by the poet.
>
> Scott McFarlane 156

organizing a performance, the materiality of his family and artistic life contributes to the montage effect in his letters.

Saying it again—the same as different

Perhaps it is because of the seriality epitomizing Kiyooka's writing process that his letters—sometimes in their entirety, sometimes in part—re-appear in his other writings. Or perhaps the opposite is the case—his poetry is subsumed by his letter-writing. This repetition is echoed within the letters themselves, for frequently an entire incident or a set of ideas recurs from one letter to another. A recurring feature in letter-writing, repetition draws the loci of these instances into focus, a way of embodying in the text the data of cultural history, showing how permeable the boundary is between life and art, history and artifice. A re-assemblage that teases the Kiyooka reader with its familiarity, a requisite manifestation of what is of deep concern to him, this repetition presents in relief what matters. But what matters, what is repeated, is not always the same. As the mise en scène changes from letter to letter, especially in letters written to different addressees, so does the meaning of what is repeated. The reciprocity that binds Kiyooka's letter-writing to his correspondents inevitably affects what is repeated. Repetition in *Pacific Rim Letters* is not mere re-citation; it belongs to the living archive composed letter by letter, but also becomes a transcription of the same into something different.

Editing Kiyooka

In his re-reading of *Transcanada Letters*, Douglas Barbour expresses his gratitude that this book 'exists,' and 'hope[s] that at least one more such volume may appear some day (although, without Kiyooka's highly specific editing, there will be some kind of loss in terms of the 'shape' of the whole).'[23] Barbour does not explain what he has in mind when he refers to 'Kiyooka's highly specific editing.' Nor has it become clear to me, after working with Kiyooka's Papers at Simon Fraser University's Special Collections, what 'specific' editorial principles Kiyooka employed to edit his voluminous correspondence that became *Transcanada Letters*, or to prepare *Pacific Rim Letters*. In the absence of direct instructions from him about the latter volume, I had hoped that finding out how he edited the former would have served as my guide in this project. No sooner had I begun working with his archive than I realized

> For me, the letters in some actual sense supercede my poetry. [. . . They] enabled me to speak at levels my poems left out. [. . .] I was putting almost all of my writing energy into letters and my best ideas got into them.
> Kiyooka, 'Laughter' 12

> an old man sits minding his perfervid p's and q's. he is nothing if not a simple-minded poet practicing a bread and butter journalism: his specialty insofar as special 'isms' gripped him had a lot to do with the activist's sense of 'vigilance at the ramparts of ideology.' as for his own heart's circumlocutions: of all the distraught buried in the pages of the Book-of-Desire, he knew virtually nothing, nothing but the grasp etymology had on him: thus claspt all the clandestine-syllables lifted him up by the seat of his pants into the realm of their wakeful morning estate and sat the alphabet upright on his head.
> *Pacific Windows* 278

that discovering how he edited *Transcanada Letters* would have been a project all by itself. Nor did I find any unambiguous indications—perhaps, it would be more accurate to say that I failed to discern an explicit method—about any further editing plans he might have had about *Pacific Rim Letters*, and so, inevitably, a sense of loss is etched in this text.

For Kiyooka, writing, re-writing, and editing were, I have come to believe, if not quite synonymous, part of the same process of creation and composition. He may have left no specific instructions as to how he intended, or expected someone else, to edit *Pacific Rim Letters*, but he spoke and wrote about his gathering of his letters on and off, including in the letters published in his life time. 'Dear Correspondent /s,' he writes towards the end of *Transcanada*,

——thinking to 'collect'
all my Letters to you I have without your
permission/s   re-read/ alter'd/ a—
mended/ and re-written them . if I tell you
its all for the sake of the 'I'/'ME'/'WE'
revealed in and thru the litter——
with you believe in my good intentions ?
TCL 355

His intentions were, no doubt, good, but he did not always practise what he said. While he stated that the *Transcanada*-to-be 'letters have been a thorough involv[e]ment since the fall of '71—that is, the actual editing, revising, rewriting and re-ordering of them' ('Laughter' 12), he did not, as far as I was able to determine, rewrite them substantially. As for re-ordering them, if there is one thing certain about his intentions is his desire to privilege in *Pacific Rim Letters*, as he did in *Transcanada Letters*, the chronological order in which he wrote them. How, then, did I proceed?

Early in the editing process, I decided that the first edition of *Pacific Rim Letters* ought to remain as unencumbered by editorial interventions as possible. Any critical apparatus would have inadvertently drawn attention to the auto/biographical aspects of the text, thus privileging their documentary nature at the expense of their other qualities. Someone else may wish to undertake such a critical edition in the future that would situate the letters in their historical and cultural context. As for the

> [H]ow could he handle the conundrum of re-reading all the poems? It seemed an apparently overwhelming task for RK, a writer whose practice of revision inevitably became a re/vision in which a new text was produced. Simply preparing the 'collected' could easily become a self-consuming disappearance into the 'past.'
> Miki, 'Afterword,'
> *Pacific Windows* 302

editorial principles I have adopted, they respond to Kiyooka's own appeals for editing in many of the letters here, notably to Michael Ondaatje and bpNichol, with regard to *Wheels*, *The Fontainebleau Dream Machine*, and *Pear Tree Pomes*, three books he was in the process of completing and editing in the period *Pacific Rim Letters* covers. He was obviously not averse to being edited, and his plan to collaborate with Miki on the editing of his collected poetry is further evidence of the importance of this kind of 'collaboration' for him.

The typescript

The typescript of *Pacific Rim Letters* I had to work with was prepared, at Kiyooka's request, by his friend, Linda Gilbert, who had also helped Kiyooka prepare, and typeset for Talonbooks, the first edition of *Transcanada Letters*. The typescript she produced, however, was in no way a final draft. [24] Instead, it was Kiyooka's first systematic attempt to select and gather together the letters, the few poems and other textual material, that would comprise *Pacific Rim*. His references to this project in some of the letters in *Pacific Rim*, as well as in his Papers at Simon Fraser, suggest that he never entertained the possibility of publishing his entire voluminous correspondence. It was a 'selected letters' he was preparing. Editing for him, then, definitely included choosing certain letters as opposed to others, although it is difficult to ascertain what precisely informed this selection process. The typescript also included different versions of a few letters and of poems (e.g., the undated letter to Joy Kogawa, circa 1976, and the poem 'summer and smoke'). While some of the letters he selected were never mailed, I found many letters he had mailed but not selected for *Pacific Rim* to be as intriguing and important as those he had included in it. [26]

The original, the copy, and the print scroll

If Kiyooka's Papers at Simon Fraser University did not reveal to me any obvious revision or editorial patterns, they did pose a host of questions as to what was an original, or a copied, photocopied, and amended letter.

I did not find the computer disks the typescript had been printed from. Instead, I found two different computer printouts; in scroll form, they included amendments and corrections not all of which were incorporated in the typescript I

a small 'i' thinks
it is thinking in Japanese
<u>even</u> as he recognizes
he doesn't see a single ideogram . . . [. . .
. . .] –tongue 'it'
sets down a [?] vagrant
   english equivalent: callit
a home-spun   Romaji

'i' hear
a consummate
   legerdemain
      of alpha-bets in
wind's
   [?]
           concatenations[25]

running the old words thru again
& again, as in the notion of
'a draft.' the offtimes
impossible impulse to make it better.
                PRL 164

had. To determine which one of the printouts was the most recent version, I compared the letters in the typescript against the text of the printouts, as well as against the 'actual' letters in Kiyooka's Papers. The typescript I had was, I concluded, the most recent version.

The 'actual' letters in his Papers were carbon copies and photocopies. But I also found letters that—judging by the paper on which they were written, penned comments in Kiyooka's handwriting, and his signature—appeared to be original. The archive, rather than disclosing information that could have resolved doubts, confounded the notion of what was 'original.' Kiyooka must have often composed different 'originals,' variants of the same letter, mailing one of them, while keeping the others. Still working on a typewriter those days, he was able to preserve intact different versions of a letter. I did not see my task as determining the 'authenticity' of the letters as such, and so I proceeded to consult the variants strictly for editorial purposes.[27]

The copies or 'originals' also included suggestions for corrections, in someone else's handwriting (I am inclined to assume Gilbert's), of Kiyooka's typographical errors and abbreviations (e.g., *rememberd* was to become *remembered*, *cant can't*), as well as guesses at the right words when his typing had mangled, or when he had coined, a word (e.g., *palapleness* was to be rendered as *palpableness*, *soups soaps*, and should *conscienceness* be *conscience* or *consciousness*?).

The scroll printouts incorporate many of Kiyooka's changes made directly on individual letters, but also include marginal comments about modifications still to be made, some of them in Kiyooka's handwriting, others in someone else's, presumably Gilbert's.[28] They consisted of corrections of typing errors made in the process of Gilbert's producing the digital text; corrections of Kiyooka's own typing errors in the 'original' letters that had been reproduced while being copied; notes indicating an attempt at guessing the date of undated letters; a line running across some letters or paragraphs indicating they were to be deleted;[29] and Kiyooka's notation 'run on,' specifying that some letters were to appear as prose, that is, not follow the short lines of the original texts.

Considering the size of this project, these changes were sparse. Nor were all of them incorporated in the typescript I had. What's more, not all cases of misspelling or typographical

when you asked me
when you were here—
to take off my mask,
I have done so
again and again I
stared at this face
that was hidden
behind the other one

you thought you recognized
but could not place.
when has the mirror
stripped away what is not

there but present
in another's eyes? since
you left it is
not the same face ever
          Pacific Windows 32

errors had been corrected, some of the dates guessed at were wrong, phrases and words in some instances were missing, and some letters were out of chronological order. In sum, the typescript in my hands had not been edited thoroughly or consistently. No doubt, had Kiyooka had the opportunity to revisit this project, he would have continued to make more amendments.

Editing the typescript

Certain that Kiyooka intended the letters to appear in chronological order, I have rearranged the letters that had been misplaced while they were being retyped by Gilbert or had been incorrectly dated by Kiyooka.[30] Since he had not dated a large number of his letters at the time that he wrote them, he could not have recalled accurately their exact dates. However, in preparing *Pacific Rim Letters*, he was obviously eager to identify them by year and, when possible, by month or season. The letters in his archive are held in folders organized by year, each folder including at the start a handwritten index of its contents on lined pad pages,[31] but I found many letters and other texts in folders to which they did not belong chronologically. Nevertheless, events, projects, exhibitions, and trips within Canada and to Japan mentioned in the letters, and other information in his Papers, made it possible to identify the year, and in some cases the month, of the undated letters. I have inserted, in shaded format, the exact or approximate date only when the interval of time between undated letters could have caused uncertainty or ambiguity as to when they were written.

> 'nobody owns words'
> 'nobody can put a price on them'
> *Pacific Windows* 72

There is, however, one instance involving the letters' order that departs from the editing process I describe here. What opens *Pacific Rim Letters* now, following the epigraph from Vico, was placed four pages later in the typescript. While all the letters in his Papers are, as I have mentioned, assembled in folders organized by year, this text, 'some thoughts concerning / a 2nd Book of Letters titled / *The Pacific Rim Letters*,' is in a folder by itself. Undated, it could have been written at any time during the long period that this project was in progress. Not only because its original position in the typescript seemed to me to be arbitrary, but also because it is Kiyooka's most extensive account of how he understands the nature of this project, I have decided to place it as the frontpiece of *Pacific Rim Letters*, at once inside and outside the text proper.

The large size of the typescript made it necessary to delete a number of letters. However, the content of most of the letters I have edited out is repeated, sometimes virtually verbatim, elsewhere in the book. In the case of a few letters and poems included in the typescript in different versions, I have kept only one version. Other texts I have edited out fall into the categories of reports, budgets, press releases, curriculum vitae, and project descriptions that had been attached to the letters when they were mailed out. Some of this omitted material still appears in *Pacific Rim*, accompanying different letters.

With regard to Kiyooka's eccentric use of language, I have deleted but also added apostrophes, removed stray commas but also inserted commas when necessary. As his letter to bpNichol indicates, on the one hand, he wanted to maintain 'the casualness of lower case' and, on the other, he was eager to do something about this. About these matters, as well as with regard to the capital or lower case of nouns and pronouns, I have kept in mind his ambivalent relationship with English.

While *Transcanada Letters* replicates the notation of the short lines of the original letters, Kiyooka, as I have already mentioned, planned to have many of the letters in *Pacific Rim* 'run on.' As with his other re-writes, he did not indicate this with any degree of consistency. I have adopted this 'run on' form for letters that resemble in tone and style those he marked as such.

I have corrected Kiyooka's spelling of many proper names, though I have not changed his phonetic spelling of such proper nouns as *Americun*. Similarly, I have corrected mistakes I found in the epigraph and in some of the quotations,[32] but I have not removed the quotation marks which, for the sake of emphasis or nuance, Kiyooka often surrounds words with. All ellipses are his, and they do not indicate omissions; a frequent feature of his writing, similar to the space he often leaves before and after a period, they reflect the disjunctures in his thinking, echoing the 'ellipses' in his painting.

Although it is customary to offer at least a synopsis of the life of an author one edits, I have decided, instead, to compile a chronology of the bare facts in Kiyooka's life. The reader can find a brief narrative account of Kiyooka's life in Miki's 'Afterword' in *Pacific Windows*, and read *Mothertalk* for a more in-depth depiction of his childhood and adolescence in the context of his family. Even though there is considerable biographical information available about him in reference sources, the

> you will find a number of inconsistencies like using both upper & lower case 'I's' not to mention uncapitalized nouns. i've left it that way 'cause i couldn't make up my mind & you could advise me on this. a part of me wants the formality of caps thru-out & a part of me doesn't. i want the casualness of lower case. so what do you think i ought to do about it? please advise Stan before it goes to press. i'll take your word for what suits the occasion.
> Letter to bpNichol, PRL 39

information provided there tends to privilege the arc of his life as a visual artist or, conversely, to focus primarily on his writing. Not exhaustive (I do not, for example, include all of his exhibitions or list all of his travels), the inventory of events I provide in this book sketches the outlines of the variously interlaced paths of Kiyooka's life. While I have relied on a number of reference sources,[33] I have also benefited from information that I have received from Fumiko Kiyooka, one of his daughters.

Although Kiyooka left no instructions as to what photographs he wanted included in this book, I have no doubt photographs would have been part of his overall design for *Pacific Rim Letters*. I have selected *Okinawa*, the 1984 grid of silver prints, because it overlaps with the time frame of the letters, but also because it reflects the powerful and complex ways in which Japan beckoned him during that period. The portrait of the elderly man included in this grid is the Oji-san, the retired fisherman and folk singer who sang 'the tales of his tribe during a 5 day typhoon' (PRL 117) in Kohama (also called Obama), an event Kiyooka witnessed and which had a profound impact on him.

Postscript

Dear Roy was how this afterword began at some point, a letter I felt compelled to write in response to the ones I often thought he was writing just for me. There is a special kind of knowledge—the kind of non-knowledge Bataille says lays bare what you have known—that comes from the intimacy that grows between an editor and the edited text. An act of intervention and negotiation, editing is also a labor of love. Editing Kiyooka's *Pacific Rim Letters* has been like a lingering love affair—now maddening, now elating—the kind of relationship you know you have to put an end to, but you cannot, for it keeps you hooked, wanting more of the pleasure and anguish you are wrapped in.

So, I feel both a sense of relief for having completed this project, but also a requisite sadness. It was my memory of his laughter—which, must be said, was not always a sign of mirth—that kept me going when I had to make difficult editorial decisions, when, not without guilt, I abandoned his text for a while to take on other things. My relationship with him—his letters and poems—will continue unabated, albeit in a different way. I only hope that the result of this intense engagement, even if it cannot be what he would have 'completed' himself, is at least an approximation of his own good intentions.

All amazed
Smaro Kamboureli
Victoria, BC, 2002—Guelph, ON, 2005

NOTES

[1] Roy K. Kiyooka, *Transcanada Letters* (1975), with an Afterword by Glen Lowry (Edmonton: NeWest Press, 2005), 256. All references to *Transcanada Letters*, henceforth abbreviated as TCL, are to this edition. Though not a second edition as such, it is paginated, and includes my corrections of typographical errors.

[2] The number of the letters varies depending on whether one's count includes the poems, letters to himself, the various 'documents' attached to some of the letters, and the couple of letters by Daphne Marlatt Kiyooka includes in the collection.

[3] Kiyooka in conversation with Alvin Balkind, Chief Curator at the Vancouver Art Gallery that exhibited 'Roy Kiyooka: 25 Years' in 1975. In 'Laughter: Five Conversations with Roy Kiyooka,' recorded and edited by Gerry Gilbert, *artscanada*, 32, 4 (Winter 1975-76), 12. Further references to Kiyooka's 'Five Conversations' are cited in the text as 'Laughter.'

[4] n.p. From a chapbook self-published by Kiyooka (not included in *Pacific Windows*). Citations from this text in the 'Afterword' include my editing of typographical errors and punctuation. Following Miki's method of acknowledging Kiyooka's chapbooks in *Pacific Windows*, I provide here its entire colophon.

March : Prose : Works
<u>A Concatenation of</u>
<u>Pacific Rim Vernacular/s</u>
  a hank of seaweed
        flotsam in brine
an erstwhile Coupling of the Auguries
of a dilapidated Pacific Rim Synchronicity:
for the 8th Annual Literary Conference
at St. Michael's College   March 20 21 22nd——
but especially for Smaro Kamboureli and
Robert Kroetsch who both know that the Writing
Life adds Levity to Pleasure and Strife
written
copied, 30 times
collated
stapled & signed
at 648 Keefer st.
Vancouver
b.c. V6A 1Y4
between march 1st
& the ides '86
under the sign
of The Blue Mule

[5] *Pacific Windows: Collected Poems of Roy K. Kiyooka*, Roy K. Kiyooka, edited by Roy Miki (Vancouver: Talonbooks, 1997), with an 'Afterword' by Miki, 301-20.

[6] Roy Miki, 'Inter-Face: Roy Kiyooka's Writing: A Commentary/Interview,' *Roy Kiyooka*, a catalogue of Roy Kiyooka's 'mini-retrospective' (Vancouver: Artspeak Gallery and Or Gallery, 1991), 53-4.

[7] Henry Tsang, a Vancouver multi-media artist and one of Kiyooka's students at the University of British Columbia in the early 1980s, remembers Kiyooka speaking 'of immersing [himself] into a process which is and should be a personal exploration [. . .]. . . being an artist is not a career but a quest' (86). Tsang also writes that 'In mid-1980s Canada, [Kiyooka] figured that about 200 actively followed his work. Given that much of his artistic output of that period involved homemade limited edition chapbooks and prints, hand-delivered or mailed, it is not surprising that he could gauge his constituency in such a de facto manner. He was in control of both the means of production and the distribution of his work' (91). Tsang, 'Art Calling Fool Scold: The Discursive Pedagogy of Roy Kiyooka,' in *All Amazed: For Roy Kiyooka*, eds. John O'Brian,

Naomi Sawada, and Scott Watson (Vancouver: Arsenal Pulp Press, Morris and Helen Belkin Art Gallery, and *Collapse*, 2002), 84-93.

[8] All references in this paragraph are to Roy K. Kiyooka, *Mothertalk: Life Stories of Mary Kiyoshi Kiyooka*, edited by Daphne Marlatt (Edmonton: NeWest Press, 1997).

[9] An excerpt from this manuscript, 'from *The Artist and the Moose: A Fable to Forget*,' edited and introduced by Roy Miki, appears in the special 'O' issue, 'new writing, critical essays, photography on the work of Roy Kiyooka,' *dandelion*, edited by Jill Hartman and derek beaulieu, 29, 1 (2003): 127-39.

[10] Henceforth cited in the text as PRL.

[11] See Edward Said's interview with Israeli journalist Ari Shavit conducted in August 2000, 'My Right to Return,' chapter 29 in his *Power, Politics, and Culture* (New York: Pantheon 2001).

[12] See Kiyooka's letter, 'Dear Lucy Fumi: c/o Japanese Canadian Redress Secretariat,' in *Mothertalk*, 187-190, in which he offers an account of this experience.

[13] See Francis Fukuyama, *The End of History and the Last Man* (New York: Avon Books, 1993) and Tony Judt, 'The End of History,' *New Republic*, May 14, 2001, 36-41.

[14] *13 Cameras* (Ottawa: National Film Board of Canada, Stills Division, 1979). Kiyooka's Preface, 'Stalking a Silver-image,' appears in *Pacific Rim Letters*.

[15] The last letter in *Transcanada Letters* is not dated, but the previous letter, also addressed to Marlatt, is dated Monday, April 14, and was evidently written the day before the last letter. Regarding the opening of *Pacific Rim Letters*, see later in the 'Afterword.'

[16] 'Transcript of Roy Kiyooka Conference,' *All Amazed*, 64.

[17] I am referring to the Vancouver Poetry Conference in 1963, organized by Warren Tallman. There are many references to this event and its impact on the Vancouver poetry scene in a variety of sources. See for example, Pauline Butling and Susan Rudy, *Writing in Our Time: Canada's Radical Poetries in English (1957-2003)* (Waterloo: Wilfrid Laurier University Press, 2005), 144-45.

[18] References in this paragraph are to Kiyooka's interview with Roy Miki, 'Inter-Face,' 50, 49, and 51 respectively. 'inglish,' Kiyooka's word, appears often in his writing; see, for example, *Pacific Windows*, 141, 241, 260 and 273.

[19] 'October's Piebald Skies & Other Lacunae,' *Pacific Windows*, 277.

[20] 'Transcript of Roy Kiyooka Conference,' *All Amazed*, 24.

[21] Scott McFarlane, 'The Beguiled Air of Astonishment' (a review of *Pacific Windows*), *West Coast Line*, 25, 32/1 (Spring-Summer 1998), 153-57.

[22] Letter to Carolle Itter, TCL 23.

[23] Douglas Barbour, 'Roy Kiyooka: Writing the 'trans' in *transcanada letters*,' *West Coast Line*, 16, 29/1 (Spring/Summer 1995), 11.

[24] Though she lived in Vancouver, it proved very difficult to locate Linda Gilbert for a long time. It was in the spring of 2003, by which time I had already begun editing, that I managed to have a single, long conversation with her over the phone. Further communication with her, however, was prevented by the illness she was battling at the time, and to which she succumbed in 2004. She did not tell me anything that required I review my editorial approach.

[25] Kiyooka, untitled poem found in one of his notebooks included in his Papers. Question marks inside square brackets indicate words I could not decipher.

[26] According to Gilbert, Kiyooka had asked her and a couple of women friends to give him feedback on this project. They felt that the letters of 1976-1985 were substantially different from those included in *Transcanada Letters*—more revelatory about him and some of his correspondents—and, therefore, strongly recommended that he eliminate or substantially edit a good number of them. Always according to Gilbert, Kiyooka was reluctant to adopt this kind of editing.

[27] Whether an 'authentic' letter is a letter mailed out or another version of that same letter kept for inclusion in *Pacific Rim Letters* is an intriguing question, but not one that could be resolved, if that would be possible,

without access to letters received by Kiyooka's correspondents. Moreover, I did not deem this to be a question relevant to editing this project.

[28] I had difficulty determining some times whether the corrections penciled in handwriting different from Kiyooka's were all made by the same person, i.e., Gilbert.

[29] Judging by the color of the pen used, those deletions were Kiyooka's.

[30] The scroll printouts include some marginal comments by, I assume, Gilbert who raises questions as to the date attributed by Kiyooka to some undated letters. She was right in most instances. In a few instances, letters addressed to the same recipients were grouped together.

[31] The index in the folders lists the contents according to the correspondents' names, but also provides brief annotations and cross-references within the body of this correspondence; it does not, however, identify the full identities of the letters' recipients.

[32] My random check of his quotations—'random' in the sense that I checked only those sources that I recognized and those that were relatively easy to locate—revealed errors in them, as well as various kinds of embellishments.

[33] These sources, too many to list them here, are widely available. Not all of them, however, have proven to be utterly reliable. There are discrepancies in them about dates, while the entries on Kiyooka in the two main literary reference volumes about Canadian literature, *Encyclopedia of Literature in Canada* and *The Oxford Companion to Canadian Literature* (second edition), erroneously attribute titles to him. A more detailed list of Kiyooka's exhibitions, albeit still 'selected,' is available on the web site of Catriona Jeffries Gallery, www3.telus.net/cat_jef/roy_kiy_bib.html.

ROY KENZIE KIYOOKA—A CHRONOLOGY

1926   Born Roy Kenzie Kiyooka, January 18, in Moose Jaw, Saskatchewan, to Mary Kiyoshi Oe from Tosa (Kochi City) and Harry Shigekiyo Kiyooka (meaning 'nice clean hill'), from Umagi-mura on the island of Shikoku. Maternal grandfather, Masaji Oe, a samurai and the 'last great master of the Hasegawa school of Iai,' dies. Family moves to Calgary the same year where it settles close to Victoria Park by the CPR railway tracks. Parents run a vegetable stand.

1930   Travels to Japan with his mother where 'relatives were all astonished that [he] could speak both Japanese and English.' Circa 1930s, badly burns his back in accident at home.

1941   Pearl Harbor 'ends his adolescence' and formal schooling at Western Canada High School.

1942-46 Fingerprinted and registered as 'enemy alien.' Family forced to move to Opal, Alberta, 'about a dozen home,' '3 grain elevator' hamlet north-east of Edmonton, 'the only Japanese Canadian community in northern Alberta.' First live in a one-room log house with no running water or electricity. Father buys a 'quarter section farm' where RKK builds 'a small 2 room log house.' While father is employed as a bull cook in a logging camp 'run with German and Japanese prisoners,' RKK works on the farm, and as a forty-five-cents-an-hour fish processor in a fishing camp on Great Slave Lake, Northwest Territories. Reads Sherlock Holmes, *Tales of Genji*, and pocket books. Develops interest in art through 'grade school art [and] comic books.' Brother George's 'still life in charcoal/pencil . . . would have been Roy's only early exposure to original art.'

1946-49 In Calgary to study art at the Provincial Institute of Technology and Art (now Alberta College of Arts) where J.W.G. Macdonald and I.H. Kerr were his teachers. Rooms with George Self, Professor of History, whose large collection of jazz, classic, and folk records is RKK's 'first exposure to the world of music.' Owes Marion and Jim Nicoll 'all the literacy' he has. Receives a Diploma in Fine Arts from the Institute in 1949.

1949-50 Joins Ron Spickett in Toronto where he lives on 272 Parliament Street for nine months. Paints.

1950   Wins the O'Keefe Award for Painters Under Thirty. Returns to Calgary to teach evening classes at Coste House while working full time as window trimmer and show card man at The Bay.

1951   Included in the National Gallery of Canada's Biennial. Family moves from Opal to Edmonton.

1953	Teaches full time at Institute of Technology and Art, Calgary (1953-55).
1954	Monica Dealtry Barker, his wife-to-be, a graduate of the University of Manitoba, works at the Calgary Planning Department, and takes RKK's evening class. His painting *Pastoral* wins the Calgary Golden Prize.
1955	Monica, who has moved to Nelson, B.C., to work as an architect, invites RKK to join her. They marry in April. RKK works as a sign writer for a supermarket firm; wins Scholarship to the Instituto Allende, Mexico.
1956	RKK and Monice live in San Miguel de Allende, Mexico, where RKK studies with James Pinto, paints, parties, and travels around the country to look at art (Orozco, Rivera) and the Aztec, Inca, and Mayan ruins.
1956-60	The Kiyookas move to Saskatachewan where RKK teaches full time at the Regina College of Art. Before they move, not having storage space, RKK 'tak[es] an ax to the paintings and bur[ies] the remnants' in his brother George's back yard. The Kiyookas live in the College's basement suite, while RKK uses a tower room at the College as his studio. RKK participates in the Emma Lake Artists' Workshops, summer school, University of Saskatchewan, where he works with Joe Plaskett, Will Barnet (1957) and Barnett Newman (1959). Exhibits widely in many solo (at least ten by this point) and group exhibitions.
1958	Work selected for the Walker Biennial exhibition in Minneapolis Art Gallery; wins Minneapolis Center Arts Council Award; work represented at the Winnipeg Art Gallery for which he receives First Prize.
1960-65	Moves to Vancouver to teach at the Vancouver School of Art (now Emily Car College of Art and Design).
1963	Travels to Japan 'in search of [his] origins' and to visit sister Mariko. Attends the Vancouver Poetry conference organized by Warren Tallman where he is exposed to the Black Mountain poetics. Begins writing.
1964	Publishes first book, *Kyoto Airs* (Periwinkle Press, designed and printed by Takao Tanabe). Awarded senior art fellowship from the Canada Council; exhibits, together with brother Harry, at the Alberta College of Art, Calgary.
1965	Participates in the Eighth São Paulo Bienale, Brazil, where he wins Silver Medal and Honourable mention. Solo exhibition at Grippi-Waddell Gallery, New York. Joins the faculty at the Sir George Williams (now Concordia) University, Montreal (1965-70). Member of Royal Canadian Academy of Arts.
1966	Mosaic murals commissioned for the First Presbyterian Church in Regina and the Biology Building of the University Saskatchewan. With dancer Vicki Tansey, RKK performs first 'happening' in Montreal.

1967	Participates in World Expo 67, Montreal, and virtually every major centennial show. Publishes *Nevertheless These Eyes* (Coach House Press). Begins work on a series of ten cedar laminate fiberglass sculptures.
1968	Included in *Canada 101*, Edinburgh International Festival Exhibition. Participates in group exhibition, *Seven Montreal Painters, Mollinari, Barbeau, Tousignant, Goguen, Kiyooka, Hurtubise, Juneau*, Washington Gallery of Modern Art and Hayden Gallery at M.I.T., Boston.
1969	Wins commission to make sculpture for the Canadian Pavilion at the International Expo in Osaka, Japan. Lives in Kyoto for four months; commutes daily to Osaka. Ceases to paint. Begins multidisciplinary work, inaugurated with his 'mania for photography viz Stonedgloves and subsequent images' while working on his sculpture at the Expo site in Osaka. Travels in October through Honshu's backcountry with father and Syuzo Fujimoto ('our intrepid guide'), and begins writing what will become *Wheels*. Resumes work on cedar laminate sculptures upon his return to Vancouver.
1970	*Abu Ben Adam's Vinyl Dream*, his sculpture at World Expo 70, Osaka, Japan. *StoneDGloves: alms for soft palms*, solo exhibition at the National Gallery, Ottawa. (Exhibition travels to 14 other cities in the course of 1970-71.) Publishes *StoneDGloves* (Coach House Press). Moves to Vancouver. Cuts off finger on Boxing Day while working on sculptures. Coordinates and participates in group exhibition, *B.C. Almanac(h) C.B.*, National Film Board, Stills Division, Ottawa. Marriage breaks down.
1971	*B.C. Almanac(h) C.B.* shown at the Vancouver Art Gallery, Edmonton Art Gallery, and the Museum of Modern Art, New York.
1971-72	Embarks on his trans-Canada journey in a van; destination, Halifax, Nova Scotia. Teaches at the Nova Scotia College of Art and Design. Divorce.
1972	*StoneDGloves* exhibited at Centre Culturel Canadien, Paris, France. Back in Vancouver where he spends the rest of his life. Joins the faculty of Fine Arts Department, University of British Columbia.
1973	Represented in the group exhibition, *Japanese Artists of the Americas*, Kyoto, Japan. (Exhibition travels to Tokyo the following year.) Visits Kyoto in the fall, and travels in Kyoto's backcountry.
1974	RKK's father dies in Edmonton. Moves in, 'with three cast-iron skillets,' with Daphne Marlatt and Kit, her son, in Kitsilano, Vancouver.
1975	*Transcanada Letters* (Talonbooks). *Roy Kiyooka: 25 Years*, exhibition at the Vancouver Art Gallery, travels to the University of Calgary Art Gallery, Windsor Art Gallery, and the Robert McLaughlin Gallery, Oshawa. Richard Sommer gives

	RKK a child's dulcimer as a gift; RKK starts playing music. Circa mid 1970s, at Véhicule Art Inc. gallery, Montreal, RKK and Vicki Tansey do a performance/improvisation during which he tears up an issue of *artscanada* and puts up the pieces on the windows while she performs on a ladder.
1977	Publishes *The Fontainebleau Dream Machine* (Coach House)
1978	Officer of the Order of Canada—attends the investiture in green tuxedo.
1979	Group exhibition, *13 Cameras*, at the National Film Board, Ottawa.
1980	*Powell Street Promenade*, photoglyph. Lacking any formal training in music, RKK initiates an 'apprenticeship' with New Music composer (now playwright) Don Druick; they meet weekly for about two years, RKK playing his 'inexpensive zither' and taping every session. Interested in 'self-structured improvisation,' a kind of 'shamanistic sound-making,' he refuses to 'learn musical skills or how to tune.'
1981	Visits Kohama, Okinawa, Japan in the summer. Begins to improvise on a jamisen after witnessing an Okinawan elder's performance. Starts writing the subsequently 'abandoned' novel on Tom Thomson. Presents 'We Asian North Americanos' in the Japanese Canadian / Japanese American Symposium, Seattle, Washington, May 2. Exhibition of photographs, with 'dulcimer/dance performance' (with Vicki Tansey), and reading from *Wheels* at Scarborough College. RKK and Daphne Marlatt separate.
1982	Publishes manuscript edition of *Wheels* (Coach House Press).
1983	Visits Japan (Tokyo, Kochi City, Kyoto, Osaka, Yokohama, Nomi, Gotenyama, Kohama) for 60 days in early May; his mother accompanies him for the first part of the trip. Goes to Portugal on a two-week vacation with Jenny Shaw, his first and last trip to Europe. Continues with, and tapes, his musical improvisations, 'self-generated bardic' creations that now involve collaboration with Howard Broomfield and Trudi Rubenfeld.
1984	Visits Japan (Kochi City, Umagi-mura, Yokohama, Kohama) in April for about two months.
1985	*In/Around/My Japan: A Canadian/Japanese Artist's Color Prints taken between 1969-1984*, solo exhibition, Richmond Art Gallery, Richmond, B.C. Musican performance of RKK, Broomfield, and Rubenfeld at Coburg Gallery, Vancouver. Following Broomfield's death, Rhoda Rosenfeld and Maxine Gadd join RKK's collaborative musical sessions on Saturdays at his house or Blue Mule Gallery. Travels to Kyoto, Hirakata, Nagoya, and Kohama.
1986	Returns to Japan in July (perhaps his last trip there) and visits Kochi City.
1987	Publishes *Pear Tree Pomes* (Coach House), short-listed for the Governor General Award for Poetry.

1990	'Pacific Windows: A Photoglyphic Narrative . . .' published in *Capilano Review*. 'Roy Kiyooka,' a retrospective exhibition at Artspeak and Or Galleries. Participates in group exhibition, *Yellow Peril Reconsidered*, which travels (1990-91) to seven Canadian cities.
1991	Retires from his position at the University of British Columbia.
1993	Major by-pass surgery for a clogged artery.
1994	Dies on Keefer Street, Vancouver, first week of January.
1996	His mother dies at age 100 in Edmonton.
1997	*Pacific Windows: The Collected Poems of Roy K. Kiyooka*, edited, and with an Afterword, by Roy Miki (Talonbooks); *Mothertalk: Life Stories of Mary Kiyoshi Kiyooka* (NeWest) edited, and with an Introduction, by Daphne Marlatt.
1998	*Pacific Windows* receives Outstanding Book Award in Poetry from the Association for Asian American Studies. *Photographic Works 1970-1994*, solo exhibition, Catriona Jeffies Gallery, Vancouver.
1999	'Roy Kiyooka Conference,' October 1-2, Emily Carr College for Art and Design, organized by the Morris and Helen Belkin Art Gallery in collaboration with the Vancouver Art Forum Society and the Charles H. Scott Gallery.
2000	*Filmic Works 1978-80*, solo exhibition, Catriona Jeffries Gallery, Vancouver.
2001	Fumiko Kiyooka, RKK's daughter, makes two films based on his art, *The Return* and *Longed-for Knowing*. *Kenzie Kiyooka: '71—the penultimate year*, solo exhibition curated by his brother, Harry Kiyooka, Triangle Gallery of Visual Arts, Calgary.
2002	*All Amazed for Roy Kiyooka*, (transcript of the 1999 conference) edited by John O' Brian, Naomi Sawada, and Scott Watson (Vancouver: Arsenal Pulp, Morris and Helen Belkin Gallery, and *Collapse*).
2005	Fumiko Kiyooka at work on *Reed*, a feature film based on *Mothertalk*. *Transcanada Letters*, corrected edition edited by Smaro Kamboureli, with an Afterword by Glen Lowry (NeWest); *Pacific Rim Letters*, edited, and with an Afterword, by Smaro Kamboureli (NeWest).

* Citations in this chronology about RKK's early years come from 'Roy Kenzie Kiyooka: Life/Times' by Harry Kiyooka, included in the catalogue that accompanied the 2001 Calgary exhibition, and Monica D. (formerly Barker and Kiyooka) Robb (e-mail). Citations about RKK's improvisational music come from Don Druick (telephone conversation). Other information about RKK's musical sessions comes from Rhoda Rosenfeld (telephone conversation), while references to his first dulcimer and performances in Montreal come from Vicki Tansey (personal interview). The reference to the 'three cast-iron skillets' is courtesy of Daphne Marlatt (e-mail).

Index of Correspondents

(When last name is not known, correspondents are listed by their first name.)

Akino, Fuko 287, 322

Akino, Kazuko and Isamu 48, 140, 160, 161, 162, 206, 220, 250, 281, 327

Akino, Michun (Michiko) 223, 287, 322

Amer, Liz 223

Arntzen, Sonja 114, 151, 187, 191, 194, 197, 213, 317

Arntzen, Samantha (Sam) 115, 181

Bates, Max and Charlotte 174

Beaulieu, Victor-Lévy, 26

Beaulieu, Michel 190, 200

Bell, Lynne 9

Bevington, Stan 43, 49, 93, 208, 276, 290, 310, 318

Bolduc, David 207, 278, 279, 293

Bowering, George 270

Candelaria, Fred 113

Carney, Lora, 117, 118, 119, 120, 124, 137, 138, 215, 227, 245

Caswell, James (Jim) 132, 168, 180, 192, 201, 210, 244, 264

Coleman, Victor 129, 135, 224, 236, 258, 259

Curnoe, Greg 23, 232

Dawson, Fee (Fielding) 288

Dery, Francois (and Katrina) 127

Deverell, Tim 311

Dragland, Stan 275

Farkas, Endre 240

Faucet, Brian 35

Fertig, Evelyn 234

Fujimoto, Syuzo and Sachiko 130, 157, 158, 159, 160, 162, 163, 211

[ ], Geoffrey 67

[ ], George 68

[], George and June 95

Gomez, Ricardo (Rick) 147

Gordon, Tom 84

Hanbury, Mary Rose (Rosy – a.k.a. Bloodoff) 46

Hayes, Martha 71, 80, 94

Hindmarch, (Maria) Gladys 10, 47

Holden, Richard 328

Hoover, Gwen 38

Hope-Smith, Page 295

Ireland, Ann 311

Johnson, Charmaine (Char) 219

Kemp, Penny 45, 62

Kiyooka, Fumiko (Fumi) 266

Kiyooka, Kiyo 266

Kiyooka, Mariko 42, 228, 229, 251

Kogawa, Joy 6, 153

Koizumi, Maya 88, 183, 214

Kroetsch, Robert 225

Kubota, Noburo (Nobby) 230, 257

Langford, Martha 81

Lapp, Claudia 19, 282

Lefko, Elliot 169

Leroy, Hugh 52

McKinnon, Barry 34

Macdonald, Joan 111

Marlatt, Daphne 1, 4, 29, 154, 170, 171, 193

Marlatt, Kit 1, 8, 97, 143, 238

McClelland & Stewart (Editors) 55

Mellen, Peter 58

[ ], Michael 65

Miles, Sharon 113

Mitchell, Peter 107

Monk, Lorraine 63, 64

Moore, Kathleen 99

Murray, Joan 111

Nichol, bp [Barry] 33, 40, 188

Ondaatje, Kim 12

Ondaatje, Michael 12, 106, 131, 165, 167, 172, 182, 188, 195, 196, 198, 202, 218, 231, 247, 274, 276, 280, 284, 292, 298, 312

Padgham, Terry 28

[ ], Phil 139

Pickering, Dale 226

Reid, Dennis 36, 54, 89

Rivard Le Moyne, Suzanne 21

Rombout, Luke 22, 70, 271

Rosenfeld, Rhoda, 321

Rubenfeld, Trudi (Trudy), 263

Ryley, Nancy 58

Schreyer, Edward 79

Sheard, Sarah 78, 85, 92, 133, 149, 208, 248, 277, 283, 291, 294

Shikatani, Gerry 31, 39, 44, 98, 102, 104, 112, 148

Siegler, Karl, 59

Simmins, Richard and Karen 96, 103, 105, 116, 221

Sommer, Richard 19, 69, 123, 136, 199, 217, 300

Sorenson, Dave 30

Spalding, Linda 131, 172, 196, 198, 218, 231, 247, 280, 312, 320

Spend, John and Susan 86

Sumimoto, Minoru 209

Takaji, Kyoko 61

Tansey, Vicki 19, 123, 124, 125, 126, 134, 199, 212, 217, 300

Townshend, Nancy 173

Trudeau, Yves 32, 100

Uchida, Bart 315, 316

Vanesse, Linney (Linda) 184, 216, 233, 246

Wah, Fred 147

Walters, Louise 37, 41

Watson, Scott 252

Watson, Sheila 20, 52, 304

Watson, Wilfred 20, 52, 304

Webb, Phyllis 17, 50, 57, 150, 186

Will, Robert 192, 203, 210

Yoshihara, Mayumi and Hiro 241, 249, 373

Young, David 49, 78, 85, 92, 283

ACKNOWLEDGEMENTS

I have accrued many debts in the long process of editing this manuscript. Dianna Rutherford proved to be as unflappable a secretary in my former Department of English at the University of Victoria as the secretary in Kiyooka's Fine Arts Department. She helped scan the typescript, and carried out the first proofreading of it. Marika Strobl, my assistant at the University of Victoria, was immensely helpful at the preliminary stages of work on this project: she proofread the scanned text and conducted various kinds of research. Gregory Plakonouris, my assistant at Simon Fraser University for a short term, also contributed to the preliminary research stage: he compiled a bibliography of Kiyooka's works, provided annotations, and located some material in Kiyooka's Papers. I am also grateful to him for giving me, for keeps, a precious copy of *Transcanada Letters* at a time when my library was in disarray as I was getting ready to relocate to Ontario.

Moving from one side of the country to the other interrupted the completion of this project. Sandy Sabatini, at the University of Guelph, performed what can only be a miracle by finding and giving me access to a Macintosh computer in a campus that is officially set against Macs; I was then able to resume work on the text before my belongings made their trip from the West Coast to Southern Ontario. Her unwavering good spirits, efficiency, and moral support made me feel "at home," and thus possible to begin work anew. Lynne Van Luven and Andrew McWhinnie offered hospitality and good cheer in Victoria. Jodey Castricano offered hospitality in Elora and helped me unpack the first boxes. Mark McCutcheon, my assistant at the University of Guelph, was instrumental in my carrying out the final stages of this project. Whether he was helping me find books that were still randomly shelved or conducting research to locate missing information, he proved to be utterly dependable, a paragon of efficiency and ingenuity. My thanks to Alan Shepard, Director of my new department, for his support during my period of adjustment, and for providing the funds necessary to employ Mark. I also owe thanks to my brother, Kostas, who returned to Ontario early from a well-deserved family vacation to help me set up my study at home. My mother, who came from Greece to help, managed to locate some of Kiyooka's books in a stack of boxes when I most needed them.

Special thanks to Pauline Butling and Fred Wah, and to Douglas Barbour and Sharon Barbour, for their personal and intellectual support and valuable insights. I am grateful to Harry Kiyooka, Kiyooka's brother, for taking me, along with Roy Miki, on a guided tour of the old Kiyooka neighborhood in Calgary. My deep thanks to the late Linda Gilbert for talking with me at a time that was most difficult for her. David Aylword promptly provided the translation for the poems in Japanese. Ruth Abrahamson, George Bowering, Jim Caswell, Glen Lowry, Tani Miki, Laurie Ricou, Gerry Shikatani, and Whipple Steinkrauss facilitated, in a prompt fashion, various aspects of my search for information. Catriona Jeffries also provided useful links, as well as helpful insights, about Kiyooka's photo-archive, and facilitated the inclusion of the Okinawa photographs in this book. Tony Power at the Special Collections, Simon Fraser University, was most accommodating while I worked on Kiyooka's Papers. It was always a pleasure and a privilege listening to Glen Lowry in Vancouver talk about Kiyooka's work. Special thanks to Slavia Miki for her gracious and generous hospitality in Vancouver while I was working on Kiyooka's Papers—for other things as well. I am particularly grateful to Ed and Lesley Pechter for their various kinds of intellectual support about the project and for their hospitality and friendship—they practise friendship with inimitable grace and generosity. Fumiko Kiyooka has been instrumental in the final stages of this project; she put me in touch with her mother, Monica D. Robb, and other friends of her father's, and clarified details about the chronology of his life. I am especially obliged to Don Druick, Rhoda Rosenfeld, and Vicki Tansey for the invaluable information and insights they offered. I owe my deepest gratitude—for their long-standing friendship and for their intellectual guidance and support with this project—to Daphne Marlatt, Roy Miki, and Phyllis Webb. Needless to say, despite the generous help I have received along the way, I remain responsible for any slip-ups that may have marred *Pacific Rim Letters*.

Three research grants from the University of Victoria made it possible for me to hire my assistants Marika Stroble and Greg Plakonouris, and visit the Simon Fraser University's Special Collections. My research fund at the University of Guelph has helped with preparing the final manuscript, including the reproduction of the Okinawa photographs. A grant from the National Association of Japanese Canadians Endowment Fund has made it possible for NeWest Press to publish this book. Finally, I owe thanks to the Estate of Roy Kiyooka for permission to undertake this project, and Ruth Linka, Manager of NeWest Press, for her patience and various kinds of support.

The founder and Editor of NeWest's 'The Writer as Critic' series, Smaro Kamboureli taught Canadian literature at the University of Victoria for many years. She joined the School of English and Theatre Studies at the University of Guelph as University Research Chair in 2004. Her most recent book is *Scandalous Bodies: Diasporic Literature in English Canada* (2000).